Theory of
Psychoanalytic Technique

THEORY

OF

PSYCHOANALYTIC

TECHNIQUE

Karl A. ^{ugustus} *Menninger*

AND

Philip S. Holzman

SECOND EDITION

Basic Books, Inc., Publishers

NEW YORK

Second Edition

© 1973 by Basic Books, Inc.

First Edition © 1958 by Basic Books, Inc.

Library of Congress Catalog Card Number: 72-89277

SBN 465-08488-5

Manufactured in the United States of America

73 74 75 76 77 10 9 8 7 6 5 4 3 2 1

PREFACE

To the Second Edition

FOURTEEN YEARS AGO THIS BOOK WAS DIFFIDENTLY SUBMITTED FOR THE assistance of students of psychoanalysis in their efforts to get a grasp of the theory underlying the treatment procedure they were studying. It proved to be more popular than expected and has been used not only in psychoanalytic Training Institutes all over the world, but in university and medical school courses. This attests to its partial fulfillment at least of a certain need.

But every author discovers errors and omissions in what he has written the day his book comes off the press. Thereafter, friends and students kindly call his attention to various defects and deficiencies. Taking advantage of the author's narcissism, these spur a renewed effort at achieving perfection, at least improvement.

And then, too, an author changes his mind, and occasionally he is fortunate in discovering a collaborator to help him do so, as in this instance. One of his most brilliant students, subsequently his assistant in teaching, kindly became his coauthor and to Dr. Philip Holzman belongs the credit for initiating and propelling and pushing through this revision. To have changed all of the first person singular references in this edition to "we," "our" and "us" would have been awkward and even inaccurate since the original text included some personal experiences and views which have been retained in the original version. These will probably be self-explanatory to the reader.

There are numerous major and a few minor changes. The schema of the legal formula for parties to a contract has been retained because we have found it helpful in emphasizing the element of reciprocity in the "therapeutic alliance" and the cooperative diagnostic investigation which the psychoanalytic experience really is. On the other hand, the importance attached in the first edition to the payment of a fee for services now grates harshly on the ears of the authors, related as it is to two of the great present dangers of psychoanalysis—its expensiveness and its exploitation. The fee discussion has accordingly been altered.

A final chapter has been added to afford an overview of the field, taking account of some recent changes in stance and emphasis. For while the theory changes little, other aspects of psychoanalysis have changed much since the time of the first edition.

To further grasp this change, the reader is urged to read again the Preface to the First Edition, bearing in mind the date. It is of the greatest importance for the candidate undertaking psychoanalytic training to get a historical *feel* for his discipline. Those unfamiliar with history are doomed to blindly repeat it. Hence, we hope that the recurrent cycles of the reader's development will be helical rather than circular, with a persistent centrifugal trend. Onward and outward, but with a constant relevancy to the central nucleus!

We wish to acknowledge our indebtedness and gratitude to our most patient and indefatigable assistants Mrs. Beverlee Hayes, Mrs. La June Whitney, and Mrs. Marilyn Kollath.

KARL MENNINGER, M.D.
PHILIP HOLZMAN, PH.D.

Chicago
1973

PREFACE

To the First Edition

"It is amazing how small a proportion of the very extensive psychoanalytic literature is devoted to psychoanalytic technique and how much less to the theory of technique."—OTTO FENICHEL

NEARLY TWENTY YEARS HAVE ELAPSED SINCE THE LATE OTTO FENICHEL recorded these words of astonishment. The situation he described then still obtains, although training in psychoanalysis, including technique, has expanded manyfold. The formal teaching of psychoanalytic theory and practice was inaugurated in 1920 in Berlin. The New York Institute was founded in 1929, the Chicago Institute in 1932, and the Topeka Institute in 1938. Today there are twenty-one such institutes in America, in addition to those of England, Austria, Holland, Belgium, France, Germany, Italy, Sweden, Switzerland, India, Israel, Japan, Argentina, Brazil, and Chile.

All over the world, in these small, hard-working units, psychoanalytic theory and practice are systematically presented by carefully selected teachers to carefully selected students. This educational edifice has been the envy and the model of educators in other fields, particularly in medicine. Repeatedly idealists have urged the assimilation of psychoanalytic training into the graduate programs of medical schools, but with few exceptions this has been resisted—first because of the peculiar nature of the content and of the teaching method, and second, because of the intensity of the teaching program, which is so much greater than in other graduate medical curricula.

Almost from the beginning it was recognized that the process to be fully understood had to be experienced. However beneficial it might be in the training of the budding surgeon for him to be obliged to undergo a major operation in order really to know some important aspects of the process, it is not as yet required anywhere, so far as I know. In psychoanalytic training this experience is considered to be of the essence. It precedes all theoretical training and all practice. But it does not replace them.

The general theory and practical methods of psychoanalysis are now common knowledge in scientific circles. They have been expounded in a hundred volumes, best of all in the collected works of the founder. All psychiatrists become familiar with them in the course of their basic psychiatric training. But one who has undergone the experience of a personal analysis studies and comprehends psychoanalytic theory in a different way. It further illumines the past—his own experience—as well as the future—beginning with the experiences of his practice. Psychoanalytic practice begins as a supervised training, but it is based on the theory that has been studied and the process that has been experienced.

This book is about theory—the theory of the therapy. It is not a manual of practice, but an examination of some of the psychodynamic principles operative in the practice. It is the product of subjective experience and of objective experience—the latter with both patients and students. These experiences were shaped and enlightened by the guiding words of the many who have written for us to read. It has long been one of my functions in the Topeka Institute for Psychoanalysis to teach a course on the subject of technique; what follows in the pages to come is a written version of my seminar presentations. I have revised and enlarged my notes each year, and in doing so I have had the invaluable assistance of many students and faculty colleagues. I shall expressly acknowledge the assistance of some of these later.

But first I feel that I should say something more general to set the tone for the teaching spirit in which this material was prepared.

It was my good fortune to grow up with psychoanalysis in America. The year the Berlin Institute was being formed, I was a young psychiatrist getting acquainted with such leaders as Adolf Meyer, Smith Ely Jelliffe, A. A. Brill, Adolph Stern, C. P. Oberndorf, William Alanson White, and many others. My great teacher, Elmer Ernest Southard, had just died. Although he approved of the emphasis that psychoanalysis gave to psychology, which was ignored by most scientists of the time, he felt that psychoanalysis was pessimistic, that it dealt too little with constructive, practical, directive techniques. Had he lived longer I am sure he would have changed his mind, for he was the most open-minded man I ever knew, and saw in 1920 a vision of the potentialities of psychiatry that we are only now beginning to realize.

I can recall hearing one of our most promising young colleagues, just back from Vienna, describe to a small group of us at one of the annual meetings of the American Psychiatric Association his personal experiences in being psychoanalyzed by Freud. There were very few psychiatrists in those days, and few of these few would admit to an interest in psychoanalysis. We were all "neurologists," or "neuropsychiatrists" perhaps, or state hospital superintendents, or assistant physicians! Neurosyphilis rather than neuroses or "schizophrenia" was our most exciting area of interest. New diagnostic techniques had just been introduced, and those of us who could use these and who knew something about how to administer the wonder drug of the day (not penicillin, not chlorpromazine, not Salk vaccine —but arsphenamine!) were busy indeed. Untreated syphilis was then very common, and hence both acquired and congenital neurosyphilis were also abundant, although frequently masked. The reader will recall that Freud commented upon the large number of his neurotic patients who came from syphilitic parents, with the implication that congenital syphilis was a contributing etiological factor.

Psychotherapy of various sorts, although undoubtedly administered with good effect to many patients by the neurologists, was not regarded as really scientific. The neuroses were neatly packaged into "psychasthenia," "neurasthenia" and "hysteria." The reader will recall here how much Freud was influenced at first by this classification. And as for treatment, the Weir-Mitchell complete-rest-and-force-feeding regimen was far better known than the more rational programs of Janet, Dubois, Ribot, and others. Various placebo procedures—electrical, thermal, and mechanical—were prescribed and administered in the good faith that their suggestive value accomplished good in some mysterious way. The state hospitals were in a most pessimistic mood of therapeutic nihilism; no one was expected to recover from mental illness of any kind, and when recovery did occur, it was considered a miracle or a misdiagnosis.

And then, under the influence of Brill, Jones, Jelliffe, and others, psychoanalysis came to America where the psychology of William James, the philosophy of Josiah Royce, the psychiatry of Ernest Southard, and the psychiatry of Adolf Meyer were all developing. William Alanson White had much to do with the constructive fusion of these points of view through his diplomacy and leadership. He was friendly with everyone—the conservative hospital superintendents, the dignified neurologists, the effervescent and often provocative psychoanalysts, and the youngsters like myself who didn't know *what* they were. It was he who engineered the affiliation of the American Psychoanalytic and the American Psychiatric Associations and, with Brill, fathered the psychoanalytic section in the latter organization.

Nevertheless, it was a long time before psychoanalysis was really accepted. Ridicule, scorn, and denunciation met any attempt to discuss the new theories. No doctor with academic aspirations could afford to be associated with psychoanalysis or "the psychoanalysts." This, of course, made it all the more attractive to some alert and independent—and, we must add, rebellious—souls, and an element of martyrdom furthered the spirit of adventure in investigating the new theories and practices.

Here and there physicians over the country were, like myself, becoming "convinced" about the new method and wondering how and where (and whether) to obtain systematic training in its modus operandi. Everywhere—in psychiatric circles—it was being debated whether or not a personal analysis was a necessary prerequisite of the use of the method. The New York Psychoanalytic Society was almost torn asunder over the question, "with one crisis after another for five years," as Oberndorf described it in his history. My "success" with a few patients had almost convinced me that this special training was unnecessary, but it was being recommended. A few young psychiatrists undertook the trip to Europe, but formal training was begun in this country in New York, in 1929. In 1930 Franz Alexander came to Chicago as the first full-time psychoanalytic teacher (and university professor of psychoanalysis) in America. He offered didactic analysis to a group of us who two years later assisted him and Lionel Blitzsten and Ralph Hamill in organizing the second American psychoanalytic institute in 1932.

The prerequisite of a personal analysis, which so disturbed our psychoanalytic beginnings, has turned out to be the keystone of psychoanalytic training. More and more clearly we recognize that Freud's decisive step toward his greatest achievement was his courageous self-examination, his unparalleled self-psychoanalysis. More than anyone who ever lived, he followed those great historic adjurations, "Know thyself" and "Physician, heal thyself." Because of what Freud discovered, no psychiatrist today need be quite so much at the mercy of his own unconscious as in the days before Freud undertook this historic task and unveiled his revolutionary findings about the human personality for us all to see, and to test and to work from.

This book was written for students of the psychoanalytic method. Most of these will be candidates in psychoanalytic institutes. But there are many others who want to know what mysteries go on in the consulting rooms of the psychoanalyst! Time was when we would have considered it very bad indeed for prospective psychoanalytic patients to be told explicitly "what goes on"; we considered that it would work against the very effects of the treatment, by arming such readers with intellectual resistances. Today, however, such procedures of psychoanalytic sessions are so well known to most literate people from innumerable case reports that anything as dry and technical as these pages can scarcely make matters worse. Knowing from a book on botany that a green persimmon is astringent is quite different from knowing it by biting into one. Indeed, the essence of the psychoanalytic process is that reading about it and experiencing it are two quite different ways of "knowing."

Furthermore, I think the attitude of psychoanalysts has changed in regard to who should be given the experience of being psychoanalyzed. I am sure my own opinion has changed. I once regarded it not only as a great educational experience but also as a therapeutic program par excellence. True, Freud warned us against the emphasis on the therapeutic effect. Now I know he was right; therapeutic effect it does have, but, in my opinion, this is not its chief value. Surely there are quicker and less expensive ways of relieving symptoms and re-routing misdirected travellers. Psychoanalysis essays to change the structure of a patient's mind, to change his view of things, to change his motivations, to strengthen his sincerity; it strives, not just to diminish his sufferings, but to enable him to learn from them.

The educational value of psychoanalysis grows, in my mind. It is an intensive post-academic education, albeit an expensive one. We used to discuss whether or not it would be desirable for all those who could afford it to be psychoanalyzed. The better question is how to make it financially possible for all those who teach psychiatry and the social sciences to have the experience. I think it is more important for them to get a new concept of themselves, of human beings, and of the world so as better to guide their students than for a similar number of sufferers to be relieved of their symptoms. I trust this will not be taken to indicate hardness of heart; I have spent a lifetime attempting to relieve suffering. But as I see it now, the greatest good for the grestest number depends upon the application of the principles and knowledge gained from the science of psychoanalysis rather than upon its therapeutic applications in particular instances. To the educational value of psychoanalysis we must add its value as a research tool. No other therapeutic method has taught us so much about the human mind.

I shall, therefore, continue to teach and to search. This implies my continuance as a student. I am indebted to the teachings and counsel of my fellow workers Otto Fleischmann, Director of the Topeka Institute for Psychoanalysis, Rudolf Ekstein, Herbert Schlesinger, and H. G. van der Waals of our faculty who have sat in on the seminar discussions and have also gone over various drafts of the manuscript with helpful suggestions. Earlier drafts were carefully examined by Maxwell Gitelson of Chicago, Norman Reider of San Francisco, and Ralph W. Gerard of Ann Arbor. And when I think of the help I have had in various ways from other present and past associates—Robert Knight, Frederick Hacker, Jan Frank, William Pious, Merton Gill, Elizabeth Geleerd Loewenstein, my brother Will, and many others—I am loath to close these brief words of acknowledgment without naming many more. But the reality principle must prevail!

I give particular thanks to Philip S. Holzman of our faculty, who for the past two years has led the discussions of assignments which follow my sessions of the technique seminar. Doctor Holzman went over the manuscript carefully and made numerous suggestions and corrections.

Harry Roth, himself an author as well as an artist (and the husband of a psychoanalyst!), attended innumerable sessions of our seminar in order to grasp my intentions in the use of the blackboard and many colored chalks. The beautiful color transformations which he made of my highly schematic diagrams had to be abandoned for black and white drawings. These please me, and will—I trust—be helpful for some readers; by others they can be ignored.

The references and quotations will be found accurate, I believe, because they were conscientiously checked by librarians Vesta Walker of the Menninger Clinic Library and Elizabeth Rubendall and Bernice Stone of the Winter VA Hospital Medical Library. Mary Douglas Lee of our Publications Division helped me indefatigably with the proofs and index.

My final words of gratitude must be to Kathleen Bryan, who has typed each page of this book no less than ten times, but each time with care and alertness for repetitousness and other blunders. Those that remain will, I hope, be forgiven us and called to our attention for elimination in a later printing. With such fond hopes of a gentle, corrective reception, I join that great company of wistful authors who diffidently commit their fledglings to the skyways.

KARL MENNINGER, M.D.

Topeka
March 17, 1958

CONTENTS

Theory of
Psychoanalytic Technique

I

INTRODUCTION
AND
HISTORICAL REVIEW

IT IS A QUESTION WHETHER TO SAY THAT FREUD *invented* THE TECH-
nique of psychoanalysis, or that he *discovered* it.

He began with simple tools—a consulting office, a chair, a couch,
an attitude of concern regarding the sufferer's problem, an avowed
effort to help solve it. He listened. He listened and occasionally
questioned, without criticizing. Gradually he realized that he was
hearing more than the patient had intended to say, and was actually
gaining access to previously unconscious material. As he and his
patients learned more, they improved and he improved. He put
together a theory to explain the facts he discovered, then he collected more facts and corrected and extended the theory. Freud
differed from both his predecessors and his contemporaries in his
basic premise that the patients' symptoms were determined by, or
related to, earlier as well as current psychological experiences, in
addition to reflecting hereditary, constitutional, and physical factors.
He applied his method of inquiry and exploration even to himself,
and believed that it was from this experience that he learned most.

From the beginning he followed the scientific protocol of describing his procedures to colleagues as accurately as he could, hoping that they would make use of them and confirm or refute his findings. His original advice to those who would learn the technique was that they should follow the road that he had traveled, analyzing their own dreams, but it was not until 1913 that he explicitly recommended that those who aspired to become psychoanalysts should themselves be psychoanalyzed.* It was much later that he cautioned that acquiring the technique required considerable training.

Freud's earliest expressed theory of technique accompanied the therapeutic explorations he reported in 1895.[65] At that time he believed that in hysteria an idea becomes painful because it conflicts with the patient's values, ideals, and moral standards. The "ego" then exerts a counterforce or "defense," which pushes the idea out of awareness. The idea becomes pathogenic *because* it is repelled.† Treatment is, hence, properly directed toward overcoming the repelling force, the defensive "resistance." The idea then emerges, and the symptom disappears.

Freud's technique for overcoming resistances was to insist that an idea would come to mind, accompanying his words by pressure with his hand upon the patient's forehead. When a link to the forgotten experience emerged, as a fantasy, idea, or memory, it was then discussed with the patient.

Freud lectured on his technique of psychoanalysis before the College of Physicians in Vienna in December 1904. He described what he and Dr. Breuer had observed and gave Breuer credit for introducing a "novel therapy for the neuroses." Freud admitted with some pride that the theory, if not the practice, had gained ground with the profession. The technique, he said, had not been developed to the point that he could give systematic directions. He reminded

---

* "I count it one of the valuable services of the Zurich School of Analysis that they have emphasized this necessity and laid it down as a requisition that anyone who wishes to practice analysis of others should first submit to be analyzed himself by a competent person . . . not only is the purpose of learning to know what is hidden in one's own mind far more quickly attained and with less expense of affect, but impressions and convictions are received in one's own person which may be sought in vain by studying books and attending lectures."[59]

† One year later Freud believed that the repelled idea became pathogenic only if it could be associatively connected with childhood.

them that physicians could not dispense with psychotherapy, since patients have no intention of permitting that. He spoke well of hypnosis, encouragement, suggestion "exercise," and other types of psychotherapy but gave preference to his own "cathartic" method, which, like sculpture, "does not seek to add or to introduce anything new but to take away something, to bring out something." He assured them that it was not an easy technique, "to be practiced offhand, as it were." He reminded them that Hamlet's stepfather appointed two psychotherapists who were so clumsy in their efforts that Hamlet exclaimed, " 'Sblood, do you think I am easier to be played on than a pipe? Call me what instrument you will, though you can fret me you cannot play upon me."[63]

The most important thing about this early paper was Freud's explicit statement that psychoanalytic treatment makes great demands upon the patient as well as upon the physician—from the former, sincerity, time, and money and from the latter, laborious application and study. Some psychoanalysts have forgotten his next statement, which should be emphasized: "*I consider it quite justifiable to resort to more convenient methods of healing as long as there is any prospect of attaining anything by their means.*"

There are indeed some conditions for which psychoanalysis is the most effective treatment. Some conditions which in Freud's day were regarded as incurable can be ameliorated, if not entirely cured, by psychoanalytic treatment. But there are other conditions for which we are not sure that psychoanalysis is the best treatment, and still others for which we are quite sure that it is not the best treatment. Psychoanalysis is a major procedure in that it involves great changes in one's living habits. It is a long treatment, and an expensive one. The burdens it imposes sometimes cause more distress to the members of the family, if not to the patient himself, than did the original symptoms. The magic of the word *psychoanalysis* attracts patients and gives them a secret hope that if they can only be psychoanalyzed they can be cured of all their ills and troubles. The combination of a patient eager to be analyzed and a psychoanalyst eager to assist may lead to a scotomatization of the practical fact that the patient may not benefit clinically and unfortunately will have to spend a great deal of time and money finding this out.

This problem of length and expense of treatment has been a

thorn in the flesh of psychoanalysis since the earliest days. Time after time exponents of brief or briefer methods of psychoanalysis have appeared and, after a temporary spate of interest and notoriety, disappeared. Some may remember the three-month analyses promised and dispensed, for a time, by Otto Rank. On the other hand, psychoanalysis has been sharply criticized for its duration. Macalpine and Hunter[133] point out that as we learn more about a theory we should be able to make the practice shorter and more effective. Instead, analyses which formerly averaged a year or two now average twice that long. The treatment of tuberculosis, pneumonia, and other medical and many surgical conditions has been shortened as more has been learned about them. The same is true of most hospitalized psychiatric illnesses. But psychoanalytic treatment has lengthened.*

It was to be some years before Freud and other psychoanalysts became more specific about who might advantageously be psychoanalyzed and who might advantageously psychoanalyze. Freud published no more papers on technique until six years later, when he ventured a view of the "future prospects" of his therapy and mentioned countertransference and modifications of the technique required for certain conditions.[53, 68]

To resume our historical review, Freud's paper on dream interpretation in 1912 was a reprise of the famous study published in 1900. It emphasized again the fact that not every dream can or should be interpreted, but that probably each dream contains an image or a reflection of the total neurosis. In the same year he turned his attention to the relation between patient and analyst, no longer regarding transference as only a resistance to treatment as he had two years previously,[49] but as the most powerful force in the treatment process. "It is undeniable that the subjugation of the transference-manifestations provides the greatest difficulties for the

* Piers, Bornstein, E. Sterba, and others have addressed themselves to this problem, well summarized by Rudolf Ekstein.[27] In his second paper on technique, a section on psychotherapy in a textbook by Loewenfeld (1904), Freud himself took the position that psychoanalysis should be considered an after-education and mentioned that it might require from six months to three years. It was in this paper that he first described the basic rule specifically.[52] For an excellent discussion of the relationship of psychiatry to psychoanalysis see Hill.[96]

psychoanalyst; but it must not be forgotten that they only render the invaluable service of making the patient's buried and forgotten love emotions actual and manifest. . . ." Although Freud had already discussed positive and negative aspects of transference, he dealt at length only with the positive manifestations of the phenomenon and particularly with the erotic component in the positive transference.

In 1912 and 1913 Freud discussed in some detail a number of very important matters, such as the trial period of analysis, the effect of long preliminary discussions, difficulties encountered when friendship already exists between patient or his family and the analyst, the evaluation of the patient's attitude toward treatment, the frequency of appointments, the length of treatment, the use of the couch, the first communications, the wording of the fundamental rule, and the use of medical treatments during an analysis.* He had also begun to observe the influence of the patient's behavior and thoughts on the analyst's feelings for the patient. Whereas in 1910 he had recommended that the analyst "begin his practice with a self-analysis" to "overcome his counter-transference in himself," two years later he advocated that "anyone who wishes to practice analysis of others should first submit to be analyzed himself by a competent person," in order to become aware of those aspects of himself that would affect his understanding of his patient's disclosures.

In 1914 there appeared his important paper, "Recollection, Repetition and Working Through,"[61] in which he discussed the role of insight in the treatment. He had come to believe that merely understanding past events did not effect a cure, since people persistently tend to repeat their past over and over in their present actions and in the transference, despite "understanding." Interpretation was better directed toward understanding the repeating of past experiences that have become part of one's "general character," instead of just recalling them.

Then came a long silence regarding technique, except for the paper, "Lines of Advance in Psychoanalytic Therapy" in 1919,[66] which stressed abstinence as a fundamental requirement of

---

* Many of these considerations are contained in a series of papers on technique written between 1912 and 1915. See, for example, 60, 49, 59, and 61 in the Bibliography.

analysis,* and two papers on dreams. In the latter he emphasized that psychoanalysts must attend not only to the unconscious significance of the dream thoughts, but to the appearance in dreams of conscious preoccupations such as the analytic process itself or thoughts and events from the day before. The analysis of those conscious or preconscious thoughts, he reminded his readers, is as important as that of the repressed unconscious wishes that make dreams possible. "It is only too easy to forget that a dream is as a rule merely a thought like any other, made possible by the easing up of the censorship and by unconscious intensification and distorted by the operation of the censorship by unconscious elaboration."

Freud wrote no papers on technique for nearly twenty years, when he published "Analysis Terminable and Interminable," another shorter paper, "Constructions," and the chapter on technique in his book *An Outline of Psychoanalysis*. In these, his latter writings, while granting that psychoanalysis, like most forms of psychotherapy, helps many people, he acknowledged the limits of its achievements. It is neither definitely prophylactic nor permanently curative.

Thus technique, as such, was an early—and then a late—preoccupation of its discoverer. This is the more interesting in view of the fact that it may be this—the creation of an instrument of investigation—that will ultimately rank as his most important single contribution. Freud never devoted a book to technique, although several of his followers have done so. The first of these was Smith Ely Jelliffe, whose *The Technique of Psychoanalysis* was published in 1920. Jelliffe was a vigorous, forceful, articulate American leader whose basic training and early practice had been in neurology and whose prodigious acquaintance with both the literature and the leaders of the profession in all countries gave him a place of preeminence. He was early alerted to the importance of psychoanalysis and was per-

---

* "In order to secure these ideas and associations he asks the patient to let himself go in what he says, 'as you would do in a conversation which leads you from cabbages to kings.' Before he asks them for a detailed account of their case history he admonishes them to relate everything that passes through their minds, even if they think it unimportant or irrelevant or nonsensical; he lays special stress on their not omitting any thought or idea from their story because to relate it might be embarrassing or painful to them."[52]

sonally acquainted with Freud, Jung, and the early psychoanalysts. His written productions had a quality of condensation and elision that never quite did justice to his profound grasp of the subject matter, and his textbook, although occupying a primary position, never quite caught on. The same year Ernest Jones of England published a book on the technique of psychoanalysis; two years later came David Forsyth's clear, popular, but evanescent book. Ferenczi then published a collection of papers on the subject appearing in English in 1926 as *Further Contributions to the Theory and Technique of Psychoanalysis*. It was followed by the first edition of Glover's book in 1928, which again had the same title as Jelliffe's and Forsyth's.*

For nearly ten years no books on psychoanalytic technique appeared. Then the eminently practical manual by Lawrence Kubie, *Practical Aspects of Psychoanalysis*, was brought out as a guide to candidates, intelligent laymen, and colleagues to justify certain of the apparent rigidities and novel conventions of psychoanalytic procedures. Some of these still excite comment and dispute —for example, the fluctuating fee scale and the charging of medical colleagues for therapeutic assistance, which some consider to be in violation of the Hippocratic oath.

Since then many books on technique have appeared, emphasizing the principles and describing the practices of technique.† Most of them discuss the theory implicitly and, of course, it is also dealt with in various textbooks. But certain aspects of the theory behind the technique, although implicit in all these books, have not been dealt with sufficiently. The second and third generation of psychoanalysts developed here and there certain special points of view or emphases in the utilization of the basic psychoanalytic principles. These made for slightly differing concepts of the technique of psychoanalysis, sometimes overemphasized as unique departures (which they rarely were). Some of these systems have become so

---

* An excellent review, "The History of Development of Psychoanalytic Technique" was published by Sylvia Payne in 1946.

† Books in English are by Alexander,[1] Balint,[4] Berg,[10] Braatöy,[15] Deutsch,[18] Fenichel,[33] Ferenczi,[35] Forsyth,[43] Anna Freud,[46] Fromm-Reichmann,[71] Glover,[82] Greenson,[86] Jelliffe,[101] Jones,[103] Kubie,[114] Lorand,[129] Nunberg,[149] Reich,[164] Reik,[167, 168] Sharpe,[183] and Stone.[188]

divergent as to pass beyond the definition of psychoanalysis originally formulated by Freud and adhered to by the great majority of
psychoanalysts.

Having reviewed sketchily the history and bibliography of psychoanalytic technique, we will plunge directly into the subject
matter of our text—the theory involved in, and assumed by, the
procedure. We have tried to show how psychoanalytic procedure
developed prior to a comprehensive theory. The theory was only
formulated—and many times reformulated—as Freud and other
psychoanalysts had more and more experience with the empirical
method. No theory is ever complete, and the theory of why and how
psychoanalysis works will surely continue to undergo modifications.

The procedure of psychoanalytic treatment involves the classical medical model of patient and therapist, meeting in a one-to-one
relationship, and parting to meet again on succeeding days. A situation and an interrelationship develop, which we propose to examine
dynamically.

The psychoanalyst, unlike the medical physician, is not prepared to give help or relief to the patient as quickly as possible. It
was perhaps essential to the discovery of the psychoanalytic method
that Freud was so little driven by a *furor sanandi* that he was able to
restrain himself from the compulsion to do (or even to say) things
to the patient groaning, struggling through the various steps of self-
discovery. This restraint is very hard for the average young psychiatrist to exercise—with the exception of some very passive individuals
who seem to operate on the theory that healing rays emanate from
them so that patients should get well by sheer exposure to them.

Groddeck had a wisdom in this respect that paralleled Freud's.
Durrell quotes and paraphrases him in the following eloquent
words:

> The illness, then, bears the same relation to the patient as does
> his handwriting, his ability to write poetry, his ability to make
> money; creation, whether in a poem or a cancer, was still crea-
> tion, for Groddeck, and the life of the patient betrayed for him
> the language of a mysterious force at work under the surface—
> behind the ideological scaffolding which the ego had run up
> around itself. Disease, then, had its own language no less than
> health, and when the question of the cure came up, Groddeck

insisted on approaching his patient, not to meddle with his "disease" but to try and interpret what his It might be trying to express through the disease. The cure, as we have seen above, is for Groddeck always a result of having influenced the It, of having taught it a less painful mode of self-expression. The doctor's role is that of a catalyst, and more often than not his successful intervention is an accident. Thus the art of healing for Groddeck was a sort of spiritual athletic for both doctor and patient, the one through self-knowledge learning to cure his It of its maladjustments, the other learning from the discipline of interpretation how to use what Graham Howe has so magnificently called "The will-power of desirelessness": in other words, how to free himself from *the desire to cure*.[21]

To know when to wait, to know when to clarify, to know when to answer or to remind or to emphasize or to question—these are torturing problems for the beginning analyst. Most of them melt if this attitude which Groddeck has verbalized can be acquired and if the theoretical framework of the treatment can be grasped in a totality.

One cannot expect to find definite answers to such questions in books. Indeed, Glover[82] and again Bellak and Smith[7] have amply demonstrated that, although certain general principles and conceptions are held in common by most psychoanalysts, they do not agree very closely on specific matters of formulation, definition, prediction, and procedure. All the more reason, therefore, that a theoretical schema be set forth, as we are trying to do, that serves to map the way for the student. Older travelers will neither follow it nor need it.

There is another attitude which it is important for students to acquire. We regard the patient as telling us about himself when he talks, but we may take the view that the patient, during silences or other periods of strong resistance, is concealing information from us and from himself. *The patient is always communicating something,* always revealing himself,* even during periods of silence and even

* The following remarkable comment on the patient-physician relationship occurs in *The Scarlet Letter* by Nathaniel Hawthorne,

"He deemed it essential, it would seem, to know the man, before attempting to do him good. Wherever there is a heart and an intellect, the diseases of the physical frame are tinged with the peculiarities of these. In Arthur Dimmesdale, thought and imagination were so active, and sensibility so intense, that the

when he is less than candid. It is part of the art and technique of psychoanalysis to be able to divine what the patient is "really" saying when he is not "saying" anything or saying "something else." Together the patient and the analyst seek to discover what conflicts, impulses, defenses, resistances, attitudes, and themes are behind or within these various verbal and nonverbal forms of communication. The analyst remains the ally of the patient's ego as it struggles with the id and with various artifacts and defensive structures. This alliance is essential to psychoanalytic treatment. Although it is not curative in itself, it is a necessary condition for the melioration to occur.

The question is, how can one help candidates to acquire a proper "attitude"? Can it be taught? If so, how? Is the example of their own analysts sufficient to instruct them? One sound basis for learning is for the candidate to get an overall understanding of what he is trying to do and what the process is and where it is going, as one might belatedly acquire a map of an area that had been traversed in a cross-country trip. Learning to "do" analysis is not like learning to ride a bicycle that moves over familiar *terra firma*; it is more like learning to fly an airplane (or to soar in a sail plane). Air is very different from solid ground, and one must get a sense of the new and relatively strange medium in which he is operating. He must learn to think in terms of the unconscious motivation and "un-

---

bodily infirmity would be likely to have its ground work there. So Roger Chillingworth—the man of skill, the kind and friendly physician—strove to go deep into his patient's bosom, delving among his principles, prying into his recollections, and probing everything with a cautious touch, like a treasure-seeker in a dark cavern. Few secrets can escape an investigator who has opportunity and licence to undertake such a quest, and skill to follow it up. A man burdened with a secret should especially avoid the intimacy of his physician. If the latter possess native sagacity, and a nameless something more,—let us call it intuition; if he show no intrusive egotism, nor disagreeably prominent characteristics of his own; if he have the power, which must be born with him, to bring his mind into such affinity with his patients, that this last shall unawares have spoken what he imagines himself only to have thought; if such revelations be received without tumult, and acknowledged not so often by an uttered sympathy as by silence, an articulate breath, and here and there a word, to indicate that all is understood; if to these qualifications of a confidant be joined the advantages afforded by his recognized character as a physician,—then, at some inevitable moment, will the soul of the sufferer be dissolved, and flow forth in a dark, but transparent stream, bringing all its mystery into the daylight."

conscious language" of the patient and his own unconscious—as well as conscious—reactions to this language and the communications made to him. Freud himself compared analysis to learning to play a game of chess, with certain concepts of power and movement to be learned and fairly stereotyped opening and closing moves to be memorized but increasing originality required in mid-game. One very helpful adjunct might be the availability for careful study and responsible discussion of a library of recorded complete psychoanalyses such as Merton Gill[75] is attempting to compile. Such a library would permit a comparison of psychoanalytic techniques and thus force clarification of methods and results.

Another very helpful device in teaching is to provide a working model of the way psychoanalytic therapy operates. To do this requires one to resort to certain schematizations in the interests of developing a consistent skeleton of theory and practice. We shall make no effort to develop the many subtle implications and variations and complications of the psychoanalytic process, referring the student and the reader to some of the literature on these, and leaving them for subsequent study in the course of the candidate's maturation.

We propose to examine the essential dynamics of the interpersonal situation involved in the two-party contract or of psychoanalytic treatment. The late Dr. Maxwell Gitelson preferred the word *compact*, and Dr. Ralph Greenson prefers *alliance*. We shall apply these dynamic principles to the psychoanalytic treatment situation, pointing out the pressures and values that can be mobilized to favor verbalization by the patient to the listening therapist. These verbalizations are accompanied or followed by gratifications and frustrations that alter the balance of the relationship in such a way as to determine a "progressive" course. If the reader will note the topics of the chapters listed he will observe that the interactive reactions of both patient and therapist to each other in the process—compact, contract, alliance—are presented systematically and successively from their initiation to a point where the process terminates and separation occurs.

This overall view will permit us to examine the phenomena of transference, transference neurosis, regression, resistance, interpretation, and so on in a perspective that gives them a clearer meaning.

Some may object that this sharpness or clarity involves certain distortions or misrepresentations that result from oversimplification. But this is a perennial dilemma for the teacher: whether to make something clear or to make it completely accurate. To convey a model, a teacher must declare and diagram clearly what actually cannot be seen at all. The student must "learn" that things are so and so and such and such in order to be able to realize subsequently that they are *not* quite the way he learned them. But by that time he will have gotten into the spirit of the matter, and from this he may arrive at some approximation of the truth. And if he is a real student, he will continue to revise this approximation all his life.

II

THE CONTRACT

The Psychoanalytic Treatment Situation
as a Two-Party Transaction

THE WORD PSYCHOANALYSIS HAS COME TO HAVE TREMENDOUS VALENCE.
It is often casually misused by laymen to mean an interview with a
psychiatrist or a session of psychological testing or a course of psychotherapy. We overlook such blunders indulgently, but it should alert
us to the magic implications of the word. Although given a specific
definition by Freud, it is used in all kinds of ways and carries with
it an aura of mystery and transformation.

Any word of such profound implication, such varied applications, and such undisputed popularity can be exploited, and it is to
the credit of some dissidents like Adler and Jung that they made
explicit declarations that what they were doing and thinking was
not psychoanalysis. The word is, to be sure, not copyrighted, although the British Medical Society long ago made a definite pronouncement that clarified the meaning as being the Freudian
interpretation of personology and the Freudian technique of treatment. This book is in that tradition.

FOUR MEANINGS OF PSYCHOANALYSIS

Historically, psychoanalysis referred to a mode or technique of gaining access to the unconscious content of the mind. In this sense it was comparable to dissection or, more accurately, visceral explorations in the living human being. From such explorations there gradually accumulated a body of knowledge based on the data that had been obtained by this method. In this sense psychoanalysis might be said to correspond to anatomy or histology. Extending this knowledge further, a system of hypotheses has been developing to describe all psychological functioning more broadly, a science of personology, as it were, which perhaps corresponds, by analogy, to physiology. Finally, there is what most people think of first when the word is used, namely, the use of this approach to unconscious processes and this knowledge of psychological functioning and this concept of personology in a rationale and technique for treating certain kinds of patients in a certain way.*

Psychoanalysis as a treatment method falls logically within the broader genus of psychotherapy. Psychotherapy is the formal treatment of patients using psychological rather than physical or chemical agents, principally verbal communication.

Psychotherapy and psychoanalysis, like all treatments, are transactional and contractual in the sense that a sufferer petitions a therapist for help and, as the object of the latter's professional efforts, assumes the obligations of a client or patient. He contracts to cooperate with the therapist in ways to be mentioned, and to compensate him in terms mutually agreed upon. The therapist contracts to treat him in ways regarded as accepted and approved. Psychoanalysis, like other forms of psychotherapy, is based upon such a

---

* The adjective *psychoanalytic* is often used loosely to describe psychological approaches that emphasize motivation, and more precisely the viewpoint in psychology and in psychiatry that unconscious psychological forces, mechanisms, and processes are the basic material of the "mind." Perhaps the common factor in all these meanings or uses is the assumed existence and importance as well as the availability of unconscious motives and memories. Since we consider psychoanalytic treatment to be something essentially scientific, although not excluding art and skill in its application, we must do everything possible to exclude the element of magic.

compact and since this contract is a very important part of the treatment, we shall study it in detail.

TWO-PARTY CONTRACTS

Let us examine a few typical two-party interchanges or compacts of this sort. Suppose a vendor, whom we shall call V, is offering for sale only some apples. He is approached by a potential customer, C. We must assume, of course, that V actually possesses some apples and is relatively short of money; the purchaser, on the other hand, presumably wants apples (*e.g.*, he is hungry) and is not so short of money.

A transaction usually begins in a tentative way when the purchaser notices and approaches the vendor. It is continued, still without commitment, when the apples are exhibited and offered, when they are inspected by C, and when they are priced by V. But there is still no contract.

If it is mutually agreed that a fair exchange can be effected, the transaction is definitely consummated: The vendor gives an apple to the purchaser; the purchaser, in exchange, gives the vendor something of value, real or symbolic (*e.g.*, money). The purchaser is now in a position to relieve his hunger; the vendor is now in a position to increase his stock. The vendor now has fewer apples but more money; the purchaser now has less money but more nutriment. An even exchange has taken place; a balance has been struck; needs have been reciprocally satisfied. The transaction is closed, and the vendor and purchaser part company.* (See Figure 1.) †

Let us change the situation slightly now and assume that the vendor possesses not goods but certain skills, plus the ability and

* Even in such a simple bargain as this, various abstruse and recondite problems in psychology are involved such as the theory of decision-making in risky choice and in riskless choice, and the theory of games. For a discussion of these, see Ward Edwards[21], and Rapaport.[159]

† Here and later on we shall refer to and include diagrams that have been useful in visualizing in abstract form the principles to be described or emphasized. For some people diagrams like this are clarifying; for others they are confusing. The reader (or the teacher or the student) may therefore "take it or leave it."[158] The diagrams are not essential to the text.

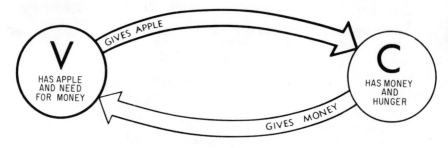

FIGURE 1

willingness to use them. Whether such services are as menial as scrubbing floors or as highly technical as surgery of the heart valves, the structure of the contract is the same. Let us assume that the services to be rendered are those of barbering. A general announcement has presumably been made that Barber *B* is able and willing to perform such services for a price. Customer *C* finds he needs a haircut. He approaches the barber, submits to the physical requirements of sitting in a barber chair and holding still; the barber wields his scissors. The performance finished, the barber accepts money and the transaction is completed (Figure 2).

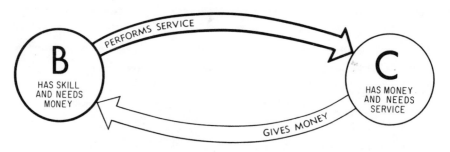

FIGURE 2

Here again we can assume that an even balance has been achieved. Each has gained by the transaction. The barber had an opportunity to exercise his skill and in addition he had the pleasure or prestige of the association. In addition he received money. The customer, on the other hand, was improved in looks and hence, presumably, in self-esteem. He also had the pleasure of companionship and a few minutes' rest. Both are presumably satisfied with the exchange.

Now the perspicacious reader may have been faintly troubled as he was reading the preceding pages by some fleeting thoughts that something was left out. Perhaps one may buy an apple that he doesn't very much need just because he likes the apple vendor. Some barbers depend upon their gossip or their funny stories to enhance the value of their services, while others are proud of providing restful silence for their customers. These important intangibles are dismissed lightly in economic theory as good will; they cannot be so lightly dismissed in the study of psychological contracts, nor are they as simple as the illustration suggests. Some of the intangible exchanges in psychotherapy contracts are completely irrational and irrelevant, defeating or assisting the purpose for which the contract was established.

Conscious factors of liking and disliking certainly enter the picture, but one of Freud's greatest discoveries was that unconscious factors quite at odds with the conscious ones are always operating in a transaction, in both directions. The complexity of the interplay is visible in an examination of the relationship of hypnotist to subject, concerning which Gill and Brenman wrote, ". . . hypnosis is a complex dovetailing relationship between the two participants wherein the overt role taken by the one is the covert (*i.e.*, secret) fantasy of the other. Thus while the hypnotist *overtly* seems the powerful figure, whether as a domineering tyrant or a boundless source of 'supplies,' he is *covertly* on the receiving end of this power and/or bounty. . . ."[77]

For several reasons the contract between a patient and a therapist is more complicated than that of the client and the barber. For one thing, the customer (patient) is—in this case—never so sure of just what he wants or of what he gets. For this reason, in part, the physician must have announced that he is qualified (medically trained), authorized (certified by the state), prepared (in the way of equipment and time), and willing to render services to anyone considering himself "sick," including the service of diagnosing the sickness and prescribing the treatment. Learning this, a sick man then approaches the physician and states his problem or complaint. In a sense this is a preliminary and tentative step in the contract. The physician gives the patient his attention, and having heard the patient's complaints, makes a decision as to whether he—the doctor

—can justifiably accept the responsibility of attempting to help this person as a patient. If the physician's decision is in the negative, no further contract exists; if he accepts the petitioner as a patient, he has, as we say, taken the case. He promises to seek the best way to help the patient. He will proceed, then, to get a history of the illness and of the patient; he will make various examinations. To questions and examinations the patient responds or submits, contributing his cooperation to the utmost of his ability. Except in pediatrics and psychiatry the refusal of this cooperation automatically terminates the contract.

As a result of the information obtained both by inquiry and by examination, the physician comes to certain conclusions. In the vernacular, he has "found out what is the matter." He then calls upon his experience and his knowledge of the procedure indicated by the pathology that he has discovered and formulates a plan of action. This is usually put in the form of a proposition. This proposition may be called an opinion, recommendation, prescription, medical order, or something else, but whatever it is called, it amounts substantially to recommendations regarding a procedure of intervention. The intent is to relieve the patient of suffering or disability. The doctor says, "I have found so-and-so about you; on the basis of these findings it is my conclusion that such and such a condition is present; for the treatment of such a condition, such and such a procedure has been found effective."

The procedure may require further services from this physician or may require the services of another physician or may be something the patient himself can carry out. In the first instance the contract continues; in the latter two cases it usually terminates after the advice is given.

Thus the patient-physician contract is usually not specifically and solely for the removal of symptoms, an eventuality that actually may not occur. The patient buys a "package"—the examination, the information translated to him by the physician from the latter's findings in that examination, and the advice drawn from the physician's knowledge about what can be done. If he accepts the treatment plan and the treatment actually is administered, he will pay for these services. The similarity and the differences between this con-

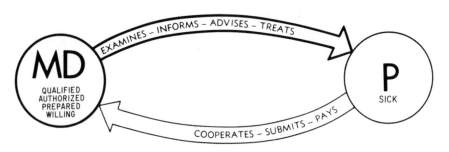

FIGURE 3

tract and those previously described are apparent in Figure 3. (The intangibles are again omitted for the time being.)

The purpose of all that we have been saying (and drawing) is to emphasize the following points: In any engagement between two individuals in which a transaction occurs there is an exchange, a giving and a gain of something by both parties with a consequent meeting of needs in a reciprocal, mutual way. When this balance is not achieved, either because one does not need what the other has to offer or because one does not give what the other needs or because there is the feeling on the part of one or the other that the exchange is not a fair one, the contract tends to break up prematurely. This is not to say it breaks up immediately, because the first effect of the awareness of dissatisfaction will be for one or both parties to attempt an improvement of the fault. In one sense, therefore, its incompleteness and unsatisfactoriness may be the bases for its continuance.

If one goes to a doctor to have a boil lanced or to a barber for a haircut, though the boil recur and though the hair grow long again, there is no sense of dissatisfaction with the contract. In the case of the man with tuberculosis or some other chronic illness, the treatment is a long, drawn-out affair in which presumably the doctor is paid not so much for doing something as for advising and trying to arrange and maintain a health-favoring situation. It may even be that while the doctor gains something, the patient gains nothing he had hoped for. But he does (did) receive the attention, counsel, and continuing effort of the physician, even if not a "cure." The patient comes to realize that it is for these intangibles that he has been paying and not for the relief of suffering or the dispelling of his affliction. And this is often applicable to the psychoanalytic contract.

THE PSYCHOTHERAPY CONTRACT

Of the four things which a patient buys from a doctor—examination, information, advice about treatment, and actual treatment—it is only the last one that we are going to discuss in this book. Our topic is not diagnosis, not the selection of patients best adapted for psychoanalysis, not the large problem of whether psychoanalysis should be the treatment of choice, not even the practical management of the treatment, but only the *theory* of one special kind of treatment. Some like to think of the psychoanalytic process as a long, continued *diagnostic* study, one in which the patient himself discovers the best thing for him to do for himself.

Although psychoanalytic treatment is conducted on the basis of a contract, it is an implicit one, rarely thought of in legalistic language. Nevertheless there is an advantage in doing so. One of our esteemed colleagues was much offended that in the first edition of this book we made use of legal terminology. We have done so purposely. The relationship *is* an implied contract and should be recognized as such; and has the essential features of *quid pro quo* that hold in all contracts. It *differs* from other contracts in several respects:

1. In a sales transaction, be it of goods, services or advice, the relations between the two parties are incidental to the goal. When one buys an apple, gets a haircut, or obtains an X-ray, whether one feels friendly or unfriendly toward the vendor is of no great moment. But in psychotherapy these relations are by no means incidental; they are basic elements in the transaction.

2. Ordinarily, transactions between people have defined time limits. A contract starts at some time and ends at another, specified time. When the apple has been bought, when the X-ray has been taken and paid for, when the lawyer's advice has been obtained, the contract is consummated—it ends then and there. When the need is felt anew, another transaction may be planned, and a new contract

made. Not so with psychotherapy. By definition, the goal of psychotherapy is betterment—amelioration, or growth, or maturation. It is
an open-ended process. It is essentially interminable, since there is
no predetermined specification of "mature," "healthy," or "comfortable." The termination of the contract in psychotherapy is decided
when the patient decides that from then on he can manage alone.
Even then this decision will be no more than a venture. In this
respect, psychotherapy is very much like learning: Even when one
may set a seemingly defined goal such as "the doctoral degree" or
"finishing college," the essence of learning is that it is an open-
ended experience—it can never be consummated.

3. Most contractual relations are confined to two parties, who
are named and described in the contract. The transaction between a
psychotherapist and his patient need not be confined to these two;
it may often involve other people to whom the patient is related.
The major part of all psychotherapy is focused on the patient's
relationship with others, and the transaction between the two parties
of the contract consists largely of an examination of the patient's
extracontractual relations. Often, the therapist must also relate himself directly or indirectly to some of the people in the patient's
sphere of living: spouse, parents, employer, physician, and so on.
Though the focus is on the two parties, the transactions are not
limited to a two-party space. In modern psychiatric therapy the
"case work" done by the social worker with various persons in the
environment serves this function of making the one-time two-party
contract into a triangular or polygonal one. (See Figure 4.)

All treatment can be classified into *subtractive* (*e.g.*, the removal
from the patient of something unwanted such as a tumor from a
woman's breast, or a cinder from a man's eye) ; *additive*, in which
the doctor, instead of taking something away from the patient, gives
the patient something to nullify the symptom (*e.g.*, a capsule of
medicine or a pair of spectacles); and *manipulative* or *alterative*,
in which the doctor neither gives anything to the patient nor takes
anything from him but does something that changes him (*e.g.*, the
doctor may reduce a dislocation or massage stiff muscles).

Psychotherapy partakes of these same modalities. It may be
additive in the sense of giving a patient hope, *subtractive* in the
sense of removing a fear, or *alterative* in the sense of redirecting

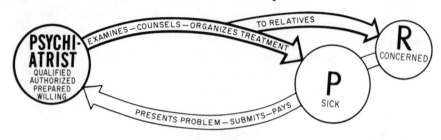

FIGURE 4

a patient in regard to a goal. But nothing *material* is given or taken away from the patient, and nothing tangible is done to him physically. There is no laying on of hands,* no utilization of instruments, no administration of medicines. What passes between the doctor and the patient are such things as words, gestures, smiles, nonverbal sounds, and the like. Patients sometimes distinguish between "talking doctors" and "real doctors," doctors whose contracts with the patient are physical and material. Even some physicians scarcely consider psychotherapy "treatment"; it seems to them more accurately a kind of "counsel" or "reeducation." But it is more than that.

Psychoanalysis, like all other psychotherapy, like the employment of a dermatologist or of a barber, or like the purchase of an apple from a street vendor, involves a certain balance of giving and of taking. And like all these other transactions, it also involves unconscious exchanges. In these everyday transactions, the intangibles cannot always be studied; in psychoanalysis they *must* be studied. Indeed, the observation and understanding of these intangibles constitute the essential uniqueness of psychoanalytic treatment, the way in which it differs from all other transactions. As we shall see, it is in respect to these intangibles, and particularly the extended unconscious meanings of them, that the psychoanalytic patient discovers himself increasingly frustrated in certain respects by the treatment, in contrast to the tendency in all other forms of treatment to be increasingly satisfied in the normal progress of the treatment. Of this we shall have much more to say in the next chapter.

---

* As the reader will recall, Freud originally used pressure on the forehead, and Groddeck and others used massage *with* the psychoanalytic listening.

PSYCHOTHERAPEUTIC DYNAMICS

It is necessary at this point to describe briefly one aspect of the dynamics of psychotherapy in general, to serve as a background for the subsequent discussion of the psychodynamics of the special form of psychotherapy represented by psychoanalysis.

Psychotherapy is of many kinds, not sharply differentiated from one another. The basic principle in all of them, however, is something like this: A patient comes to a person trained as a psychotherapist because of some kind of distress which the patient has been advised (or has come spontaneously to recognize) to be referable to the area that we call psychological. His symptoms may be psychological or they may not be; they may be physical symptoms or social ineptnesses. But the patient realizes or is told that these symptoms are connected with his thinking and feeling—in short, with his psychology. He is prepared, therefore, to accept treatment in psychological terms, to have certain false ideas taken from him, new ideas given to him, certain other ideas modified. (The word "ideas" is used with the understanding, of course, that emotions and behavior are always associated with them.)

Usually the patient does not clearly understand just how this ameliorative process is to occur or to be effected. But having told the doctor the nature of his distress, he is prepared for a response from the doctor in the direction of identifying or explaining psychological connections with this distress. The patient complains, for example, of attacks of headache; the physician may not need to say that perhaps these headaches are associated with disturbing experiences; the patient often takes this for granted or, if he does not, will assume it as a hypothesis. When the doctor asks him what events seem to have precipitated the headaches, the patient does not (usually) describe falling down the stairs or being hit on the head with a brick; he mentions the visit of his mother-in-law, or the approach of certain examinations. This gives the doctor a clue, and he asks more pointed questions, which in turn give the patient directives for further recollection or organization of his experiences in a way that leads to an explanation of the symptom.

It is very difficult to dispel the logical fallacy that one thus discovers the "cause" for a symptom. We know (but often forget) that no one thing, such as a symptom, is ever *caused* by any one other thing, such as an event. In the alphabet, *C* follows *B* but is not caused by *B*, nor *B* by *A*. Many things contribute to a totality of stress, which is sometimes relieved by "symptoms" and sometimes by other means. When headaches are found to be related to an inexpressible hostility felt for the mother-in-law, this means to the patient that the mother-in-law "causes" the headaches, or at least that his hatred for the mother-in-law "causes" them. Of course, both statements are false, as Tolstoy[194] eloquently expressed in his intuitive perception of all that Hume arrived at so elaborately: "The combination of causes of phenomena is beyond the grasp of the human intellect. But the impulse to seek causes is innate in the soul of man."

It is an empirical observation that a patient will frequently come to "understand" the origins and meaning of a symptom and, simultaneously, feel better to an astonishing degree. Is the process of discovery the "cause" of the improvement or the "result" of an improvement already in process? Something must have changed in his defensive structure to permit the formerly forgotten or neglected unconscious bit to become conscious. And then the discovery may assist him in rearranging his life in such a way as to avoid the precipitant or handle it better. Or he may go on to further discoveries.

This, to be sure, is a greatly oversimplified illustration. Most psychotherapy is a *continuing* process, rather than a single-step event. The typical medical patient, having accepted a treatment program in medication that has presumably accomplished its effect, recovers, pays his bill, and separates himself from the physician—and the transaction is closed. In psychotherapy, however, the treatment is not a passive submission but a give-and-take exercise which is apt to be a long, drawn out—if not, indeed, interminable—process, and might be experienced at times as a kind of extended examination. The "irritating points" have to be sought mutually by the patient and the psychotherapist in order for a change to occur.

We would not leave the impression that psychotherapy consists only in such a search. As everyone knows, much of the activity of psychotherapy has to do with the repeated correction of certain patterns of reaction (behavior) which lead to the production of the "symptom." We sometimes refer to this in rather grandiose unclarified terms; we speak of strengthening, expanding, or reinforcing the ego, making it more elastic and better able to handle the inevitable tensions of variable life experiences. This involves such things as repeated clarifications of purpose, pointing to unrecognized self-destructiveness, recalling neglected considerations, freeing oneself for constructive activities and more expeditious planning for the future.

But the process of doing this can, we insist, be brought back to a kind of continuous, progressive, mutual exchange and stimulation. The patient presents the doctor with a fact—let us say, a complaint; the therapist is given thereby a certain partial orientation and is enabled to ask a more pointed question of the patient. This directs the patient's attention and thinking toward a further self-exploration, the communication of which may enable the therapist to make another comment. This comment throws a new light on something for the patient and enables him to add further material that then still further enlightens the physician, who may then still further assist the patient objectively to appraise himself, and so on.

This differs from an ordinary conversational dialogue in that both the physician and the patient have a definite and identical purpose, that purpose being to change the patient's ideas or emotional reactions or behavior or all of these in such a way as to diminish his suffering. In this, it is the therapist's responsibility to watch the compass and guide the direction of the process. He is, at all times, "in charge" of the general situation; how he manages this relationship, including the verbal interchange, differs in psychoanalysis most conspicuously in his much greater relative inactivity. (See Figure 5.)

In a personal communication, our colleague, Dr. Herbert Schlesinger, says:

> One of the difficulties in teaching analytic technique stems from the series of dilemmas in which the would-be psychoanalyst is placed. These represent paradoxes, or as I prefer to think about them, "dialectics," the synthesis of which must be accomplished individually by each psychoanalyst. For example, you state here that the physician is "in charge" and yet, of

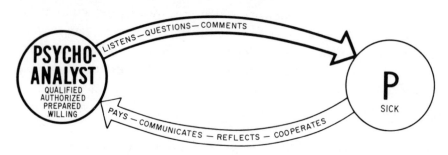

FIGURE 5

course, his purpose is to demonstrate to the patient that he (the latter) is really in charge not just of the treatment but of his life. Elsewhere it was implied that the physician must sincerely want to get the patient "well." Yet, to accomplish this, he must achieve an attitude of "desirelessness." There are, I believe, a number of such paradoxes, the continuous effort at resolution of which leaves its mark on the self-concept of the psychoanalyst. Incidentally, I believe it is the last mentioned "dialectic" that perhaps makes many "old-time psychoanalysts" suspect the orthodoxy of those analysts who also do psychotherapy, as if to do mere psychotherapy would imply too much "wanting the patient to get well" on the part of the psychoanalyst.

The whole question of the meaning of activity and passivity (or inactivity), with respect to the analyst's functioning deserves a careful discussion. I think one must distinguish sharply the analyst's relative inactivity, meaning that he does not often say or do very much that could be identified as such by an outsider, from the enormous effects that his judicious abstention from interfering can have. By way of an extravagant analogy, a person who watches another commit suicide without interfering would not be adjudged to have been "inactive."

Even though the psychotherapeutic process is continuous, each separate session is a partially completed contract. The patient pays his money and presents his problems and answers the questions posed; in return he is listened to, questioned further, and instructed, advised, or at least talked to. He may or may not feel any better, but in this respect he is no different from many medical or surgical patients who go to their physicians for treatment. It should be remembered that he is not paying money for relief; relief is what he wants, but what he pays for are the professional services of the psychotherapist.

THE PSYCHOANALYTIC CONTRACT

The indefiniteness of this time period is one of the greatest complications in the psychoanalytic contract. It makes it necessary for the party of the first part to pay his money (which is admittedly not *all* of his contribution to the contract) in divided portions against the expectation of an *ultimate* fulfillment of obligation by the party of the second part. This is not a simple case of open-end contract, because the party of the first part pays in full, hour by hour, as he goes along, but the party of the second part seems not to! The party of the second part delivers immediately and from the beginning one very essential factor in the fulfillment of the contract: he sets up the unique situation of psychoanalytic treatment. The audience room, the couch, the insured privacy, and so on, are the mechanical elements in this. Then and thereafter the psychoanalyst stands by, *ready* to serve and doing so largely by listening, occasionally by speaking, always attempting to "understand" the patient. He endeavors to see all of the given facts in a perspective that gives them a rational relationship. His verbal participation is relatively sporadic and irregular, and its full value depends upon a continued, developing process in which he participates through empathy all the time.

All this is well known to every psychoanalyst, but it is not known (or clearly understood) by the patient at the time he starts. Thus the patient enters into the contract more than a little blind, which makes it all the more important that the established "rules of the game" be conscientiously adhered to by the psychoanalyst.

These "rules" were worked out empirically by Freud, and they have been little improved upon or changed since his formulations of 1913, in "The Further Recommendations on the Technique of Psychoanalysis,"[59] a paper that every candidate should almost memorize. The tentativeness of the contract, the avoidance of lengthy discussions of the prognosis, the minimizing of conscious favorable or unfavorable attitudes toward analysis and the analyst, the definiteness regarding time and money arrangements, the clear option of the patient to stop whenever he wishes, the use of the couch and the elimination of the analyst from the patient's vision, the assignment of complicating medical problems to a colleague, and finally, the clear enunciation of the basic rule—these are features that the candidate will have learned by precept and example. But in spite of such instruction, the beginning analyst will often fumble the preliminary arrangements through a failure to understand the peculiar nature of the contract involved in psychoanalytic treatment. For this reason it is my (K.A.M.'s) own teaching practice to use role-playing by various pairs of candidates in seminars. Various practical problems are assigned them for solution, and each candidate acts as prospective therapist and prospective patient.* An excellent didactic method would be the examination of recorded psychoanalyses conducted by skilled, experienced psychoanalysts. Gill *et al.* argue that the endangerment of confidentiality and the existence of a goal in addition to a therapeutic one are not *prima facie* objections to recording psychoanalyses and using them subsequently for teaching purposes. Indeed, similar features are shared by the didactic analysis of every candidate. In theory, there is no contradiction to such teaching procedures, and they have much to recommend them.[78]

Perhaps the most important rule is that the psychoanalyst must be careful about what he promises to deliver. From one point of view the essence of psychoanalytic treatment is intellectual honesty, and no one honestly can predict with definiteness what the future will bring. Yet if the analyst did not expect to see improvement, he would not start—and so taking the case is an implied prediction. The analyst cannot promise cure; he cannot even promise relief. He can only promise to try to help the patient by a method that has helped others and on the condition that the patient try to help himself.

In this sense, every psychoanalysis is a "trial analysis." But while this should be made clear to the patient before he starts, to empha-

---

* The reader is referred to Kubie's excellent book[114] on the practical aspects of treatment, Greenson's longer and more theoretical book[86] and Greenacre's wise counsel in her article on transference.[85]

size it sounds too threatening, and certainly no special point needs to be made about it. In making the preliminary arrangement, discussing the probable length of treatment, and so on, the analyst should be careful not to give the impression that although he calls the first months of the treatment a trial period, he has actually made up his mind already.

MONEY

An important problem in the setting up of the original contract is the question of money. Freud reminded us of how hypocritical and evasive we all are about payment for getting and giving help. This is less of a problem today than it was thirty years ago, because patients have learned about what to expect in the way of psychoanalytic fees, and a rough standard prevails in most communities. It is the departure from these standards and the complications of the now common practice of third-party payment that will tax the skill of the young analyst. For the purposes of this text, which has to do with theory rather than the practice of analysis, it is sufficient to emphasize a few basic principles.

The analysis will not go well if the patient is paying considerably less than he can reasonably afford to pay. It should be a definite sacrifice for him, for *him* and not for someone else. Sometimes it is inevitable that someone else will have to make a sacrifice too, such as a wife or parent, in order for the treatment to be paid for, but innumerable complications arise if a patient pays for analysis with the largesse of a relative, a friend, or a Foundation to which he has no effective responsibility for repayment of some sort.

On the other hand, complications also arise if the patient pays more than he can afford. In an effort to please the analyst or to make a good impression, some patients will agree to a higher fee at the beginning of an analysis than they are able to continue paying as the analysis runs on longer and longer. Some analysts take the position that usually, if money is a serious problem, psychoanalysis is not the treatment of choice. Most patients should not expect to pay for analysis out of current earnings (although some do) ; it is a capital investment, and justifies borrowing. All sorts of occurrences—the unexpected illness of a wife, the loss of a job, and so forth—make this slightly risky, to be sure. The time may come when the patient cannot pay anything, and the analyst will then have to decide whether he can afford to continue treatment without compensation or whether he can afford, for reasons of professional obligation and human concern, to do otherwise. This is not just a question of the therapist's generosity, because a free treatment is apt to be more difficult because the patient tends to feel under obligation. However, Lorand and others have reported success with nonpaying patients.[130, 121]

It is generally agreed to be undesirable for the patient to be permitted to run into debt to the analyst. Bills should be rendered monthly and paid monthly. There is no need to go into a long discussion of this with the patient but he should be told that it is one of the "rules" of the treatment. Chronic failure to pay the analyst's fee usually represents "acting out," that is, the tendency for certain unconscious tendencies to manifest themselves in action rather than in consciousness.*

The analyst should at some time explain that psychoanalytic appointments cannot be cancelled, that telephoning a prospective nonappearance does not imply the cancellation of the fee for that particular hour. This may come as a surprise to some patients. The reason for this measure is to forestall the use of "excused" absences as resistance of a sort difficult to analyze. Of course, the analyst must also keep his absences to a minimum to reduce the objective basis for resistance, and to avoid interruption of the analytic work process.

RELATIVES

Among the problems often arising in the initiation of an analysis is the matter of spouses, relatives, and close friends of the patient. In order to protect the peculiar patient-therapist relationship char-

---

* From a study of thirty-six patients who failed to pay their psychoanalytic fees, Gedo had concluded that withholding of payment represented an unanalyzed desire to retain a symbolic tie to the analyst and thus to deny the separateness of patient and therapist.[73] Allen and Hilles essentially confirmed Gedo's general observation.[97, 2]

acteristic of psychoanalysis nonanalytic contacts with the patient are avoided. But the question will arise whether the analyst should see the wife or the husband or the mother, who are very often worried and eager to meet the patient's doctor. All the young analyst has to remember about this is that such meetings may impair or complicate the patient-therapist relationship, but to omit them may impair the relationship even more! It seems absurd to stand on the principle that one has nothing to say to anyone but the patient. Our impression is that it is often out of laziness, or lack of self-confidence, that many analysts refuse to see close relatives, thereby handicapping their efforts with the patient.

Some analysts make it a routine practice to see the husband or wife early and explain to the patient the reasons for this.* It provides an opportunity to see what the spouse "looks like" (which is often very different from the impression given by the patient), and to warn him against premature reactions to the patient's behavior during the treatment. This often gives great reassurance, especially to insecure, apprehensive, and troubled relatives. But it is only fair to add that sometimes it "contaminates the field," as Greenacre[85] put it, impairing the surgical asepsis of the process.

Analysts sometimes forget that psychoanalysis may involve considerable sacrifice and suffering to the relatives of the patient, over and beyond the burden to the family treasury. Sometimes, as Henri Ellenberger put it, they experience an unpleasant "one-way-vision-room" effect; that is, they feel themselves seen and heard about in a distorted way, by an unseen psychoanalyst to whom they cannot explain and refute.

Then there are always the "acting out" episodes, in which the patient takes out on relatives what he should talk out to the psychoanalyst, and it cannot be expected that relatives unfamiliar with the theories of psychoanalysis can be as tolerant or understanding of such acts as is the analyst. Finally, there is always some envy of the patient's opportunity to be listened to, understood, and helped. Must one get "sick" to have this boon?

* My own practice has been to see the relative, at the patient's request, during one of the hours usually occupied by the patient, reporting the interview briefly to the patient afterwards. Usually I tell the patient beforehand what I intend to say or not say. [K.A.M.]

FREQUENCY OF TREATMENT SESSIONS

Another initial question is that of how frequently the analytic session should occur. This has undergone much discussion in recent years, partly because of the greatly increased number of patients seeking psychoanalytic treatment, partly because of the (American) trend to shorten the work week, and partly because of certain theoretical propositions made by one group of analysts who hold that the frequency of visits should be variable at the discretion of the analyst. Originally patients were seen six times a week. Five times a week is now perhaps the prevalent standard in this country, and four times a week a minimum.

Dr. Phyllis Greenacre has stated precisely what most of us believe about the frequency of treatment sessions and stated it so clearly and well that I would like to quote the passage in full:

> It is well to have analytic sessions spaced sufficiently close together that a sense of continuity of relationship (between analyst and analysand) and of content of material produced may be sustained. It would seem then that as nearly as possible a daily contact avoiding frequent or long gaps in treatment is desirable. In the setting of the organization of most lives, the analysis takes its place in the work of the week and accordingly five or six sessions are allocated to it. Later in many analyses it may be desirable to reduce the number of sessions, after the relationship between analyst and analysand has been consolidated, and the analyst has been able to determine the analysand's reactions to interruptions, first apparent in the reactions to week ends. If the analysand carries over a day's interruption well, without the relationship cooling off too much or the content being lost sight of, then it may be possible to carry the analysis on a three- or four-session-a-week basis, keeping a good rhythm of work with the patient. The desirability of this, however, can only be determined after the analyst has had a chance to gauge the patient's natural tempo and needs and the character of his important defenses; and this must vary from patient to patient. This initial period is generally at least a year, and more often longer.
>
> There are three additional unfavorable factors here, however, which are seldom mentioned: (1) The actual prolongation of the treatment by spreading or infrequent spacing of ses-

sions, in analytic work as well as in other psychotherapeutic approaches. If this prolongation is great, there is that much longer impact on other arrangements of the patient's life. "Brief psychotherapies" are sometimes paradoxically extended over very long times indeed, being repeatedly ended and reopened, because little was consolidated in the treatment and all sorts of extraneous and unnecessary interferences entered. (2) The larger the number of analytic patients possible at any given time when sessions per patient are less frequent, the greater the tax on the analyst in keeping at his mental fingertips the full range of facts and reactions belonging to each patient. The monetary recompense may, however, be greatly increased. Here again the feasibility of spacing must depend on some factors belonging to the analyst's special equipment and demands, combined with the patient's ability to "carry over," and there will inevitably be considerable variability in these. (3) The less frequent the therapeutic sessions the greater may be the risk of inadequate analysis of the negative transference. Especially with those patients where hours are made less frequent because the patient is thought by the analyst to be "wasting the hour" by what appears as unproductive talk or by silence, or where the analyst fears that the patient is feeling guilty over his silences, it has sometimes been recommended that the patient be given a vacation from treatment or that sessions be made less frequent. From my experience in the reanalysis of a number of patients, it has seemed to me rather that many of these periods are due to the patient's difficulty in expressing hostile or erotic feelings. It is about these feelings, rather than about his silence, that he feels guilty. Too often if he is given a rest or hours are made infrequent, these emotional attitudes are never brought out to be analyzed, and appear later on in disturbing forms. I am further impressed with the fact that those analysts who talk most about the dangers of dependence seem rarely to consider the reciprocal relationship between tenacious dependency and unanalyzed negative transference. In so far as negative attitudes toward the analyst are not analyzed or even expressed, the need of the patient to be reassured of the love and protection of the analyst becomes enormously increased and demanding. The analyst may see only this side of the picture and erroneously attempt to deal with it by greater spacing of contacts.

The length of the hour is, as a matter of practice, generally maintained at forty-five to sixty minutes. Certainly it is desirable that a sufficient span of time be permitted for a kind of natural organic pattern of productivity to occur during many of the sessions. The hour is our time unit in general use, perhaps because it does involve some kind of natural span of this kind, and is a feasible unit fitting into the working day. While there have been many experiments of speeding up analytic sessions to two a day or increasing the length to two hours at one session, no such practice has generally taken hold. It is my belief, however, that a regular allotment of time—the same duration and so far as possible on a prearranged and constant week-by-week schedule (in contrast to varying spans of time in sessions at irregular periods not expected in advance)—generally aids in the rhythm and continuity of the work and minimizes utilization of external situations as ressitance by the patients.[85]

For reasons that will become increasingly clear as we go on, the psychoanalyst must *try* (and it is not easy) to remain neutral and "aseptic." This means that one doesn't "side" with either the drive aspect of the patient's conflicts, or with the inhibition of them. Nor does one socialize with patients, touch them unnecessarily, ask favors of them or accept favors or gifts from them.*

OTHER DETAILS

An important detail in practice relates to necessary interruption of treatment by the analyst. These are of several kinds. A brief absence, unless it occurs at a very critical period, can be explained to the patient as it arises (at the end of an hour several days before the analyst is leaving). The analyst who "begins" a patient's hour by an announcement violates his own statement of wanting to hear the spontaneous free association material of the patient's mind. It is bad manners, and it is a technical error. The exception to this is the situation developing when the patient consistently suppresses or

* Comments Dr. H. G. van der Waals:

"I think every analyst in Europe, at least every analyst I know, shakes hands with his patient at the beginning and the end of the hour. It gives valuable information about the mood of the patient, his reaction to the hour, etc. In Europe it would be a technical error not to do this; patients would think it very queer.

"As a general rule an analyst should not accept gifts, but he should also know when to make an exception. When a patient who has great difficulty in giving anything is able in the course of his treatment to make the analyst a small present, it would be a serious mistake not to accept the gift."

represses his reactions to "end-of-the-hour" events, such as receiving his bill. This makes it necessary for the analyst to take it up, artificially, in subsequent sessions. Longer absences, such as vacations, the patient will half expect. But no patient should be abandoned for a month a few weeks after beginning an analysis. If this is unavoidable, as in the case of emergency, the analyst should recognize that he is breaking the terms of the contract, and make the best compromise he can in reparation. Sometimes this involves finding another analyst for the patient. Sometimes it involves keeping in nonanalytic contact with the patient during the absence. Analysts who get married or divorced during the course of the analysis of a patient can expect plenty of trouble. It is impossible to keep knowledge of these things from the patient, and they always cause serious, sometimes devastating, reactions.

The psychoanalyst is a psychotherapist, and the fact that he is also a psychiatrist and a physician or a psychologist is less important now. *As far as this patient is concerned,* the psychoanalyst is a specialist and not a general medical practitioner. He has not contracted, and should not undertake, either to diagnose or treat intercurrent physical affections. The patient may be justified in expecting him to have medical knowledge and to answer some other types of relevant questions within his competence; but if the patient needs much medical information or examination or treatment of physical diseases, he should be referred to a colleague. This keeps the emphasis of the analysis on the psychological plane.

There are a few other matters of importance in connection with the sealing of the original contract. The patient does not know exactly what the treatment is like. He may believe that he will be immediately and progressively better and wiser. He should be warned, therefore, that this is not necessarily true, that analysis can be an upsetting and *then* a restorative process, and that important moves and decisions in the life program should be deferred until the analysis is complete or thoroughly discussed in the analysis. This applies to such things as marriage or divorce, change of occupation, and so on.

In spite of all the preparatory instruction, which should be minimal, and in spite of the (now) widespread popular familiarity with some features of the treatment, the patient who contracts with a therapist for psychoanalytic therapy does not really know what he is letting himself in for. To be sure, the same might be said of various surgical operations and other technical procedures in modern medicine. But the very nature of psychoanalysis, in opening a way for the direct expressions of previously unconscious material, makes it peculiarly exotic, strange, and unimaginable. What the patient is unconscious of he naturally does not know, by definition. In theory he understands this, but only *after* he has had the experience of being psychoanalyzed does he fully appreciate the depth and power of the forces and mechanisms of the unconscious.

The patient who submits himself for psychoanalytic therapy begins with a certain blind faith in the psychoanalyst, regardless of the disclaimers he may profess. He begins, too, with various hopes and expectations, regardless of the skepticism he may express. As we shall see, these are actually far more specific than he realizes, and may have little to do with "getting" or "being" well in the conventional sense of the words. And finally, he has some fears, most of which are unrealistic to be sure, but disturbing nonetheless.

But his faith is not entirely blind, if he has been well advised. For the psychoanalyst has certain scientific and ethical obligations. The patient does not know just what will happen, but he should have reason to believe that he may advantageously enter into a contract with this fellow human being and expect professional integrity and competence. The patient's fears thus tend to return to his own inadequacies, his own incompetence to fulfill a contract. And he may be right. It is the task of the analysis to forestall this failure if possible, to defeat this defeatism, or—in the occasional sad instance—to recognize that it is invincible and gently redirect the seeker toward more attainable goals.

III

THE REGRESSION

The Reaction of the Party of the First Part to the Psychoanalytic Treatment Situation

GIVEN THE PRIVILEGE OF SAYING WHATEVER ONE IS THINKING TO A listener who refrains from excessive or discouraging interruption, an individual seeking therapeutic help will experience both a gratification and a growing frustration. This process leads to the unmasking of the original wish to be cured and the appearance of more primitive, less conscious wishes and the employment of techniques that once applied to expectations of other kinds from other persons. This regressive trend includes fluctuations and variations in the self-estimate, the body image and the ego-ideal. It develops or appears in waves and cycles at variable speeds, with much alternating and frequent reformulating. By maintaining a steady position of attention and nonreaction, the analyst assists in the process, by acting as a sort of polestar, for orientation.

One undergoing psychoanalysis soon realizes that he has become involved in a most extraordinary process. It is so familiar and routine to some of us that we forget how remarkable this situation really is. A patient who has come to a doctor for relief from his pain is invited to lie down and to talk about it, or about *anything else* he chooses! He may talk about himself, he may talk about his neighbors, he may talk about his wife. He may talk about the past, present, or future. He does not have to be fair; he does not have to be considerate, he does not have to be objective. Everything is to be considered "tentative"—an opinion as of this moment only. The main object of the procedure, as it is explained to him, is that he present his uncensored thoughts and feelings to the joint observation of himself and his unseen listener. Thus he may—indeed *must*—say anything that comes into his mind, which is something he cannot do in *any other existing human situation.*

It is little wonder that patients often find difficulty in taking advantage of such opportunity immediately. But the uniqueness of the situation is apt to be preconsciously grasped so that the first few sentences spoken by a patient after the psychoanalyst has seated himself and announced his attentiveness often evade all screening and give important clues about the nature of the deepest problems. Then, after the introductory phase, the patient's "natural" resistance is aroused and he only gradually feels his way into this unparalleled situation of "free thought" and "free speech." With more or less difficulty, sometimes with eagerness and sometimes with trepidation, he starts talking.

For one hour he pours out his thoughts, helter-skelter, into the ears of the physician. To all of it the physician listens, but makes little response except to indicate his close attention. He makes no suggestion. He gives no comfort. He makes no criticism. He gives no diagnostic opinion. He only listens.*

Grateful for the attention and audience and intrigued by the new experience, the patient pays his money (in credit) and takes his leave; one unit of the transaction is completed. On the following day the patient returns, reclines, recites. Once more he gives, and gives, and gives. He tries his best to do as he thinks the analyst wants him to. He submits his "free associations," his memories, his reflections, his confidences, his intimate thoughts, his gravest fears. Again

---

* It is not quite correct to say he "only" listens or to imply that he is stiff and silent as a statue. We will clarify this later; here we are schematizing the relationship.

the analyst listens and is silent (and does *not* "give"). Again the patient pays and leaves.

This process of free association in the sense of verbalizing one's random thinking is really a most extraordinary phenomenon with a long history. Something like it appears to have been used by the Greeks, if we may judge by the sample reported in Aristophanes' comedy, *The Clouds*. They even used a couch!*

According to Freud,[58] Friedrich Schiller in his correspondence with Koerner in 1788 recommended that anyone who desired to be productive should adopt this method. Freud[58] also mentions Ludwig Boerne's article entitled "The Art of Becoming an Original Writer in Three Days," written in 1823, which pretty well described free association. Freud also referred to Havelock Ellis' discovery of the publication by Dr. J. J. Garth Wilkinson in 1857 of "A New Method" of writing poetry, which was essentially free association.† William Lecky,§ the English historian, specifically de-

---

* The story is that Strepsiades, an unhappily married, stupid, and dishonest farmer, comes to Athens to consult Socrates as to how one can successfully cheat his creditors. Socrates directs him to lie down and give free associations, which he tries to do, in spite of bedbugs, and other interruptions, while Socrates points out inconsistencies and inferences. The play thus ridiculed the teaching of Socrates. See the Benjamin Rogers translation in *Fifteen Greek Plays*.[173]

† The reader is referred to an interesting paper by Trosman[197] on the possible influence of the Boerne article on Freud's development of the free association method.

§ In *Rationalism in Europe*, Vol. II, 1865, quoted by Oberndorf[152] as follows:

"That certain facts remain hidden in the mind, that it is only by a strong act of volition they can be recalled to recollection, is a fact of daily experience, but it is now fully established that a multitude of events which are so completely forgotten that no effort of will can revive them, and that their statement calls up no reminiscence, may nevertheless be, so to speak, embedded in the memory, and may be reproduced with intense vividness under certain physical conditions.

"But not only are facts retained in the memory of which we are unconscious, the mind itself is also perpetually acting—pursuing trains of thought automatically, of which we have no consciousness. Thus it has been often observed that a subject which at night appears tangled and confused, acquires a perfect clearness and arrangement during sleep.

". . . In the course of recollection, two things will often rise in succession which appear to have no connection whatever; but a careful investigation will prove that there is some forgotten link of association which the mind had pursued, but of which we are entirely unconscious. It is in connection with these facts that we should view that reappearance of opinions, modes of thought, and emotions belonging to a former stage of our intellectual history. It is especially common (at least especially manifest) in languor, in disease, and above all, in sleep."

scribed the existence of unconscious connections between thoughts in 1865. Long before, Plotinus[155] (204–270 A.D.) and then Leibniz[118] (1646–1716) had explicitly pointed out the existence of unconscious mental connections.

Hobbes, in *Leviathan* (1651), according to Macalpine and Hunter,[133] described that

> TRAYN of thoughts [by which], I understand that succession of one Thought to another, which is called . . . *Mental Discourse.* When a man thinketh on any thing whatsoever, His next Thought after, is not altogether so casual as it seems to be. Not every Thought to every Thought succeeds indifferently. . . . Only this is certain, it shall be something that succeeded the same before, at one time or another. This Trayn of Thoughts, or Mental Discourse, is of two sorts. The first is *Unguided, without Design,* and inconstant. . . . In which case the thoughts are said to wander, and seem impertinent one to another, as in a Dream. . . . And yet in this wild ranging of the mind, a man may oft-times perceive the way of it, and the dependence of one thought upon another.

Immanuel Kant published a pamphlet, "The Power of the Mind, Through Simple Determination, to become Master over Morbid Ideas," in which he relates that while suffering with gout he performed an experiment on himself:

> In order that my sleep should not be interfered with, I at once seized upon my stoical remedy, that of directing with effort, my thoughts towards some chosen indifferent object, for example, towards the many associated ideas brought up by the word Cicero. In this way I led my attention away from every other idea. Thus these became quickly blunted so that sleepiness could overcome them. And this I am always able to repeat in attacks of this kind with a good result. That I had not dealt with imaginary pain was clearly evident the following morning when I found the toes of my left foot swollen and red.[14, 105]

Freud apparently never consciously discovered the report of Francis Galton, published in *Brain* in 1879 as "Psychometric Experiments," which Gregory Zilboorg[206, 207] has so vividly brought to our attention. Galton recorded his having become interested in what passed through his mind when he looked at certain objects or thought of certain words. He called these "associated ideas." He wrote them down and noted their number and the time it took him to register them.

> The associated ideas arise of their own accord, and we cannot, except in indirect and unperfected ways, compel them to come. My object is to show how the whole of these associated ideas, though they are for the most part exceedingly fleeting and obscure and barely cross the thresholds of our consciousness, may be seized, dragged into daylight and recorded. . . . The results well repaid the trouble. They gave me an interesting and unexpected view of the number of the operations of the mind, and of the obscure depths in which they took place, of which I had been little conscious before. . . . I was sure that samples of my whole life had passed before me, that many bygone incidents which I never suspected to have formed part of my stock of thoughts had been glanced at as objects too familiar to awaken attention.[207]

Freud discovered that this process goes on much more productively when there is a listener. But then other complications develop. For as this consciously undirected process of thinking and talking goes on with a minimum of participation by the listener except occasional indications of his attentive presence, the talker begins to develop expectations. "Perhaps," he thinks, "the doctor is accumulating sufficient information to enable him to say something to me that will solve everything." For a time the patient is sustained in this apparently one-sided transaction by such assumptions as this. Having poured out his "soul," as the expression goes, and thus enriched the analyst's knowledge about his problems, he expects from the analyst the "magic word," the oracular pronouncement.

In such generalizations as we are making, it should be remembered that different patients *begin* the course of treatment at various levels of maladjustment—that is, degrees of regression or, more frequently, lags in development of the normal pattern of psychological growth. They may be desperate; they may be only sorely troubled; they may be perplexed and uncertain; or they may be calmly resolute in the direction of improving certain self-observed deficiencies. Whichever it is, each patient will have endeavored to present to the world in everyday life a certain front. Upon beginning psychoanalytic treatment, even though it is in the privacy of the consultation office, he tends to present this habitual front to the doctor in spite of the "permission" to do otherwise.

Rado[158] described successive levels behind this initial "front." There is the relatively mature individual, who takes the position: "I am (consciously) delighted to cooperate with the doctor and to utilize this opportunity to discover how to make better use of my potentials." Another patient might take the attitude: "I have troubles which I have not been able to solve myself, and I am willing to cooperate with the doctor in order to learn how to do this." A third patient might say, "I don't know what to do. I want to find out. Perhaps by this method I can get relief from my torture." A still more regressed patient might say: "In my desperation I turn to the doctor for the help he can give me, the relief he offers me." And finally (at the lowest level), there is a state of near hopelessness and the magic-craving expectation of a miracle. Treatment of various kinds, including psychoanalysis, can be applied at any of these various levels, all of which appear in the course of any psychoanalysis.

In our presentation of the theory of psychoanalytic treatment we are apt to assume that the patient comes in at the highest level of functioning, which of course he rarely does. Behind this initial front something is wrong or the patient would not be seeking treatment. But increasingly, in the course of the treatment, he will tend to "regress" to lower levels; he will become more and more child-like in his attitudes and in his emotional dependency upon the analyst. The idea is that he will become childish and then grow up again—better than he did before now guided by his more mature intelligence and with the warnings and lessons of his unhappy experiences better understood.

This metaphorical language can be helpful in grasping the general principle of regression, but it will be confusing if one pushes it too far. Of course, in one sense the patient cannot actually become a child, but in another sense he does. He acts like one and he sees that he has always acted like one to some extent, and he can compare how he has actually acted with how he has often wanted to act and couldn't, especially when he *was* a child. An occasional patient will carry the regression back to an enactment of infantilism that is disturbing and undesirable; the prognosis is better if the extreme infantilism is merely glimpsed.

The term *regression* is one of the more ambiguous concepts of psychoanalytic theory. It refers to many phenomena that can be viewed from dynamic, economic, structural, genetic, and adaptive aspects. Kris[113] suggested an intriguing addendum to the theory of regression: the integrative functions of the ego may include self-regulated regression. Perhaps this is the regressive quality that is so apparent in most successful psychoanalytic treatment.*

This is the general thesis of psychoanalytic treatment. It involves the induction (or occurrence) of a regression, over and beyond that partial regression or developmental lag present at the start, representing the illness for which the treatment was undertaken. Psychoanalytic treatment is a little like removing an embedded fish-hook that has to be pushed farther and the barb removed before the hook can be extracted. Freud hinted at this when he spoke of neurotic illness as expressing the suffering from reminiscences which can neither be fully repressed nor fully recalled. In psychoanalytic treatment they are, first, more completely recollected and then more fully repressed or more completely integrated.

One writer has commented that "the patient may use regression as a direct defense against making progress in analysis . . . to block the analyst's endeavor to change him and bring him to a higher level of behavior."

We do not think it is the analyst's proper task to "endeavor to change" the analysand or "to bring him" anywhere, be it higher or lower. This image presents a pouting patient hanging back against

* Some of our colleagues take issue with this model of regression. They hold that what appears to be an increasing regression in the analysis describes rather the increasing accuracy of the patient's awareness of himself, of the infantile nature of his intentions, wishes, needs, moods, and so forth. They think regression does not properly describe the increasing knowledge acquired by the observing part of the ego, which is (therefore) constantly progressing, in one sense. Other colleagues object to our use of the word *induction* as attributing too much power to the analyst and implying that he can determine the form of the regression. Of course we don't mean it in this way. The regression occurs and develops. It is induced by the total situation, as explained. The analyst should not develop fantasies that it is *he* as a person who has induced it. Cf. D. W. Winnicott.[204]

the pull of a leash held in the hands of an analyst. Regression in the analytic situation is not this kind of tug of war or holding back against the pull of virtue, progress, truth, or whatever the analyst may represent. Regression, in part, describes a process of temporary surrender of contemporary reality-loyalty in favor of a replacement in fantasy of repetitions from a recollected state of existence. In the course of doing this the analysand discovers things and—if he then wishes—he can make appropriate amendments of his contemporary reaction patterns. He does not resist or regress merely to annoy, although he knows it (sometimes) teases. But some analysts do experience it in just that way and react to it negatively, or managerially.*

Psychoanalysis is not alone in making use of regression in order to favor a new development. It was recommended by Jesus to Nicodemus, who was astounded by the recommendation that he be born again and really grow up. The same idea appears in other (especially Oriental) religions.[146] Regression occurs to some degree in all hospitalization, whether for psychiatric or medical illnesses. Reports by scientific observers of various indoctrination programs by communist governments[122] involving situations of sensory deprivation[93, 94] suggest that this principle has been employed in the induction of cognitive changes that vary in extent and duration. Such reports describe extraordinary phenomena that may be conceptualized as processes of regression.[72, 122, 181]

But in psychoanalytic treatment, *for one hour a day* the regression is there, to be heard and seen and utilized and ultimately resolved. It is sometimes called the "transference neurosis," but whatever it is called, this phenomenon of regression and its technical exploitation are of the very essence of psychoanalytic treat-

---

* Alexander[1] emphasized that regression was of two types: one to an earlier, happier state, and one to an earlier traumatic state. Coincident with the regression, new integrative efforts appear and arouse further anxiety, motivating the patient to continue analytic work. Alexander's model is confusing. Whether the period to which the patient regresses is looked upon as happy or as painful depends on which aspect the patient concentrates upon, but these are not two "types" of regression. Everything in life has both happy and painful aspects. Our assumption is that something in the early life of the child that was very painful has been partially—but only partially—forgotten, and therefore remained an unsolved but disturbing enigma, reflected in many subsequent events and attitudes.

ment. (See contributions of Fisher,[40] Gill,[74] Macalpine,[132] and Nunberg.[151])

There are a few contemporaries who are skeptical about the desirability of permitting or favoring a further degree of regression to occur in psychoanalytic treatment.[104, 157, 158] The experiments of these workers in the exploration of the unconscious processes and the use of insight without the induction of regression are interesting and suggest methods of psychotherapy valuable for some conditions, but these methods are not our conception of classical, correct psychoanalysis. In this book we shall consider the regression incident to psychoanalytic treatment as an essential element. In the following material we shall offer a theoretical framework within which to explain why the regression occurs, the way it usually occurs, its therapeutic derivatives, and its ultimate recession and disappearance.

What we call regression in the psychoanalytic treatment situation refers to a very considerable retrograde process of personality functioning. There is a regression to earlier and more primitive ways of feeling, experiencing, and behaving. There is a constriction in the field of attention, a preoccupation with the self, and a simplification or reduction in the structural complexity of psychological functioning. Primary processes emerge and secondary processes diminish in importance.[76] As we shall see, the process can be described from various standpoints.

The term *regression* was a central one in the libido theory. Freud first used it to describe a retrogression of drive energy to previously fixed and therefore earlier established aims and objects. In the course of the normal development of a child, the hypothetical energy of the sexual impulse, libido, aggressively becomes invested in a series of aims, objects, and body zones. Some of the libido may remain fixed at earlier stages that no longer are age-appropriate. Freud called this phenomenon *fixation*. The early-drive theory implies that when part of the libido remained fixated at earlier aims, zones, objects, stages, or modes of response, there was an increased likelihood that at a later period some of the libido that has progressed in more mature development will return to that fixation point. Thus, under certain conditions, there will be a regression of libido from advanced positions to earlier ones. One of these conditions, according to Freud, is frustration of sexual aims. How much frustration is required to begin a regressive process depends upon prior fixation. If the fixation is minimal, a large amount of frustration will be required; and if fixations are significantly prominent, minor frustrations may begin a regressive process.*

The theory of regression has been explored in much greater depth in Gill and Brenman[77] and in Schafer.[178] Here we merely wish to indicate that the phenomenon of regression—whether or not one wishes to preserve the specific presentation of it in the older libido theory—occurs in the context of the frustration induced by the psychoanalytic situation. But this regression occurs in the setting of introspection and understanding, and it is these that provide the therapeutic use of the regression. For growth seems always to occur after periods of relative disorganization and temporary regressions. Consolidated and automatic ways of behaving, thinking and relating to the phenomenal world become deautomatized (cf. Gill and Brenman[77]) and "uncoupled," as it were, thus making possible new arrangements and organizations. The frustration-induced regression therefore makes possible further growth on the basis of the patient's discoveries within himself. For he discovers the immaturities in himself, the archaic nature of his loves and hates, and the self-defeating compromises between aspects of himself, all of which he has obscured from himself. Thus, the process of regression brings with it a breaking up of processes into their component organizations, permitting new reorganizational possibilities.

One prerequisite for this kind of growth, however, is that the analysand should never lose the attitude of curiosity, search, and

---

* The idea of fixation and regression was suggested to Freud in the course of his neural anatomical investigations in Brücke's laboratory. He wrote, "When as a young student I was engaged under Von Brücke's direction on my first piece of scientific work, I was concerned with the origin of the postganglionic nerve roots in the spinal cord of a small fish of very archaic structure; I found that the nerve fibers of these roots have their origin in large cells in the posterior horn of the gray matter, which is no longer the case in other vertebrates. But I also discovered soon afterwards that the nerve cells of this kind are present outside the gray matter the whole way to what is known as the spinal ganglion of the posterior root; and from this I inferred that the cells of these masses of ganglia had migrated from the spinal cord along the roots of the nerves. This is also shown by their evolutionary history. But in this small fish the whole path of their migration was demonstrated by the cells that had remained behind."[56]

scrutiny in collaboration with the analyst. This joint endeavor, which some have called the therapeutic or working alliance,[205, 86] remains as a steadying and guiding influence.

Why does the regression occur? This topic has been long and much discussed. We certainly must try to avoid the fallacious causality explanation. No one thing "causes"* regression—it results from numerous factors. The partial regression already present represents the patient's illness, as has been already mentioned. Applying for help is a further step backward, in a sense—a step backward in order to make a better "run" forward, later. Going to the psychoanalyst makes it possible to partially lay aside the façade or pretense of normality, so that the already existing degree of regression covered by the façade becomes immediately apparent.

Entering psychoanalytic treatment means the taking of not just *one* more step but many more steps, backward. During the analytic hour (and sometimes outside of it) the patient is definitely "worse" or "sicker" than was apparent before the treatment. From one point of view this is only apparent; he and the analyst are able to see how sick he really was, but he can cover it up. But in another sense it is real in that his pretense at being normal is diminished, made more difficult.

Freud called these phenomena to our attention. In his 1914 paper, "Recollection, Repetition and Working Through," he stated:

> He [the patient] also repeats during the treatment all his symptoms and now we see that our special insistence upon the compulsion to repeat has not yielded any new fact but is only a more comprehensive point of view. We are only making it clear to ourselves that the patient's condition of illness does not cease when the analysis begins, that we have to treat his illness as an actual force, active at the moment, and not as an event in his past life. . . . Transference thus forms a kind of intermediary realm between illness and real life, through which the journey from the one to the other must be made. The new

* For the Aristotelian theory of complex causation, the "formal cause" of the regression might be ascribed to the basic rule, the permissiveness of the analysis, the very nature of the therapeutic situation. The "material cause" would then be the very existence of the neurosis, the need of the patient for help, the already present tendencies toward regression. The "efficient cause" would be the frustration in the therapy to which we have referred. Then the "final cause" would be the assumed capacity of the patient for ultimate reintegration, resumption of growth and "cure."

state of mind has absorbed all the features of the illness; it represents, however, an artificial illness which is at every point accessible to our interventions. It is at the same time a piece of real life, but adapted to our purposes by specially favorable conditions, and it is of a provisional character.[61]

We must remember that it is precisely this more honest, even if more disturbing, behavior that the therapist must learn about in order to offer help. He has invited the patient to let himself go, to let himself be as childish as he wishes, to say whatever comes to his mind regardless of the consequences that would ensue were this not a special situation. Thus, the patient is not only permitted but encouraged to abandon those very devices he has spent a lifetime in acquiring with respect to what he might say to and about another human being. *In this situation* there is no need to be polite, no need to be considerate, no need to be fair, no need to be practical, no need to be realistic. It is only necessary to follow the original instruction: "Try only to be honest. Think whatever you wish and say whatever you think. It may be only tentative. But in any case, I promise there will be no retaliation, no passing of judgment, no definite conclusion."

Such an invitation from the therapist for the patient to become more self-preoccupied may not be needed; for many patients the urge to regress in this direction is only too strong. It occurs even outside the analytic hour. Regression is greatly favored not only by the "permissiveness" of the analyst's attitude but by the physical features of the analytic situation—the reclining posture, the invisible physician, the quietness of the chamber, the relative silence of the therapist. Gill mentions "The general atmosphere of timelessness . . . the disregard of symptoms . . . and the frequency of visits, which, metaphorically speaking, we may regard as the constant irritation necessary to keep open the wounds into the unconscious. . . ."[74] The diminution of external sensory stimuli furthers this; Hebb and his associates of the University of Montreal have shown that a considerable degree of regression can be induced by this device alone.*[12, 93, 94]

* From the recent studies in experimental isolation which followed the early study by Bexton *et al.*[12] (for example, by Lilly,[123] Macalpine,[132] and Solomon, Leiderman, Mendelson, and Wexler[185]) we are beginning to realize more and

In the opinion of one of our most thoughtful teachers, the late Bertram Lewin,[119] the regression in psychoanalysis is comparable to that which occurs in sleep, the psychoanalytic process having indeed developed from a kind of sleep therapy (hypnosis). Lewin developed the idea that traces of sleep insinuate themselves into the manifest picture. The wish to be put to sleep becomes supplanted by the wish to associate freely, and the patient lies down, not to sleep, but to associate. But in associating he tends to regress and to dream. The analyst, as Lewin pointed out in another paper,[120] contributes to a magical effect, which operates either to soothe or to arouse, to awaken the patient somewhat or to put him a little further to sleep.

Loewald, in a carefully reasoned paper, put it this way:

> An analysis can be characterized . . . as a period or periods of induced ego disorganization and reorganization. The promotion of the transference neurosis is the induction of such ego disorganization and reorganization. Analysis is thus understood as an intervention designed to set ego-development in motion, be it from a point of relative arrest, or to promote what we conceive of as a healthier direction and/or comprehensiveness of such development. This is achieved by the promotion and utilization of (controlled) regression. This regression is one important aspect under which the transference neurosis can be understood. The transference neurosis, in the sense of reactivation of the childhood neurosis, is set in motion not simply by the technical skill of the analyst, but by the fact that the analyst makes himself available for the development of a new "object-relationship" between the patient and the analyst. The patient tends to make this potentially new object-relationship into an old one. On the other hand, to the extent to which the patient develops a "positive transference" (not in the sense of transferences resistance, but in the sense in which "transference" carries the whole process of an analysis) he keeps this potentiality of a new object-relationship alive through all the various stages of resistance. The patient can dare to take the plunge into the regressive crisis of the transference neurosis

---

more how great the role of external stimulus impact is on ego functioning. In the light of these isolation experiments and accumulating data regarding solitary sailors, polar explorers, prisoners, and the deaf and blind, it is increasingly apparent that the autonomy of ego is maintained only by a balanced dependency on both the id and the external world. (See Rapaport.[161])

which brings him face to face again with his childhood anxieties and conflicts, *if* he can hold on to the potentiality of a new object relationship represented by the analyst.[5]

THE CONTROLLED FRUSTRATION

The sense of frustration experienced by the patient in the analytic situation is partially a reflection of the reality situation, but insofar as it depends upon the responsiveness of the analyst it can and will be regulated by him. Actually, of course, the patient is not denied anything except what he should not be given—as in the case of a child who cries for a shiny, loaded revolver. But the sense of frustration *experienced* by the patient is directly attributed by him (even against his better judgment) to what the analyst does and does not do—or say. Knowing this, the analyst must indeed do or not do what is necessary to control the rapidity of the retrograde process and the depth of the regression. Analysis is defeated by too rapid or too slow a regression or by too deep a regression too early in the treatment. We cannot go back on our original invitation and promise; that would be a breach of contract. But we did not promise to give the patient anything except audience, understanding, and "help." And we must decide what kind of help to give and when to give it. The analyst must learn to withhold, but he must also learn to give and to give at the right time.

One of our colleagues, Dr. Herbert J. Schlesinger, made the sage observation that

> the analyst could not, of course, fulfill the patient's anachronistic wishes even if he were to want to. While he might accede to a patient's specific requests, for instance, to speak to him more often, his action would only be such as to encourage the patient to continue to express his regressive wishes in pseudo-mature forms. The analyst need not think of himself as frustrating the patient's regressive demands; the frustration is built in to the fact that this is a transference neurosis, a re-enactment rather than a primary experience. The sense of frustration experienced by the patient is a very real phenomenon but, like the regression, it should be thought of as part of the patient's psychology, not the analyst's. I recall you saying something to some of us that is relevant here. When the analyst

finally "gives" something to the patient (an interpretation) it is something much more and different from what the patient wanted and, like a drouth-breaking cloudburst, it brings a measure of relief but also problems of its own. It is necessary to emphasize that the analyst's giving and withholding are not conceptually coordinate with, and are certainly not intended to fulfill the desires expressed by the patient. Although the analyst learns to intervene judiciously so that the patient is not unnecessarily helped to feel constantly that he gets too much or too little (a common resistance pattern that serves to reduce the analyst's comments to a common denominator of so many quantities of verbiage), the analyst must avoid becoming pre-occupied with "dosing" the patient with his offerings. To do so would be merely to meet the patient's transference expectation with a complementary countertransference attitude. (Personal communication.)

Our theory holds that a patient's illness reflects a growth, im-peded in its original, natural development by deflections incident to faulty responses to early crises. Complex emotions, chiefly rage, have followed unmanageable, unendurable situations. Hence, the oppor-tunity for better direction of long repressed rage is, in a narrow sense, an *immediate* object of the treatment. This must be not only a temporary drainage but an elimination of the basic or typical prov-ocations of the rage in order that the energy required for this inflammation and blockage can be more expediently invested. This should never blind the analyst to the *ultimate constructive* objectives of the treatment as defined above.

Thus the patient undergoing psychoanalysis can be expected to display—after a while—inappropriate and futile anger. He may not *feel* it as anger; he may want to call it resentment or depression or righteous indignation or discouragement. But whatever he calls it, he will display it, and in displaying it rather than masking or "con-trolling" it, he will manifest still further regression. His sense of frustration affords a continuing provocation to resentment. For, as the days go by, there develops in the patient a growing suspicion that there exists between him and his therapist what an economist would call "an unfavorable trade balance." The patient has "coop-erated," he has obeyed the instructions, he has given himself. He has contributed information, exposing his very heart, and in addition to all this he has paid money for the sessions in which he did it! And what in return has he gotten from the analyst? Attention, audience, toleration, yes—but no response. No "reaction." No advice. No explanation. No solution. No help. No love.

This is not quite right, of course, because there have been some responses and reactions on the part of the analyst. But they have not been what the patient expected. There was certainly no magic word. There was a minimum of reassurance. There was no indication, for the most part, that the analyst took a position in anything. The analyst was told about the enormity of the patient's wife's behavior—but he said nothing. He was told a good joke—but he didn't laugh. He was given a full account of an incident with a traffic officer—and he asked only how the *officer* felt about it! He interrupted the recounting of a most important episode to ask a seemingly most irrelevant question—something about the day of the week on which it occurred.

These unpredictable responses from the therapist are disconcerting and cannot be dealt with in ordinary logical ways. Combined with his general nonresponsiveness and silence, they favor a growing sense of frustration. This is increased by the fact that, in the course of relinquishing his self-censure and his long-used conventional habits of verbal restraint, the patient has become increasingly concerned about being approved of by the analyst. Gradually the sense of having contributed in vain, of having failed to please or satisfy or even provoke the analyst, begins to weigh upon the patient, first as mild uneasiness, then as anxiousness, and finally as frank frustration and resentment. Phyllis McGinley probably wasn't thinking of psychoanalysis when she wrote, very aptly:

> Sticks and stones are hard on bones.
> Aimed with angry art,
> Words can sting like anything.
> But silence breaks the heart.[134]

How this frustration feels, how the "transference neurosis" is experienced and rationalized by the patient is conveyed in a somewhat caricatured manner by Haley,[89] who describes it as a kind of sham battle between patient and analyst. With tongue in cheek, no doubt, but with discernible earmarks he writes:

> The patient enters analysis in the "one-down" posture by asking
> for help and promptly tries to put the therapist one-down by

building him up. . . . The patient begins to compliment the therapist on how wonderful he is and how quickly he (the patient) expects to get well. The skilled analyst is not taken in by these maneuvers. . . .

When the patient finds himself continually put one-down, he changes tactics. He becomes mean and insulting, threatens to quit analysis, and casts doubt upon the sanity of the analyst. These are the "attempts to get a human response" ploys. They meet an impassive, impersonal wall as the analyst remains silent or handles the insults with a simple statement like, "Have you noticed this is the second Tuesday afternoon you've made such a comment? I wonder what there is about Tuseday," or "You seem to be reacting to me as if I'm someone else."

Frustrated in his resistance ploys, the patient capitulates and ostensibly hands control of the situation back to the analyst. Again building the analyst up, he leans on him, hangs on his every word, insists how helpless he is and how strong the analyst is, and waits for the moment when he will lead the analyst along far enough to devastate him with a clever ploy. The skilled analyst handles this nicely with a series of "condescending" ploys, pointing out that the patient must help himself and not expect anyone to solve everything for him. Furious, the patient again switches from subservient ploys to defiant ploys. By this time he has learned techniques from the analyst and is getting better. He uses what insight he has gained to try in every way to define the relationship as one in which the analyst is one-down. This is the difficult period of the analysis. However, having carefully prepared the ground by a thorough diagnosis (listing weak points) and having instilled a succession of doubts in the patient about himself, the analyst succeeds in topping the patient again and again as the years (!) pass.

Frustration by itself is certainly not an effective form of treatment. If it were, many simpler ways could be found for frustrating a patient than the use of the psychoanalytic couch. Frustration is a condition in which the real dynamics of psychoanalytic treatment become effective. This principle stems from Freud's second "fundamental rule" of psychoanalysis:

Analytic treatment should be carried through, as far as is possible, under privation—in a state of abstinence. By abstinence, however, is not to be understood doing without any and every satisfaction—that would of course not be practicable; nor do we

mean what it popularly connotes, refraining from sexual inter-
course; it means something else which has far more to do with
the dynamics of illness and recovery.

You will remember that it was a *frustration* that made the patient ill, and that his symptoms serve him as substitutive gratifications. . . . The patient looks for his substitutive gratification
above all in the treatment itself, in his transference-relationship
with the physician, and he may even strive to compensate himself through this means for all the other privations laid upon
him. A certain amount must of course be permitted to him,
more or less according to the nature of the case and the patient's
individuality. But it is not good to let it become too much.
Any analyst who out of the fullness of his heart and the readiness to help perhaps extends to the patient all that one human
being may hope to receive from another, commits the same
economic error which our non-analytic institutions for nervous patients are guilty of. They exert themselves only to make
everything as pleasant as possible for the patient, so that he
may feel well there and gladly take flight back there again away
from the trials of life. In so doing they entirely forego making
him stronger for life and more capable of carrying out the
actual tasks of his life. In analytic treatment all such cosseting
must be avoided. As far as his relations with the physician are
concerned, the patient must have unfulfilled wishes in abun-
dance. It is expedient to deny him precisely those satisfactions
which he desires most intensely and expresses most importu-
nately.[66]

The state of abstinence, then, refers to the activity of both
patient and analyst: the analyst must abstain from responding to the
patient's pleas, charges, maneuvers, requests, and demands in the
way he would ordinarily respond were this a social relationship, *and*
the patient must experience the denied satisfaction. For so far we
have come upon no better method for allowing the patient to discover his style of, and his conditions for, loving and hating. It is this
controlled frustration in analysis that highlights the patient's typical
methods of relating himself to the significant people in his life. This
self-discovery is crucial for the process of recovery.

STEPS IN THE REGRESSION

Obviously the mounting sense of deprivation and frustration
just described cannot go on indefinitely. It provokes in the patient

certain reactions of various kinds and degrees, and the desired effect can be obtained only if the frustration tension is held within a certain optimum range. Technical skill consists in knowing at what time and in what degree and form the patient's need for response from the analyst should be ministered to in order to maintain the optimal degree of frustration, or, to put it another way, in order to keep him from becoming completely demoralized from an excessive feeling of frustration.

We can find an answer for this by examining closely just what the patient really expects or wants from the therapist at a particular time. To be sure, he wants relief from something uncomfortable. He wants to be "cured" of some affliction, or at least to have it ameliorated. This is his conscious avowal in having undertaken treatment and in the making of the two-party contract. But we soon discover that considerably more and different expectations underlie this conscious motivation.

If one listens without comment to the free associations of a patient for a series of thirty or fifty or a hundred hours and then condenses the essence of the material to the simplest possible schematic form, it would often appear something like this:

1. I am suffering (and have suffered) in this way and that way, thus and thus and thus.
2. I don't *want* to suffer thus and thus and thus. (*Analyst may inquire regarding details.*)
3. I want the analyst, once he fully understands my suffering, to cure me or relieve me. (*Analyst silent.*)
4. In order that he may do so, I will explain *more* fully how I have long suffered in this way and sometimes in that way, formerly in that way and now in this way. (*Analyst listens in silence.*)
5. Surely by now the analyst understands me and could, if he would, counsel and advise me and prevent my having to suffer in these ways. Will he? (*The analyst remains essentially silent.*)
6. I have now told him everything—well, nearly everything. He is omniscient, and he could probably take away my suffering almost by magic, if he would only speak. Surely he realizes how I suffer; surely he knows how much I want his help? But he is silent! Why?
7. *When* is he going to help me? Why doesn't he? (*Analyst still silent.*)

8. Well, then, I may as well confess. I knew I would have to tell him at last. He knew I had done such things; he must have known. He was waiting for me to tell it all. Now I have done so. I feel ashamed, but relieved. It's out!

9. I feel better. My analyst isn't too shocked, I guess. He asked a few questions, but there was no scolding.

10. He is listening, then. But am I getting anywhere? He is so good to listen, so patient, so calm, *so understanding.*

11. If he could only accept me, believe me, pity me—helpless, weak, and guilty as I am. But how can he?

12. I wish he would talk to me—scold me, praise me, tell me I'm not impossible, or even that he liked me a little. I've tried so hard to please him in ways I have always thought worked pretty well. But I don't succeed. (*Analyst comments briefly.*)

13. Regardless of his coldness, I do like him. I almost love him. But how can he love me—or even like me? No one does, no one can. No one really ever did. But I must go on, I guess.

14. I don't like this fellow at all; he is rude and crude, he is unsympathetic, he is indifferent, he is impossible to please. He doesn't understand me. He is stupid; a fraud, a quack, an ignoramus. I will tell him so. (*Analyst is essentially silent.*)

15. Well, he didn't get mad. But *I'm* still mad. I have given the doctor what he asked for; I think I have a right to *expect* something *from* him. I have given, but I do not get.

16. I might try again the techniques I have so often used—I have tried these in vain with him. Are my techniques wrong? Is the doctor wrong? Am I wrong? Surely something is wrong!

17. How *do* I get what I want? Is this the way I relate myself to other people? *What is the something I really want?*
    (What this "something" turns out to be, we shall see later.)

This is as far as we shall take the schema now. Of course, the progression is never precisely this, and rarely so clear and simple as we have represented it. There are always various furbelows, digressions, interruptions, and minor complications. But in general it is quite typical and from it several significant things can be deduced.

First, the patient's sense of frustration derives not alone from the mere unresponsiveness or unpredictableness of the party of the second part, baffling and disconcerting (and frustrating) as this may be. It is clear from even this short sample that the patient is seeking something not explicit in the original contract. He is seeking to get something (from the analyst) without being quite sure what it is. We see, too, that in the pursuit of this desideratum he uses successively various approaches, various devices or techniques to try to obtain it. In this process, too, he is able to see that it is not the analyst who frustrates, but he, the patient, who frustrates himself; that all his life he has adopted maneuvers that had "informed against" him, as it were. He begins to feel that it is his own responsibility to take charge of his life, and not the analyst's function. How this comes about we will discuss in Chapter VI.

Techniques of getting what one wants from the environment were learned, as we know, in childhood and developed as our bodies and minds developed. In all adults they have been *somewhat* modified by experience. In the "normal" adult they have been greatly modified in realistic directions. In the "neurotic" adult they are much less completely metamorphosed. Hence, under frustration even the "normal" adult may "regress" to the use of some earlier techniques. In analysis the patient will first use his customary, semi-mature techniques and then regress to those still more infantile ones used earlier in his life.

He usually begins by wanting the analyst to be sympathetic— *i.e.*, to recognize that he is really suffering—and he may interpret the analyst's audience and silence to be sympathy. Encouraged by this, he tells more about himself, including sooner or later some things of which he is ashamed. He will often interpret the analyst's silence as forgiveness. But soon he begins to wonder if the analyst is—after all—just indifferent or perhaps bored or even disgusted. But, again encouraged, or desperate, he soon goes ahead with his revelations. For a time he (again) appreciates the analyst's attentive silence but gradually succumbs again to misgivings. "Why doesn't he say something? Am I not doing just as he told me to do? Am I not trying? Am I not producing? Why doesn't he at least commend me, even—God forgive me—praise me a little? I'm trying so hard to please him. Am I failing?"

UPS AND DOWNS IN THE PROGRESSIVE REGRESSION

The function of analysis is not, of course, to have the psychoanalyst "pleased" or the patient praised. Nevertheless the patient
will, like most other human beings, do his best to be as pleasing as
possible in his particular way because this is an early learned technique which daily experience of later life confirms. He will keep
hoping that he has in some measure succeeded. The analyst's continued silence, however, is ultimately interpreted as an indication
that this technique has failed. The patient may even come out quite
frankly and ask, "When are you going to say something, Doctor? I
have come here hour after hour now, for quite a while. I've paid my
money and I've spoken my piece. I have done what you told me to
and what am I getting? I don't hear a word out of you. Isn't it
about time that you woke up and said something?"

The young analyst, no matter how much he has prepared himself by reading, is certain to be startled when he first encounters
this astonishing phenomenon—the frank "admission" by the patient
that he is not in treatment for the sake of getting better. I recall the
dismay of a candidate in connection with his analysis of an intelligent scientist who complained at length of loneliness because his
wife had gone on a brief vacation. He spoke of the way in which he
looked forward to his analytic hour as an opportunity for both companionship and sympathy. He began to describe himself as having
been "abandoned" by his wife. Apparently disappointed that his
analyst made no comment in regard to this self-pity, he mumbled
grudgingly that perhaps he wasn't doing what the analyst expected
of him. To this the analyst remarked that his only expectations
were that the patient would endeavor to say whatever came to his
mind. The patient (to the analyst's astonishment) burst out in
anger. It was, he said, a most injurious, destructive, devastating remark. It left him helpless and hopeless. It expressed clearly the
analyst's attitude of complete rejection, of utter indifference toward
the patient and his suffering. Sympathy, companionship, friendship
—these were what he needed, not interpretations and snide remarks.

Similar sentiments were expressed in a poem by Tom Prideaux:

> With half a laugh of hearty zest
> I strip me of my coat and vest.

Then heeding not the frigid air
I fling away my underwear.

So having nothing else to doff,
I rip my epidermis off.

More secrets to acquaint you with
I pare my bones to strips of pith.

And when the exposé is done
I hang, a cobweb skeleton.

While you sit there aloof, remote,
And will not shed your overcoat.*

The patient does not feel frustrated all the time. There are waves of gratitude for being listened to and understood, surprised joy in the achievement of new insights and progress, relief from oppressive guilt feelings, dawning hope for new possibilities. We have been emphasizing the patient's negative feelings because we feel that they tend to be neglected in psychoanalytic writing and teaching. But to avoid a similar blunder of one-sidedness, let us stress here that psychoanalysis is a series of ups and downs, of ebbs and flows, of little gratifications and then disappointments. One can imagine the analytic hour to be like a magnifying mirror reflecting an imaginary beam of light emanating from the oscillations of the patient's moods from day to day, as determined by all of the external and internal stimuli bearing upon him. It is often helpful to counsel patients against being depressed over the fact that they are depressed, because the time one feels the worst may be when he is making the most progress.

It is well to keep in mind the model introduced in Chapter II of a customer seeking to obtain something in an exchange. The patient really wants something; he has paid for it (or will) and he will seek in his way to get it. He may avoid asking for it explicitly, endeavoring to be agreeable, at first, and suppressing plaintive and complaintive thoughts. He may express these covertly in dreams or

---

* First published, as we learned from a reader, Miss Jessica Davidson, after its appearance in the first edition of *Creative Power*, by Hughes Mearns (Doubleday, 1929). Mr. Prideaux, an editor of *Life*, was a teenage English student at the time. This poem "was reprinted in a couple of other places, including the *Atlantic Monthly* where—imagine this—it was sent by a lad from a reformatory school, and published under his name, not mine" (personal communication from Tom Prideaux).

by various roundabout maneuvers. He may ask to be reassured or to have certain dreams interpreted, thinking that this will both please the analyst and obtain some assistance. Other patients, or the same patient at other times, will grieve and stew and worry, trying different methods to please the analyst, to bribe him, or to provoke him, whimpering, pouting, sulking, storming, sobbing—in short, using all the methods of a frustrated child, and particularly those used by this particular patient as a child. Sometimes the latter have succeeded, in times past; sometimes they have failed. But in this new and baffling situation the patient is impelled to try everything.

In good time, the origin and meaning of these techniques will be pointed out to him, if he does not recognize them himself. But first he must *experience* them, see and feel the ways in which he tries to get what he wants. He will ultimately realize that certain methods, constantly unsuccessful, nevertheless were retained by him, whereas better ones were abandoned because under certain circumstances—one particularly painful time, maybe—they didn't work. This cyclic, repetitious factor in attempts at mastery is an important feature of psychoanalytic theory, and one sees it clearly in the psychoanalytic treatment process. The neutrality of the analyst, later on his confrontations and interpretations, enables the "observing" portion of the ego to get a panoramic view of what hitherto was only felt intensely and uncomprehendingly.

Of course, the analyst does break his silence, *his* abstinence—occasionally. He too is experiencing these abortive techniques as used by the patient; he too is surveying this panorama. While helping the observing ego to see it more clearly or more comprehensively, he may also lend comfort to the regressed portion of the ego by this indication of interest and approval. The patient will then respond with signs of pleasure and encouragement. The young therapist is sometimes misled by this wave of "improvement." If the analysis goes as it should, frustration will mount again and the cycle will be repeated over and over. But each time the perspective will have been enlarged, the area of exploration widened, the penetration into the hidden part deepened.

I have often attempted to construct drawings that would indicate this oscillation of the course of analysis diagrammatically. I have never been satisfied with any that I have made, nor wholly satisfied with some of the better ones that some of my students have made, to indicate how each succeeding frustration and regression takes the patient deeper or further back, but how, with each recovery, each capturing of insight, he reconstitutes himself at a higher level, as it were. Perhaps it is a little like a mountain climber who discovers that the path he is following has not yet reached the peak but may bring him to a rise from which he sees how he must go down again in order to get on a path that will take him higher.

There is a classical experiment in gestalt psychology used to test certain forms of animal learning in which an ape is placed in a cage with an opening to the rear and a banana is placed outside the cage to the front. The animal must bring himself to surrender for a moment the exciting view of the banana, detaching himself from the stimulus of its proximity and making a direct move away from it, in order to get effectively to its actual capture.

This is comparable to the regression induced by the treatment, which is over and beyond that degree of regression—already present at the time the treatment began—represented by the patient's "illness." It is a "progressive regression"! It is a repetitious going-back to look and to remember and then coming forward to compare and perhaps correct.

We shall examine four aspects of this regression: regression in regard to the nature and substance of the thing wanted from the analyst, in respect to the techniques for getting the thing wanted, in respect to the source or indirect object of the patient's endeavors, and in respect to the nature and character of the seeker himself. This can be made clearer if we diagram the sentence: I, the patient, want from the doctor (analyst) a cure (of my illness). (See Figure 6.)

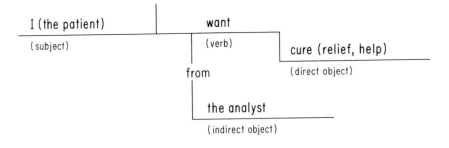

FIGURE 6

REGRESSION IN RESPECT TO THE OBJECT

Let us first examine the regression in regard to the thing wanted. When the patient first comes to the doctor, there is no question about it. He wants help, relief, cure. At least that is what he *says* he wants. But very soon he comes to realize that he wants *more* than this. Even before he gets relief, often, he wants sympathy. And in the process of getting relief he gives evidence of wanting all those signals from one's fellow man which other human beings want— approval, acceptance, and even praise. In short, he wants to be liked. He wants to be thought of as having some intrinsic likableness, in spite of his symptoms, his failures, his complaints.

Gradually the patient comes to realize that his "wants" do not stop at this. Over and beyond sympathy and help and praise and being admired, he wants to be loved. He wants to have tokens of, or proofs of, love. Slowly and painfully he proceeds to this mainstream underlying the persistent quest for some attainment in the treatment contract.

We can show this progressive substitution of a more primitive *object* of the patient's seeking as it develops in the regression by successively substituting the order of succession (*i.e.*, indicated in Figure 7 by descent in the column) for the *object* in our diagrammed sentence.

REGRESSIVE OBJECTIVES

All of these desired reactions will be recognized as intangible proofs of love from the analyst. Someone may ask why the search for love is so characteristic of the regressed state. The explanation lies in the many ways in which the word "love" is used in our vocabulary. Love as experienced by the patient when this regression has occurred is reminiscent of the yearnings of a nursing baby at the breast or a child first experiencing pleasurable skin sensations or excitement. This love is something given by someone else, like milk or a caress—not as it is expressed (given) in a mature way. It is perceived as almost magical in its powers, essential and restorative and pleasure-giving as a mother's milk. There is a little echo of this magic feeling in the ecstasy of adolescent romance,

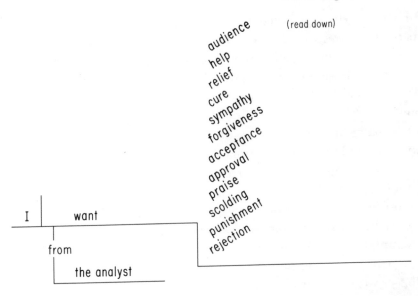

FIGURE 7

when it seems appropriate to say such things as the song title "Love me and the world is mine."

During the analysis of certain patients, this yearning for something he calls love from the analyst becomes strikingly intense. It is a simple matter for the analyst to defend himself against the impact of these passions by discounting the patient's love as "not real." We should not forget, however, Freud's warning that "One has no right to dispute the genuine nature of the love which makes its appearance in the course of analytic treatment. However lacking in normality it may seem to be, this quality is sufficiently explained when we remember that the condition of being in love in ordinary life outside analysis is also more like abnormal than normal mental phenomena. . . . It is precisely these departures from the norm that make up the essential element in the condition of being in love."[60]

We have to remember that such infantile experiences, intense and idyllic as they were, cease to be clung to by the normally developing person because of the number and breadth of adult substitute satisfactions with the maturing of the love capacity. We never abandon the wish to be loved in this magic way, but it loses its poignancy for most of us. But the patient who comes to analysis has not found these substitutes and has not experienced this development, and for him the early experiences thus have a greater relevance. Once the patient reaches the stage of "I want (from the analyst) *love* (but don't get it sufficiently) ," he begins to elaborate on the expectation. It is as if he were to say: "If you *do* love me, you will prove it. You will *give* me symbolic tokens of it, you will *do* things for me and to me."

Hence it develops that the formula "I want *love from the analyst*" undergoes metamorphosis first into "I want *verbal acknowledgments of love* from the analyst" and then into "I want *tangible proofs of love* from the analyst." These tend to become specific according to the specific needs, real or imagined, of the patient either in a past situation or in his present reality situation. Typical examples are represented in Figure 8.

Ultimately the patient will express, progressively, his wish for the *physical expressions* of love from the analyst, *e.g.*, in Figure 9.

REGRESSION IN THE VERB

Let us now return to our primary diagrammed sentence, "I (the patient) want from the doctor (analyst) a cure." Having spoken of the aspect of the regression referring to the object, we turn our attention to regression in respect to the verb of the formula (Figure 6) . We have seen what the patient wants, craves, and feels he needs. His techniques for obtaining gratification for these needs also tends to regress in quality and effectiveness to lower levels.

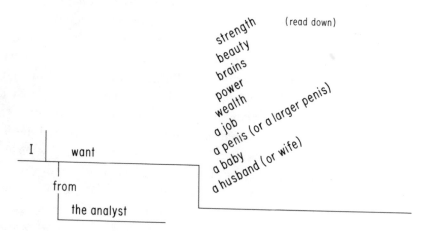

FIGURE 8

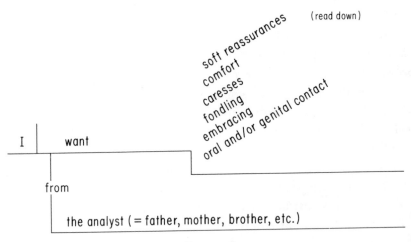

FIGURE 9

In beginning the treatment and tacitly agreeing to comply with the basic rule, the patient feels at first that he is merely performing as directed in his own best interests to obtain what he seeks. Gradually, however, his compliance in this respect comes to mean for him obedience, which, in childhood, was the price of parental help. The patient begins to use his verbalized self-examination (free associations) as a medium of exchange, a *quid pro quo*. He attempts to use his analysis as he once used various communications to or deeds for his parents, teachers, and others—*i.e.*, to get a certain desired return. Along with obedience may go a pleasant manner or a surly one, laughter or tears, joking or whining. All sorts of counterfeits may be tried out. "Obedience" may be prompt or lagging, perfunctory or enthusiastic.

Sooner or later the cumulative frustration in the analytic situation will arouse sufficient anger to make good manners (suppression) and fear (repression) no longer able to contain it. It is an illusion that the anger appears suddenly; it was there from the very beginning. It was not only suppressed because of good manners and discreet tactics; it was *repressed*, as the consequence of earlier conditioning experiences that made the betrayal of one's real feelings too great a danger. To oversimplify it somewhat, one could say that every patient is sick just because of his long present but inexpressible anger. Something happened in the patient's life that has crippled his devices for handling his own instinctual pressures; he could (can) only control his raging aggressiveness by devices that cost him too much and make him sick. The very symptoms of which he complains exist partly for the purpose of controlling that anger, suppressing it or keeping it out of consciousness by repression, and partly for the purpose of expressing it. Every one of his symptoms may be considered to be an expression of anger in which he does not feel or recognize the original emotion.

Bear in mind that the patient doesn't immediately get angry. It is unnecessary to do so; it is ill-mannered. It is even dangerous. Before he gets angry, he will have tried all sorts of things. Besides, there are many satisfactions in the regression despite the "frustration." He will have attempted to bribe the analyst, arouse his pity, tease him, trap him. No analyst is proof against being caught off guard in some of these respects. But this only makes matters worse, for the analyst will recover himself and the patient's frustration continues. He is not getting what he wants, and sooner or later he says so, and he is likely to say so the sooner just because of the extra surcharge of poorly controlled anger which he has carried around from childhood.

When, therefore, we say that anger appears in the psychoanalytic situation, we mean that the patient becomes conscious *again* of an anger that once arose in him and, unexpressed, has made him "sick." But the provocation is now not the whipping his mother once gave him or the embarrassment his father once caused him or the victory his brother once gained over him; the provocation now is his feeling that the *analyst* is disappointing him, punishing him, neglecting him. Then, the formula of "I want to please the analyst in order to insure his loving me" is changed into "I *don't* want anything from the analyst. Hence I shall not try to please him, in order to win love. Rather I would like to displease him, even to hurt him."

On this general theme there develop all sorts of variations and further regressions in the verb formula. "I want to win love by pleasing" becomes transformed into "I want to pay him back and I want to get whatever I can get from him by irritating and hurting him as he has hurt me. I want to cheat him. I want to embarrass him. I will pretend to comply with his wishes but only to make fun of him. I will try to exasperate him. I will discourage him. I will argue with him. I will baffle him. I want to humiliate him and show him up. I want to tell people lies about him. I will slander him. I will try to insult him." Or, in another direction, the formula may go, "I will seduce the analyst. I will find his weakness and prey upon it. I will destroy his power. I will castrate him. I will kill him."

All this behavior is an echo, a reenactment, a contemporized recollection of situations and events of long ago. But it is met by a reception different from that which the patient once found so cruel and hurtful. The analyst reminds himself and, if need be, the patient, that in the analytic situation all statements are tentative and are to be taken only in the perspective of *all* the material. The patient comes to see how he defeats himself, how his rage at not getting prevents him from getting. He doesn't see this immediately; he is apt to be blinded by his own angry tears.

Sooner or later, of course, there come the expressions of fury and helplessness in the form of outbursts of rage directed toward the analyst. On the one hand, the patient identifies them more or less accurately as belonging somewhere else, somewhere in the long ago. On the other hand, the influence of the conscience and of the recognition of the injustice of some of his accusations leads him to penitence and remorse. He may offer apology (which, of course, the analyst should not accept any more than he accepts the accusations). He may undertake self-imposed penance. He may redouble his efforts in whatever he thinks the analyst wants him to do, or he may swing over completely to the masochistic position of "I want the analyst to scold me for what I have done, to punish me, to attack me, to humiliate me, to assault me sexually, to castrate me, even to kill me!"

REGRESSION IN RESPECT TO THE INDIRECT OBJECT (DISPLACEMENT AND SUBSTITUTION)

All the while the analyst remains (or attempts to remain!) in a stable position. Whether the patient is up or down, whether the patient is provocative or seductive, whether he is angry or gay or flippant or sad, the analyst remains as he was. The constancy on the part of the analyst is unhuman, to be sure. It constantly surprises the patient because in ordinary life people respond to the behavior of others by corresponding changes. It is reassuring and encouraging to find someone who is both interested in and yet unaffected by one's

Significance of consistency

mood swing and one's confessions. To some extent this is the anti-dote or "healthy sequel" to the sense of frustration first experienced. This constancy in the analyst tends to stabilize the patient and enable him to orient himself in spite of his oscillations, so that gradually these oscillations diminish in frequency and latitude of excursion.

It may not be self-evident why the constancy of the analyst tends to stabilize the patient and becomes a potent therapeutic factor. By stability we do not mean aloofness and unavailability, notwithstanding the patient's protestations to the contrary. By stability we mean the readiness of the analyst *not* to respond to the patient's transferences except insofar as he recognizes them and communicates them and their meaning to the patient. This constant stance provides an increasingly stable image of what and who the analyst may actually be, freed progressively from the transference distortions. The diminishing frequency of the oscillations then reflects the patient's increasing awareness of the distorting nature of his transference. The analyst as a person becomes a point of reference for the patient, and hence available as a new object and increasingly so as the transference is analyzed.

Let us go back again to Figure 6. Thus far we have discussed aspects of the patient's regression represented by successive changes in the form of the object and of the verb. We have yet to consider the metamorphosis in the subject, I, and in the indirect object, the analyst. We shall take up the latter first.

It must be remembered that the progressive denudations of the primitive human wish to get something from someone or to have something pleasant done to one take place under the peculiar circumstances that the self-denuding patient is talking to a listener he does not see or know. He is talking in the presence of this person in a way in which he would not speak in the presence of any other human being. This unseen person is acting in a completely unexpected way in that he is not responding as any ordinary human being would to these very earnest appeals. It is just because this person who is listening cannot be seen and is rarely heard that it is possible for the patient to indulge his tendency to distort in fantasy the actual character, attitude, intentions, and even appearance of the analyst.

Hence, just as the nature of the thing desired and also the techniques of obtaining it change, so the image or prototype of the person from whom it is to be obtained also changes. It is as if the patient by mere repetition of the experience was enabled to regress back through the years so that instead of saying, "Doctor, I want relief from my headache, from my fears," the patient says, "Mother, I want to be taken into your arms."*

This phenomenon of displacement and substitution is perhaps the most familiar of all unconscious psychologic mechanisms. The veriest layman knows about kicking the dog or telling it to the chaplain or marrying on the rebound. But in the psychoanalytic situation there is more to it than mere displacement of affect and substitution of objects. There is a series of such displacements and a rainbow of affects that extend way back toward the earliest interpersonal relationships. This forms one of the most important aspects of the psychoanalytic treatment, perhaps the most important, and we shall devote a whole chapter to it later under the general heading of "transference."

REGRESSION IN RESPECT TO THE SUBJECT

We have yet to discuss the fourth aspect of regression, regression in respect to the *subject* of the formula.

One's first impression might have been that it was chiefly the "I," the subject, the analysand that does the regressing. But as we have seen, the regression also occurs in the various expressions of that I's endeavors.

But it does occur, also, in the subject itself. Any of us can experience some temporary regression at will—relapsing into memory and fantasy, imagining oneself to be a child again and experiencing pleasures or pain of long past situations. In the psychoanalytic situation this backward look becomes very vivid and productive. The

* Dr. Earl Bond, in a lecture to the Fellows of the Menninger School of Psychiatry, March 1957, described a patient afflicted with a severe mental illness of lengthy duration in the course of which she expressed overtly many sexual wishes. One day her physician in an experimental mood picked her up and held her in his arms, thrusting the nipple of a nursing bottle between her lips. She drank the milk avidly, expressing great satisfaction. "This," she said, "is what I have always wanted, this nonsexual love." This episode marked the beginning of a rapid return to recovery. Cf. also the work of Marguerite A. Sechehaye.[182]

"I" of this present moment of reality is then replaced by the I of a dozen years ago, or a score. William James pointed to the various identities or I's that performed respectively in the library, classroom, football game, the home. In psychoanalytic regression, as in hypnosis, the very manner and tone of speech may resemble those of earlier years.

It is an extraordinary and unique feature of psychoanalysis, however, that not only the doctor but the patient himself observes these phenomena. Thus while he is making this progressive retreat into the behavior and attitudes and memories of his childhood, which we have reviewed schematically, the analysand is observing it too, along with the analyst. He observes it with the unregressed part of his mind, his present-day conscious intelligence, the "healthy" part. A precondition for the therapeutic use of psychoanalysis is a certain partial intactness of the patient's ego, a part that can ally itself with the analyst, as Freud pointed out long ago. We assume that the patient's perceptions, memory, and reality-testing capacity are sufficiently intact to enable him to cooperate in this strange contract we have been describing in which he resumes, without consciously intending to, numerous previous "identities." Sterba[187] put it this way: that this alliance between the healthy part of the ego and the analyst enables the patient to overcome his resistances in the treatment! Indeed, resistance might be described as the tendency for the observing part of the ego to give up its brave aloofness and join the regressing ego.

It is natural, therefore, that every patient sometimes becomes confused about his own identity. He doesn't always know which of the various I's that comprise his total or essential self is now speaking. Is this the infantile I that is complaining, or is this the objective, adult I? Is this the four-year-old boy complaining to his mother or the eight-year-old boy reproaching his father or the twenty-five-year-old man scolding his doctor? He tries to distinguish and identify these, and one of the essential tasks of the analyst is to help the patient to obtain and maintain his orientation and to become aware of these many identities and the way and the conditions under which he employs them. This help is often best given not by official pronouncements or clever rejoinders or sharp queries but by the proper dosage of interference with or interpretation of the autistic process of the analysis, or few words of concurrence, or an indication of understanding by a chuckle or a casual comment or an expression of doubt about some "fact"—any of these may serve at one time or another to reorient the patient and start him on his way again in the further exploration.

It is the task of the analyst not only to help the patient to become conscious of the transference distortions, the substitutions and displacements, but simultaneously to help him to maintain the attitude of observer in an exploration. This joint exploration maintains the analytic work through times of painful frustration. It leads to an identification that is both conscious and unconscious. The patient tends to modify his patterns of behavior in order to be like the analyst, particularly in respect to the attitudes of introspection and self-scrutiny.

It may have seemed thus far as if nothing but blind rambling and futile frustration occurred in an analysis. But psychoanalysis is not characterized by perpetual silence on the part of the analyst. From time to time the silence is broken and the patient is helped in the direction of continuing the process by certain responses that both clarify and gratify.*

THE REVERSAL OF THE REGRESSION

We shall have more to say about the analyst's facilitation of the treatment later, under "Interpretations." For the present we must go further in schematizing the natural history of the "transference

---

* "At this point I want to introduce a new term for the reaction of the analyst to the communications, words, gestures, pauses, and so forth, of the analyzed person. I call the sum of this reaction, which includes all kinds of impressions, *response*. The analytic response is thus the emotional and intellectual reply to the speech, behavior, and appearance of the patient, and includes awareness of the inner voices of the analyst. Every interpretation, all that the analyst says, the form of his explanation and exposition, are all preceded, and to a great extent determined, by this response. The response is, so to speak, the inside experience of that which the analyst perceives, feels, senses, regarding the patient. It is clear from the preceding chapters that the main part of that response is in its nature unconscious or, to put it otherwise, that only a small part of it becomes conscious. The response is thus the dark soil in which our understanding of psychical processes is rooted. Out of these roots, which are hidden deep in the earth, emerges our intellectual, logical grasp of the problems. Out of these concealed roots grows the tree of psychoanalytic knowledge." (Theodor Reik[167])

neurosis," as it has been called traditionally, by which is meant the regression in point of subject, verb, direct object, and indirect object of the sentence, "I want help from the doctor."

Having gone back to the beginnings of all his misunderstanding and misinterpretations and mismanagements, having conceded his errors and forgiven those of others, having recognized the unrealistic nature of some of his cherished expectations and love objects and methods of procedure, the patient gradually begins to put away childish things. The "I" begins to grow up. He gradually "works through," as we say; he works his way back to reality, abandoning his inexpedient goals and techniques and attitudes for more appropriate ones, more adult expectations from more suitable love objects obtained in more effective ways. In this process of working through, the more infantile aims and goals lose much of their compulsive force; the patient is then free to choose or to develop new techniques, aims, and goals that are more adaptive and gratifying.

In this *reversal phase* of the regressive process, the psychoanalyst who has been all sorts of people in the fantasies of the patient gradually becomes increasingly a kind, friendly, incorruptible person who has stood by the patient, withstood his attacks and reactions and fulfilled the contract realistically. This objectification of the analyst characterizes the final stage of the treatment; its success is a good criterion of the patient's progress toward "health," but not the only one. We shall discuss this at greater length in the chapter on termination.

Why does the process thus reverse itself in direction, so that what was a regression becomes a progression? Is this determined by mysterious internal forces of direction like the orbit of a planet or a molecule? Or is it the result not of innate tensions but of alterations in the internal tensions? These we like to believe are effected by the clarifications, catharses, improved perspectives, and reduced anxieties that the examination of the past—in the light of the present—has achieved.

For the regression induced by the analytic situation is both frustrating and gratifying to the patient. To perceive one's own childishness is often a shock, yet the reminiscences and reexperiencing of earlier periods of life may be quite pleasurable. We assume this after a "certain period" during which the patient's regressive behavior has been emerging for both him and the analyst to observe. The painful aspects of the regressive experience begin to dominate the gratifying ones. The patient then consciously and unconsciously attempts to change his behavior to make it more congruent with his picture of maturity. Consequently, fewer and fewer regressive qualities appear or remain, and the process seems to take a progressive direction.

Yet another factor can be adduced for this. The unconscious factors of the neurotic patterns find their expression in the transference, and in the regression of the subject, object, verb, and indirect object of the formula sentence. On the level of theory, we may say that these elements, by the fact of their having been repressed and therefore unconscious, are unintegrated with preconscious and conscious experiences. Such isolation has a constricting effect on behavior, narrowing choices, and leaving to compulsive determination much of the patient's action. This permits new organizations of affects and ideas, more of which now become available to consciousness and hence under greater voluntary control. "If an interpretation is correct," Leowald stated, "it changes something in the nexus of [the patient's] psychic processes."[126]

Leowald continued: "Analysis of the patient's demands and conflicts in essence involves having him put into words, whenever possible, his feelings, thoughts, fantasies, etc. Recognizing them as manifestations and derivatives of the underlying instinctual conflicts, he would then interpret them by fitting them into a wider psychic context. This involves our linking them with the patient's past experiences and establishing or reestablishing freer communication between different levels of integration of his past experiences. Such linking has been conceptualized by Freud as hypercathexis."[126]

This new organization now makes possible greater communication between unconscious and preconscious processes, adding a significant contribution of secondary process thinking to behavior, and greater freedom in now controlled access to infantile motives and modes of response. This increasing hypercathexis is what underlies the appearance of the progressive direction in the analysis.

Some therapeutic regressions do not seem to proceed far enough; the turning point occurs too soon, and the patient abandons the process regression of treatment and turns back toward nonclinical contemporary reality. This has been called "a flight into health." The phase should be no reproach to either patient or analyst. Perhaps the patient unconsciously knows best.

The Greek work *kairos* was used in Hippocratic medicine to designate that moment at which an acute illness changed its course for the better or for the worse. It was believed that certain critical symptoms pointed to this moment and indicated the new direction, recognizable by the proficient physician. This time-honored concept has been revived in the theological field by Paul Tillich[193] and reintroduced into psychotherapy by Arthur Kielholz.[107] The implication is that such moments occur not only in the process of psychoanalytic treatment but in the process of any other deviations from a previous course of life and way of living.[28] We shall return to this point in our last chapter.

IV

TRANSFERENCE AND COUNTERTRANSFERENCE

The Involuntary Participation
of Both Parties in the Treatment Situation

IN THE COURSE OF THE CONTINUING THERAPEUTIC ALLIANCE OF THE psychoanalytic treatment situation, psychological changes occur in both parties. We have described some of these as they occur in the patient as regression. There are successive alterations in the indirect object of the patient's conscious-unconscious wish for help *from* the analyst. The analyst becomes at various times people of earlier importance to the patient—mother, brother, sister, father, grandmother, etc., in the fantasies and unconscious formulations of the patient. Although this is only one aspect of the therapeutic regression, many psychoanalysts speak, write, and even think of it as characterizing the whole process and refer to it as the "transference neurosis." There are historical and rational explanations for this, all dependent upon the fact that of the four features of the regression occurring in the treatment situation, transference is undoubtedly the most important or, at least, the best understood. But it is *not* the sum total of the regression.

For centuries, physicians and others have observed the childishness that characterizes the sick and dependent person in point of technique and objectives. Some regression accompanies almost any illness, and this is furthered by the help from the doctor. Some physicians almost consciously play the role of the "grand" father or of the jocular uncle. But rare, indeed, is the doctor who perceives that he is unintentionally filling the role of a sister, a mother, or a hated father! This type of identification is equally unrealized by the patient.

Freud himself was astonished at the discovery of this tendency. Later he recognized its existence in all therapeutic relationships, but he always considered the phenomenon to be one of the essential and distinguishing features of psychoanalysis. Greenacre put it thus:

> Human beings do not thrive well in isolation, being sustained then mostly by memories and hopes, even to the point of hallucination, or by reaching out to nonhuman living things (like Mendel and the beans).* This need for sensory contact, basically the contact of warm touch of another body but secondarily experienced in the other senses as well (even the word "contact" is significant), probably comes from the long period of care which the human infant must have before he is able to sustain himself. Lonely infants fed and cared for regularly and with sterile impersonal efficiency do not live to childhood.
>
> Even if the periods of repeated contact between two individuals do not comprise a major part of their time, still such an emotional bond develops and does so more quickly and more sensitively if the two persons are *alone* together; i.e., the more the spontaneous currents and emanations of feeling must be concentrated the one upon the other and not shared, divided, or reflected among members of a group. I have already indicated that I believe the matrix of this *is* a veritable matrix; i.e., comes largely from the original mother-infant quasi union of the first months of life. This I consider the basic transference; or one might call it the primary transference, or some part of primitive social instinct.
>
> Now if both people are adults but one is troubled and the other is versed in the ways of trouble and will endeavor to put the torchlight of his understanding at the disposal of the troubled one, to lend it to him that he may find his way more expeditiously, the situation more nearly approximates that of the

---

* Dr. G. undoubtedly meant to write "the peas." Forgive!

analytic relationship. The analyst acts then like an extra function, or set of functions, which is lent to the analysand for the latter's temporary use and benefit.

Since this relationship may, in its most primitive aspects, be based on the mother-child relationship and since the patient is a troubled person seeking help, one can see at once that the relationship will not be one of equal warming, but that there will be a tendency for the patient to develop an attitude of expectant dependent receptiveness toward the physician. It is the aim of treatment, however, to increase the patient's maturity, to realize his capacity for self-direction, his "self-possession" (in the deeper sense of the word); and *not* to augment his state of helplessness and dependence, with which he in his neurotic suffering is already burdened.[85]

Freud has been struck from the first by the curious behavior of patients in hypnosis, in that they accepted the authority of the hypnotist as if he were a far more powerful individual than he actually was. Freud sought an explanation for this, both as an observer of Charcot and in the course of his own subsequent treatment of patients with and without hypnosis. He called this curious tendency for the patient to respond to the therapist as if the latter were *someone else*, "transference." In attempting to explain it, he invoked the mechanism of displacement and the principle of the repetition compulsion.

HISTORICAL NOTE

Freud's first allusion to what later became his concept of transference[65] was made in 1895 in the comment that one of his patients made a "false connection" to the analyst when an affect became conscious which related to memories still unconscious. This use of the term *transference* to describe such displacement phenomena was used later in the theoretical section of *The Interpretation of Dreams*.[55] "We learn from the [psychology of the neuroses] that an unconscious idea is, as such, quite incapable of entering the preconscious and that it can only exercise any effect there by establishing a connection with an idea which already belongs to the preconscious, and by *transferring* [italics ours] its intensity onto it and by getting itself 'covered' by it. Here we have the fact of 'transference,' which provides an explanation of so many striking phenomena in the mental life of neurotics. The preconscious idea, which thus acquires an undeserved degree of intensity, may either be left unaltered by the transference, or it may have a modification forced upon it, derived from the content of the idea which affects the transference" (pp. 562, 563).

Such displacements effect noteworthy changes on the preconscious ideas, and this process underlies the more complex conception of transference later evolved by Freud. In 1905, in discussing the sexual nature of the impulses felt toward the analyst, he asked; "What are transferences? They are new additions or facsimiles of the tendencies and fantasies which are aroused and made conscious during the progress of the analysis. . . ."[51]

In psychoanalytic treatment, the peculiar power of such transferences to effect a reexperiencing of what was earlier felt toward important figures finds this elaboration in a 1910 paper:

> In every psychoanalytic treatment of a neurotic patient a strange phenomenon that is known as "transference" makes its appearance. The patient, that is to say, directs towards the physician a degree of affectionate feeling (mingled, often enough, with hostility) which is based on no real relation between them and which—as is shown by every detail of its emergence—can only be traced back to old, wishful fantasies of the patient's which have become unconscious. Thus the part of the patient's emotional life which he can no longer recall to memory is reexperienced by him in his relation to the physician; and it is only this re-experiencing in the "transference" that convinces him of the existence and of the power of these unconscious sexual impulses. His symptoms, taking an analogy from chemistry, are precipitates or earlier experiences in this sphere of love (in the widest sense of the word) and it is only in the raised temperature of his experience of the transference that they can be resolved and reduced to other psychical products. In this reaction the physician, if I may borrow an apt phrase from Ferenczi (1909), plays the part of a catalectic ferment, which temporarily attracts to itself the affects liberated in the process.[50]

In his earlier writings Freud repeatedly equated transference and suggestion (see Macalpine[132] for five instances). But in 1912 he attempted an explanation of the dynamics of transference in terms of the libido theory. The processes of fixation and repetition principally underlie the following description.

> It must be understood that each individual, through the combined operation of his innate disposition and the influences brought to bear on him during his early years, has acquired a specific method of his own in his conduct of his erotic life— that is, in the preconditions to falling in love which he lays down, in the instincts he satisfies and the aims he sets himself in the course of it. And this produces what might be described as a stereotyped plate (or several such), which is constantly repeated—constantly reprinted afresh—in the course of the person's life, so far as external circumstances and the nature of the love objects accessible to him permit, and which is certainly not entirely inceptible to change in the face of recent experiences. Now, our observations have shown that only a portion of these impulses which determine the course of erotic life have passed through the full process of psychical development. That portion is directed towards reality, is at the disposal of the conscious personality, and forms a part of it. Another portion of the libidinal impulses has been held up in the course of development; it has been kept away from the conscious personality and from reality, and has either been prevented from further expansion, except in fantasy, or has remained wholly in the unconscious so that it is unknown to the personality's consciousness. If someone's need for love is not entirely satisfied by reality, he is bound to approach every new person whom he meets with libidinal anticipatory ideas; and it is highly probable that both portions of his libido, the portion that is capable to becoming conscious as well as the unconscious one, have a share in forming that attitude.[49]

In this paper as well as in the important technical paper "Recollection, Repeating and Working Through"[61] he emphasized the repetitive character of the transference, and in "Beyond the Pleasure Principle,"[48] he indicated this to be the very origin of transference.

> For instance, the patient does not say that he remembers how defiant and critical he used to be in regard to the authority of his parents, but he behaves in that way towards the physician. He does not remember how he came to a helpless and hopeless deadlock in his infantile searchings after the truth of sexual matters but he produces a mass of confused dreams and associations, complains that he never succeeds at anything, and

describes it as his fate never to be able to carry anything through. He does not remember that he was intensely ashamed of certain sexual activities, but he makes it clear that he is ashamed of the treatment to which he has submitted himself, and does his upmost to keep it a secret; and so on. . . . We soon perceive that the transference is itself only a bit of repetition in that the repetition is the transference of the forgotten past, not only on to the physician, but also on to all the other aspects of the current situation.[61]

It is understandable that Freud should have been puzzled by transference and that he later modified his earlier explanations of it. We know now that certain transferences permit—indeed, greatly enhance the effect of—suggestion, but constitute something quite different in essence. There has been an increasingly clear recognition of the fact that the displacement, introjection, projection, and repetition associated with the (partial) misidentification of the analyst and the use of various attitudes and techniques toward him are all part and parcel of the total regressive process described in the preceding chapters of this book. In the years since Freud's discovery of the phenomenon, the word *transference* has been applied with confusing variability. For some it means merely an attitude toward other persons; others use the word to describe any unrealistic attitude toward another person, especially an unrealistic attitude toward a therapist. Commonly but incorrectly it is used to describe a consciously positive feeling toward a therapist.*

To cite some additional authoritative definitions, Anna Freud defines transference as "all those impulses experienced by the patient in his relation with the analyst which are not newly created by the objective analytic situation but have their source in early . . . object relations and are now merely revived under the influence of the repetition compulsion."[45] Glover[80, 81] defines it as the "capacity . . . to repeat in current situations . . . attitudes developed in early family life," which, in our opinion, is too narrow. Fenichel[33] equated transference with resistance (which in our opinion is also too narrow). Lagache[115] has defined transference as "a repetition in present-day life, and particularly in the relationship to the analyst,

---

* For a brief, lucid statement, see Waelder's "Introduction to the Discussion [of] Problems of Transference."[201]

of unconscious emotional attitudes developed during childhood within the family group and especially toward the parents." Macalpine's definition is broad: "Analytic transference may thus be defined as a person's gradual adaptation by regression to the infantile analytic setting." In other words, she includes all forms of the regression under the term *transference*.

> The analysand brings, in varying degrees, an inherent capacity, a readiness to form transferences, and this readiness is met by something which converts it into an actuality. In hypnosis the patient's inherent capacity to be hypnotized is induced by the command of the hypnotist, and the patient submits instantly. In psychoanalysis it is neither achieved in one session nor is it a matter of obeying. Psychoanalytic technique creates an infantile setting, of which the "neutrality" of the analyst is but one feature among others. . . . In their aggregate, these factors, . . . amount to a reduction of the analysand's object world and denial of object relations in the analytic room.[132]

We define transference in a much more limited way as *the unrealistic roles or identities unconsciously ascribed to an analyst by a patient in the regression of the psychoanalytic treatment and the patient's reactions to those representations, usually derived from earlier experiences.* These identities reflect unconscious fantasies and recollections that the patient reenacts in the analytic situation.

In other words, this is the aspect of the regression that relates to the indirect object of the patient's expectations and constitutes an involuntary unintentional participation of the analyst in the treatment situation. It is always irrational and to a considerable degree disagreeable to the patient.[184] It is facilitated by the total psychoanalytic treatment setup in many ways—the quiet and constancy of the environment, the analyst's silence, the encouragement of free association, and other features. (See especially Macalpine.[133]) It is not the result of suggestion on the part of the analyst, although the characteristic behavior of the analyst inevitably assists in determining aspects of it.

Our definition, given above, endeavors to describe transference as a phenomenon usually occurring in association with the regression in the psychoanalytic treatment situation called the transference neurosis. Transference, as we have defined it, eliminates (we hope) such presumptuous and mischievous notions as "manipulating" the transference. One can, to be sure, behave in certain ways that affect the frustration tension. This will, in turn, affect the depth of the regression, which will be reflected in the transference manifestations.

On the basis of our definition, also, there are no such things as "positive transference" and "negative transference," terms we hear used to mean all sorts of unrelated things. One may speak of positive and negative attitudes in the transference; one can say that the transference is at the moment such as to present a positive or a negative feeling toward the analyst. Our definition places emphasis upon the fact emphasized earlier; namely, that the analyst and the analysand are engaged in a two-party contractual relationship in which the patient makes his payment and expects a return. He gets a return, but not in the form in which he expects it. What he actually gets that is valuable in this two-party process, is the *result* of his disappointment in not immediately getting what he originally expected! In the course of his experience he relives many phases and incidents of his life in relation to a neutral figure to whom he ascribes many roles or as-if identities.

A fairly typical illustration of this can be cited. An unmarried male laboratory technician of thirty underwent psychoanalysis for the relief of his lifelong loneliness and general dissatisfaction with himself and what he was getting out of existence. Early in the analysis he described his father's reserve and aloofness. Later he made similar observations about one of his teachers and then about his employer. Ultimately, of course, it was the analyst who seemed reserved, cold and aloof. A little later, however, he recalled certain earlier experiences with a girl cousin whose warmth was a sharp contrast to the chill formalities in his own home. He felt guilty, however, because of certain of his responses to her advances and feared particularly what his father's reaction might be. Something similar was repeated with a young woman he met in college. The analyst was not surprised, accordingly, when some months later the patient dreamed of the analyst in the form of a seductress, which evoked reproach that the analyst was expecting too much of him and encouraging him in forbidden directions. Next, it developed that there had been in his childhood a particularly stern aunt whose judgments were feared by all the relatives and, indeed, by the entire neighborhood. She evidently represented to him, then, what law and order, the police court and purgatory came to represent to him later. This began to appear in the transference when the analyst, who had previously been accused both of coldness and of seductiveness, became a stern figure of retribution from whom the patient expected punishment and dismissal.

In all of these aspects of transference one sees the irrational roles in which the analyst is cast, the ways in which the earlier models are used. The little details of identification—inflections of the voice and irrelevant coincidences such as the color of a necktie worn—are always striking. Even more impressive is the way the patient takes advantage of subtle situations and even creates opportunities for some apparent actualization of the role. In this, of course, unintentional countertransferences in the analyst may unwittingly cooperate, as we shall see later.

Near the end of an analysis the analysand becomes merely a recovering patient, talking to a soon-no-longer-necessary psychoanalyst; old fantasy assignments to the analyst tend to be abandoned.* It is in this sense that one can say the transference is ultimately dissipated (although there may be continuing displacements).

This chapter was introduced with a subtitle of "The Involuntary Participation of Both Parties. . . ." This was to imply that the analyst does participate in the contract by more than his presence and the rent of his office, so to speak. He does give something to the patient beyond audience. By his noncritical attention to what the patient is saying and doing, the analyst is doing something. He is gratifying the patient as well as frustrating him. But certainly the frustration exceeds the gratification, and this is related to the patient's progressive regression, if we may use such contradiction in terms, the tendency to regress further and further. Freud ascribed this repression to the frustration alone (see Lagache[115]), knowing that some frustration is always involved in learning; but psychoanalysis is not like the regression of the Buddhist holy man, for there is constantly some correction not only from the analyst but from the hours spent outside the analysis.

As we shall see later, in the chapter on interpretation, the

---

* Lagache[115] has elaborated this interacting of regression and projection in an extension of some ideas put forward originally by Pierre Janet in regard to the dual character of all social behavior.

patient gradually becomes aware of the fact that he has responded to the analyst as if he were mother or father or someone else, and. when this is clearly understood by him, the former value of the myth is lost. The patient "corrects" his mistake, "accepts" reality and usually moves on to another phase or period of his life with other *personae.*

Old conflicts and archaic ways of responding to them are now viewed from the vantage point of a later time and a greater maturity. Loewald put it this way:

> The transference neurosis, in the technical sense of the establishment and resolution of it in the analytic process, is due to the blood of recognition* which the patient's unconscious is given to taste—so that the old ghosts may re-awaken to life. Those who know ghosts tell us that they longed to be released from their ghost-life and led to rest as ancestors. As ancestors they live forth in the present generation, while as ghosts they are compelled to haunt the present generation with their shadow-life. Transference is pathological insofar as the unconscious is a crowd of ghosts, and this is the beginning of the transference neurosis in analysis: ghosts of the unconscious imprisoned by defenses but haunting the patient in the dark of his defenses and symptoms, are allowed to taste blood, are let loose. In the daylight of analysis the ghosts of the unconscious are layed and led to rest as ancestors whose power is taken over and transformed into the newer intensity of present life, of the secondary process and contemporary objects.[125]

Yet all of these shifts and changes occur in the context of an authentic relationship between analyst and analysand, which builds upon the mutual work accomplished. The patient finds new ways of relating himself to the analyst; the analyst, by his response to those new ways, nurtures the patient's growing maturity. This is one of the meanings of "where Id was there shall Ego be."

Korzybski[112] made a vivid contribution to our understanding of this mechanism with his insistence on distinguishing the identity of any particular person or thing by precise statement of time, place, and circumstances, graphically insisting that M^b (the mother of, say,

---

* The allusion is to Freud's comparison of the immortality of unconscious processes to the Homeric ghosts of the underworld which "awoke to new life as soon as they tasted blood" (p. 553).[55]

the six-year-old Tom Jones) is *not* M^a or M^c or M^d, meaning that same woman as related to Tom Jones at the age of three, or ten or thirty.

COUNTERTRANSFERENCE

We should not forget that the psychoanalyst himself has an unconscious, and that he, too, has a persistent temptation to indulge in infantile techniques and objectives, magical thinking, and the like. But whereas the patient has many encouragements to indulge in these things, the analyst has many reasons for not doing so and much support for the resistance of his temptations. Although it is true that the analyst is involved in the analytic situation with the patient, he is not subject to the same frustrations and—theoretically—is not involved in a "transference neurosis" (regression). Nevertheless, his reactions to the patient may contain strong irrational and unconscious elements. This empirical fact must be discussed in connection with the corresponding misidentifications made by the patient. Countertransference is often linked in discussions with transference, although, since the analyst is not receiving treatment, *his* unconsciously determined reactions to the patient cannot and should not be described as if they were his therapeutic reactions to the patient's therapeutic intentions. But they *are* adventitious, unintentional, and involuntary participations by the party of the second part in the contract and they are always there and always important.

Having made the great discovery of the tendency of the patient to make a displacement upon the therapist of the emotions and feelings experienced in childhood toward his parents and other (significant) persons, Freud made the secondary and allied discovery, five years later, of what he named countertransference, "which arises in the physician as the result of the patient's influence on his [the analyst's] unconscious feelings. . . . We have noticed that every analyst's achievement is limited by what his own complexes and resistances permit. . . ."[53]*

At first, this was regarded as a troublesome and interfering phe-

---

* Thereafter, Ferenczi contributed a classical paper on the subject[35] and there were increasingly frequent references to it in the literature, with, more recently, quite a number of serious studies devoted to it. Curiously enough, most of these

nomenon, for which allowance and correction had to be made lest it "blur the transference picture."[33] Freud's recommendation was emotional aloofness and coldness, like that of a surgeon, "who puts aside all his own feelings, including that of human sympathy, and concentrates his mind on one single purpose, that of performing the operation as skillfully as possible."[65] This was an ideal that analysts, for a time, strove to achieve. Later, of course, it was realized that the analyst must not only be this surgeon, but he must also be the warm, human, friendly, helpful physician. He must be both. Freud's advice to analysts on the role of warmth and sympathy in the analytic process is rarely quoted in full. True, he urged restraint; but he also urged tact and eschewed cold rejection of his patients' confessions of their love for him. He advised against both ignoring "the transference love" and responding to it. Only in this context can the patient's conditions for loving come to light.

But regardless of what he tries, consciously, to be and do, the analyst will *tend* to react to unconscious roles he ascribes to the patient. In the words of Annie Reich, "Counter-transference is [not only an inevitable feature but also] a necessary prerequisite of analysis. If it does not exist, the necessary talent and interest is lacking. But it has to remain shadowy and in the background."[162] It is a part of the interrelationship.

More and more it is recognized that psychoanalysis is not something that happens to one person under the observing eye and with the occasional help of a second person, but that it is a two-party transactional relationship. (This is what we have attempted to emphasize throughout this manual.) Sullivan,[189, 190] Lagache,[115] Fromm-Reichmann,[70, 71] and Loewald[125, 126] have also emphasized this. We become so preoccupied with describing the reactions of the patient, and particularly the predetermined character of his reactions, that we forget that the analyst is also a person, that he, too, is a party to the contract, that he, too, is reacting, even though his predominant *overt* reaction is one of silent listening. One has to remind oneself

have been by women colleagues—Alice Balint,[5] Therese Benedek,[8] Frieda Fromm-Reichmann,[69] Paula Heiman,[95] Phyllis Greenacre,[83] Margaret Little,[124] Annie Reich,[162] and Macalpine.[100] However, the contributions of Fenichel,[32] Berman,[11] Fliess,[42] Gitelson,[79] and Winnicott[203] are also important. Recent contributions to the significance of countertransference have come from Szasz,[191] Tower,[195] Spit,[186] and Racker[156] who are strongly commended to readers.

over and over that it is never accurate to say that a certain reaction is that of person *A* to person *B*. The reaction is always a fluid process in which *A* is also reacting to the way in which *B* reacts to *A* and, to be still more accurate, *A*'s reaction is modified by the way *B* reacts to the way *A* reacts to the way *B* reacts, and so on. And likewise *B* is reacting to *A*'s reactions to the way *B* reacts to *A* and so on. One could summarize it by saying that *A* and *B* interact with each other. Paul Heiman said, aptly: "Always ask who is doing what to whom and when"![95]

On the other hand, the relationship between a psychoanalyst and a patient is not that of two participants in a fencing match who have to make constant mutual adjustments to each other's moves. The analyst is a relatively fixed point. By reasons of training, dedication, interest, experience, tradition, and other factors, he has great authority. The patient, on the other hand, has great potential freedom of motion, but relatively little power. The only thing the patient can be authoritative about is the way he feels, and he is not always very sure about this.

Now, in any adjustment between two individuals, there are—for both—certain gratifications and certain frustrations. The gratifications tend toward a closer union of the two, toward integration, toward contact, toward love; the frustrations tend toward hostile attitudes and separation. These gratifications and frustrations are, as we know, both conscious and unconscious. In our everyday life they have crystallized in habitual preferences and aversions and friendship patterns.

In a psychoanalytic treatment contract, we ask one of the two parties that he examine day after day his own reactions to a situation in which there are both gratifications and increasing frustration. The other individual is presumed to be under less frustration and of him we may seem to make no such demand; it is not a part of the didactics of psychoanalysis. Theoretically, he has merely to observe the effect of the role he plays as a silent listener and apparent frustrator upon the suppliant party. They are *both* participants in this process, and notwithstanding the fact that the patient is consciously and undeniably frustrated in the analytic situation whereas the analyst is theoretically not frustrated, what we all realize is that to some extent the patient *is* gratified and to some extent the analyst *is* frustrated. Correspondingly, the analyst, as a human being, reacts to his frustrations and makes use of various of his "defense" measures, particularly identification and projection, sometimes denial and avoidance or reaction formation and isolation. He, too, undergoes waves of temporary regression, including temporary misidentifications of his patient. His patient momentarily becomes his mother, his father, a pupil, a colleague, another patient, or even a projection of the analyst's own self.

It seems scarcely necessary to illustrate countertransference with clinical examples, because they are so abundantly available in every training center. But if we may revert for a moment to the case cited earlier in this chapter of the laboratory technician who made his analyst into a father, a cousin, and an aunt successively, we can show how the countertransference appeared there. The analyst was actually a rather warmhearted fellow, and the accusation of coldness was only somewhat amusing to him. The accusation that he was like a female seductress, however, he found a trifle disturbing. "Does the patient realize how irrational such accusations are?" he thought. A little later, when he was cast into the role of a stern female judge, he was less annoyed at being made a woman than at being regarded as a moralist. (Actually he *was* somewhat moralistic —more so than he realized.)

But he asked himself, "Why is the patient annoying me? Why would it occur to me to say, 'Find yourself another analyst, Mr. Fellow!' Of course, I won't, but. . . ."

And then he reflected that the patient was neither soliciting affection nor rejecting it but attempting, rather, to create a situation in which he (the patient) would be rejected and thus given justification for releasing the anger so long pent up against these original figures. In so doing he would sacrifice what little companionship he had had and suffer again the loneliness of complete rejection.

Racker[156] has referred to this experience in the analyst as the occurrence of "complimentary identification," by which he means the identification by the analyst with an object introjected by the patient. In this instance the analyst identified himself with the stern female figures in the patient's life. The analyst's awareness of his own discomfort permitted him to recognize what the patient was doing to whom and when. This illustration does not contradict the previous statement that countertransference is an unconscious reaction. The manifestations of countertransference may be conscious although the intrapsychic conditions resulting in its appearance are unconscious.

THE DETECTION AND CORRECTION OF COUNTERTRANSFERENCE

Some of the common ways—cognitive, affective, and behavioral —in which countertransference makes its appearance—*i.e.*, becomes an interference—may be worth listing for their didactic value. The following are some we have jotted down at various times during seminars and control sessions in which they appeared: Probably most analysts have been guilty of some of them.

Inability to understand certain kinds of material that touch on the analyst's own personal problems.

Depressed or uneasy feelings during or after analytic hours with certain patients.

Carelessness in regard to arrangements—forgetting the patient's appointment, being late for it, letting the patient's hours run overtime for no special reason.

Persistent drowsiness (of the analyst) during the analytic hour.

Over- or under-assiduousness in financial arrangements with the patient, for example, letting him become considerably indebted without analyzing it, or trying to "help" him to get a loan.

Repeatedly experiencing erotic or affectionate feelings toward a patient.

Permitting and even encouraging resistance in the form of acting-out.

Security-seeking, narcissistic devices such as trying to impress the patient in various ways, or to impress colleagues with the importance of one's patient.

Cultivating the patient's continued dependence in various ways, especially by unnecessary reassurances.

An urge to engage in professional gossip concerning a patient.

Sadistic, unnecessary sharpness in formulation of comments and interpretations, and the reverse.

Feeling that the patient must get well for the sake of the doctor's reputation and prestige.

"Hugging the case to one's bosom," *i.e.*, being too afraid of losing the patient.

Getting conscious satisfaction from the patient's praise, appreciation, and evidences of affection, and so forth.

Becoming disturbed by the patient's persistent reproaches and accusations.

Arguing with the patient.

Premature reassurances against the development of anxiety in the patient or, more accurately, finding oneself unable to gauge the point of optimum frustration tension.

Trying to help the patient in extra-analytic ways, for example, in making certain financial arrangements, or housing arrangements.

A compulsive tendency to "hammer away" at certain points.

Recurrent impulses to ask favors of the patient.

Sudden increase or decrease of interest in a certain case.*

A personal analysis, no matter how long or thorough, is never sufficient to eradicate all of one's blind spots or all of one's tendencies to find surreptitious satisfactions for infantile needs in other than realistic ways. Some of these lurk constantly as potential "neurotic" tendencies, as it were; others become organized into the personality structure. They are bound to determine certain attitudes and reactions of the analyst toward all of his patients. We have to assume that the more serious and more interfering neurotic persistences have been called to the analyst's attention by his teachers to the point that he is prepared to make the proper allowances for them in his clinical work. If not, there is nothing for it but more personal analysis.

But short of this, the conscientious young analyst may become greatly concerned over a realization of his involuntary participation, and his proper therapeutic "attitude" will be impaired by this over-concern. On the other hand, the less sensitive or less conscientious young analyst may tend to be oblivious of or indifferent to the ways in which he is deleteriously affecting his patient or impeding the patient's progress. Since countertransference is by definition an

* I confess with mixed emotions an example of my own countertransference. One of my patients busied himself for a time with stock market speculations. Day after day he came in reporting having made a thousand or five thousand or even more on the previous day's market. He seemed to be very shrewd in his selections and soon ran his surplus up to rather high figures. He made no secret of his choices or plans, and upon one occasion I privately followed his example with a commitment. Fortunately for both of us the market fell abruptly and considerably a few days later, and we were both "wiped out." [K.A.M.]

"unconscious" phenomenon, the question is how one may deal with something he doesn't know about. Some practical suggestions seem to be indicated even in a book dedicated to theory, and we have accordingly set down a few rules of thumb, each one of which deserves (and, in a teaching seminar, would receive) fuller discussion. Here they are:

1. One must be constantly alert to the existence of countertransference but not intimidated by it, recognizing both its pitfalls and its uses. It may alert the analyst to unverbalized themes and impulses in his patient. But although it may be useful and though it may be inevitable, let us not assume that the more of it the better. Think about it from time to time; reflect on it. In this one might well take a page out of the book of some religious orders. For countertransference is dangerous only when it is forgotten about.

2. Try to recognize those manifestations of a disturbing countertransference which enter into one's work generally and to analyze their meaning in the light of one's own personal self-knowledge. This refers both to those phases of countertransference that do not seem to interfere with the treatment of patients and to those that do. This is greatly facilitated by discussing the matter with a trusted colleague.

3. When you become aware of feelings of countertransference, especially if they are persistent, try to think through the analytic situation again and identify those features or acts or words of the patient that triggered off this reaction in you. "Why am I irritated? Why am I erotically aroused? Why does this come up now? What is the patient subtly trying to get me to do which I haven't seen clearly, maybe because I so much want to do it?"

4. Avoid becoming so introspective about your countertransference that the patient is forgotten; after all, it is the latter who is the primary object of the process. (A physiological study of the tensions manifested by therapist and patient in their psychotherapeutic relationships has thrown some light on countertransference from an unexpected angle. The authors conclude that there was a tendency for the therapist's heart rate and lability to follow a pattern similar to that of the patient. But in phases of antagonism on the part of the patient, his heart rather tended to slow down whereas the therapist's tended to speed up.[20])

One might go so far as to say that one of the most important functions of psychoanalytic societies is a control of countertransference tendencies. Dr. Robert Waelder emphasized this point. No analyst can see everything; each one's vision is limited by his personality. Members of a group are mutually self-corrective. As Waelder put it, "Since we are all partially blind, the best we can do is to support each other so that the vision of one may make up for the myopia of the other, and vice versa."[200]

THE CHARACTER OF THE ANALYST

We have described now how in the regression induced by the psychoanalytic treatment situation the patient reacts to the analyst in successively different ways: first, as a mysterious medical person who promises some kind of help; second, as a misidentified father, mother, brother, and so forth; third, as a human being with certain weaknesses; and, finally, as a human being with certain strengths. It is important to say more about these strengths, and about the character of the psychoanalyst. Several colleagues have written thoughtful articles on this aspect of the treatment.

We cannot ignore the fact that what the psychoanalyst believes, what he lives for, what he loves, what he considers to be the purpose of life and the joy of life, what he considers to be good and what he considers to be evil, become known to the patient and influence him enormously not as "suggestion" but as inspiration. A degree of such identification with the analyst is inevitable, although not necessarily permanent. However, for that longer or shorter postanalytic period during which identification with the analyst is operative, the patient shows forth the analyst—or at least some aspects of him—to the world. No matter how skillful the analyst is in certain technical maneuvers, his ultimate product, like Galatea, will reflect not only his handicraft but his character. Waelder well put it that analysts are taught to discard the overestimates made of them by their patients as less than sound reflections of mature judgment but rather the consequences of a situation of regression, but there is always the possibility of forgetting this.

> No doubt all psychoanalysts withstand the danger of flattery
> for some time; but if flattery continues as a daily fare year in

year out, there is a danger that some people may eventually be persuaded to accept part of it as a reality. It is a great danger to be trapped in self-overvaluation and complacency

for as you know securitie

is mortal's chiefest enemie.

[Furthermore, Waelder continued] psychoanalysis is an occupation in which practitioners work alone with nobody observing them and without any controls. If a surgeon operates on a patient, the result is known immediately among many people in the hospital. What happens in a psychoanalytic situation remains between analyst and patient and reaches out from this closed situation only in instances of extreme emergency. In this way the analyst works without checks other than those imposed by his sense of responsibility. There is always a danger of deterioration in the work of people who do not have the benefit of comparison with the work of others and who are in no way supervised. I do not think of deterioration in the crude meaning of a blurring of the sense of responsibility—such instances, happily, are very rare—but in a more subtle sense. An analyst knows what he has seen in a patient but he cannot know what he has not seen but might have seen, and he may get an exaggerated idea of the completeness of his observations and the adequacy of his interpretations.[200]

Waelder made these observations in connection with demonstrating the usefulness of psychoanalytic societies, but in the same article he went on to speak of the pitfalls and dangers of psychoanalytic societies. It was inevitable that, in a young and growing science such as psychoanalysis has been, there would be great zeal and intensity and almost evangelistic defensiveness. It is difficult for today's analysts to recognize the prejudice and suspicion with which those of us who are older were once surrounded. Freud ascribed this to the nature of the subject matter and the injury it inflicted upon our narcissism to realize that we are not quite so free or so masterful as we had assumed. But we suspect that it goes beyond this. The dissection of human bodies met with the same general aversion, as did numerous other medical innovations. The mysteriousness of psychoanalysis and the closed group principle have offended many scientists. Perhaps to an extent larger than we realize, some of us were guilty of just plain bad manners. Some analysts seem to assume that having learned about the unconscious motivation of a dozen patients, they now *understand* human nature—and understand it *their way.* Some of us, however, feel that excluding nonanalysts from psychoanalytic meetings inhibits a valuable source of stimuli for the self-correction of psychoanalytic ideas. We regard as a helpful development the fact that some societies now regularly open some of their meetings to medical and psychological colleagues and interested laymen.

Humility and modesty are always becoming and are more than necessary as a part of a psychoanalyst's equipment. This is not to say that patients cannot benefit sometimes even by the most ill-mannered assertions or the most condescending explanations. But the very spirit of psychoanalytic work is to help an afflicted person to realize his *own* potentialities, to let a patient discover what *he* can really do—not because he is commanded to, not because it is diagrammed for him, but because he is acquiring a new view of himself.

NEUTRALITY AND ETHICS OF THE ANALYST

Neutrality in the analyst is one of the essentials of psychoanalytic treatment. But neutrality does not mean wooden aloofness. It means, rather, a hovering attention to what the patient says, with a suspension of expressed moral judgment. The material presented is to be considered tentative and contemporary. No analyst should pretend that he takes no moral position in regard to what the patient may do. He will refrain from passing a moral judgment prematurely on what a patient mentions or fantasies or even contemplates doing. If it approaches enactment, and if it is dangerous to the patient's life or welfare or that of other people, the analyst will *of course* express disapproval. He will not announce a position of moral condemnation regarding what the patient has already done, but neither will he approve it nor condone it. It is probably something that the patient does not fully understand anymore than the analyst, and both wish to try to understand why the particular act came about. As members of the same culture it is very likely that both the analyst and the patient know that what the patient did is socially disapproved, but this must not preclude, indeed may further stimulate, the search for the reasons for it. Freud spoke very definitely and frequently to the effect that "the analyst respects the patient's individuality and does not seek to remould him in accordance with his own—that is, according to the physician's—personal ideals; he is glad to avoid giving advice and instead to arouse the patient's power of initiative."[67]

What is important for the patient is the analyst's ethic, his consistent fairness, his intellectual and economic honesty, his genuineness, his concern for the patient's best interests.* The analyst is a "model of a highly interested, sympathetic observer and participant in the search for that *objectivity* that will reveal psychic reality with a minimum of distortion, and thus allow the more efficient recognition of 'external' reality in the broadest sense. The 'neutral,' non-committed analyst is no analyst at all. He is at best a technician, too paralyzed by anxiety to be involved with his patient—and at worst, a destructive bungler who may be quite exploiting under cover of neutrality."†

Some years ago we participated in a seminar and panel discussion with some theologians, some professors of philosophy and of ethics, and some practicing psychoanalysts, who discussed the topic "Do the Psychiatrist's Moral Convictions Play a Significant Part in His Psychiatric Therapy?" (Gallahue Conference, Topeka, 1955). All of the speakers made definitely affirmative replies to the topical question. All of them felt that no psychiatrist would be able to avoid impart-

---

* It is odd that so excellent a clinician as Otto Fenichel[33] could write "If we do not break off the analysis too soon and if we consistently show the patient his intrapsychic reality, he will recognize that clinging to inappropriate ideals and moralities [*i.e.,* those disavowed by the analyst—] has a resistance function. . . . It has been said that religious people in analysis remain uninfluenced in their religious philosophies since analysis itself is supposed to be philosophically neutral. . . . Repeatedly I have seen that with analysis of the sexual anxieties and with the maturing of the personality, the attachment to religion has ended." *Of course,* Fenichel saw it (as a temporary phenomenon, at least). His personal preoccupation with and devotion to psychoanalysis were well known. And his patients strove to please. I have seen the *reverse* of Fenichel's observation, for *my* patients strive to please, too. In the long run the ex-patient finds his own attachments and commitments. I like what Ella Freeman Sharpe has said about the analyst and the analysand as persons and I recommend especially Chapters I and II of her book to all students. I also like the reflections offered to students of psychoanalysis in the article, prepared shortly before her death, entitled "The Psychoanalyst." All of these appear in her *Collected Papers on Psycho-Analysis.*[183] [K.A.M.]

† Van Buren O. Hammett, Correspondence with Martin H. Stein, *American Journal of Psychiatry*, 122: 830, 1966.

ing his value system to his patients. One of us [K.A.M.] discussed this problem at the forum in the following words:

"We have heard these eloquent and capable colleagues, representing various fields of human thought, give it as their opinion that no psychiatrist would be able to avoid imparting his value system to his patients in the course of therapy. It would seem from this to be quite obviously so. But this is a somewhat paradoxical fact and remarkable enough perhaps to be emphasized as indicative of an important change in the concept of treatment.

"Let me review certain aspects of the history of this matter. In the course of discovering and applying his new techniques of listening without reproach or censure or revulsion to the 'confessions' of patients regarding their fantasies and behavior, Freud was accused of encouraging socially improper behavior in the name of treatment. I and many others vigorously and explicitly refuted this, emphasizing that the whole philosophy of psychoanalysis was based on intelligent control of behavior and not wanton, profligate, and aggressive indulgence.

"Nevertheless the public still has a vague impression that there is some truth in the allegation, that in some way or other we psychoanalysts have a different moral code from the rest of society, a code that says that people may do anything they want to. Now do we?

"Remember that at the time when Freud began to discover what he did about human actions, certain kinds of behavior were not considered to be indicative of illness but rather of wickedness. I am speaking now not only of the viewpoint of society but of the viewpoint of physicians and of medical science. Anyone who would undertake to treat such a condition was *prima facie* guilty of abetting crime, like Dr. Mudd, who was imprisoned for years because he set the broken leg of the fleeing assassin who shot Lincoln. The attitude towards may psychiatric illnesses was: 'Those are not sick people, those are bad people.' Freud was publicly admonished that the case material he was presenting belonged in the police court, not in a scientific meeting!

"But Freud said in essence, 'Let us listen to what people have to tell us of their behavior and not take a position too quickly until we hear all the facts.' He had to say this with great emphasis because it was so customary for physicians to say, 'If *those* are your symptoms,

I don't want to treat you.' Freud said: 'Let us treat psychiatric ill-nesses like medical and surgical illnesses. Let us not condemn the sinner, but try to remedy the symptom. It is something he does not want, either; that is why he comes to us. We may be able to help him to get rid of the necessity of repeating it. But we can't get the thorn out of his flesh if we chase him out of the door before we get hold of it!'

"It was in this spirit that great emphasis was put on the psycho-analyst's neutrality in the early days of the science, his refraining from moral judgment of the patient without resigning the hope that it would ultimately be possible for the patient to accept a different point of view and 'behave himself.' The early-day psychoanalysts hence put much stress on not *telling* the patient what the proper ideals of life should be.

"One of their reasons for this was in reaction to the prevalent medical attitude. They realized better than some of their colleagues how strongly value systems have been influenced by traditions, going back as far as Hammurabi, which are more vengeful and punitive than moral. They realized too that it is often from a very excess of such self-imposed morality that the patient is suffering. The theory of psychoanalytic technique is that the analyst not advise the patient, not sympathize with him, not make decisions for him or try to make him happy. The psychoanalyst does not presume to remove the patient's conflicts.

"And so, in spite of the general agreement in this forum, it should be made clear that many colleagues do feel that there is a technical danger that the psychiatrist, the psychoanalyst, *will* exhibit moral attitude and thus occlude the treatment, thereby hurting the patient instead of helping him. Therefore, psychoanalysts tend to lean over a little bit the other way. They do not deny that penalties follow error, whether the error be called sin or stupidity. But they do not regard themselves as responsible for inflicting an artificial penalty, a tailored punishment.

"In some psychoanalysts this attitude of nonjudgment becomes almost a religion. Such individuals get themselves into absurd and illogical predicaments in their zeal to supplant social vengeance with social understanding. But it is just as absurd to scold society and punish it for its stupidity as it is to scold a patient and punish him, and this attitude leads some analysts to espouse a *laissez faire* philosophy in regard to patients' 'outside' behavior which in practice is dangerous to their patients and dangerous to the good name of psychoanalysis. The most free-thinking and modern young mother would probably not leave a two-year-old child to do as it likes in an ammunition factory, and for some patients the everyday social community is more dangerous than an ammunition factory.

"A more rational position would be to concede the point of view of society and of the law and of religion—that 'sin' is alluring and that, if we yield to it, we have to pay for the 'fun.' But the psychiatrist's further assumption is that sin is not nearly as much fun as it is made out to be, that it is usually painful and in a large sense unwanted by the individual, and that there are better ways than punishment to influence people to avoid it.

"Perhaps all of this could be said in a much simpler way: There have been many attempts to explain behavior of ourselves and other people which is not propitious or comfortable. Once it was all blamed on the devil; it was assumed that in some way or other we made pacts with the devil or yielded to his persuasions. Misbehavior was sin. Then for a while, in the days of enlightenment and even more recently, misbehavior was ignorance and required not a priest or a penance but a better education. Today both priests and educators are agreed that in some individuals, though they be both sinful and ignorant, the misbehavior can be seen also as evidence of a sickness—*i.e.*, a symptom.

"Now it is quite possible that it can be all three of these. But the practical problem is, which kind of help is most available and most effective with a particular sufferer or misbehaver? To some extent this is determined by the social and philosophical atmosphere of the place and the time and the people. We can only speak in the last analysis for the immediate time and place in which we live and with which we are most familiar. I have no idea what position I would take on many questions that might arise were I attempting the psychoanalysis of an Eskimo woman in Alaska or of one of Socrates' disciples in ancient Greece. I have difficulty enough trying to keep my finger on the pulse of social thought and feeling in the culture and congregation in which I have grown up, which are those of only one country in a big world."

V

RESISTANCE

The Involuntary Paradoxical Reactions
of the Party of the First Part to the
Psychoanalytic Treatment Situation

IN THE PRECEDING CHAPTER WE DISCUSSED THE *involuntary* PARTICIPA-
tion of the analyst in the contract. It might seem logical to discuss
next his *voluntary* participation, the furtherance he intentionally
gives to the process. However we shall defer this to the next
chapter, because from another standpoint it is more logical to continue the portrayal of the natural history of the reactions of the
patient to the process, the therapeutic situation, as it continues.

In our account of the patient's "progressive regression" during
the course of treatment, with various transference phenomena all
along the way, we have spoken thus far as if he were "all for it,"
consistently eager to participate, to "tell all," to observe his past
with one eye and his present with the other eye, comparing the
views. We may have implied that, once started, the patient easily
and progressively puts aside his natural reluctance to communicate
the unpleasant, the embarrassing, and the compromising data of his
life (if, indeed, such material should occur to him) and hews to
a line of candor and straightforward "confession."

But, of course, as everyone who tries it discovers, this is not what happens! Almost from the very start the patient realizes that telling one's mind, even though it relieves something, requires effort, and proceeds against certain counterpressures. Sometimes it seems irrelevant and scarcely worth the breath to relate a passing thought; sometimes it occurs to him that to speak his thought might reflect on the appearance or skill of the analyst or on the reputation of some "innocent bystander"—or otherwise offend canons of good taste. Sometimes it is just "too embarrassing."

This is true in spite of the extraordinary situation that the psychoanalytic treatment creates in which one person is permitted— is *expected*—to say whatever comes into his mind to another person without suffering consequences for having done so. The patient enters into the contract with hope, but also with misgivings, and usually with considerable fear. To be sure, he also welcomes the opportunity to talk about himself and to discharge a certain pressure of confession. In the early days of analysis this relief by confessing was spoken of figuratively as "catharsis" and the expression still persists in psychiatry. The implication was that some kind of blocking of communication had occurred comparable to constipation, so that pressure from an accumulation of unspoken, emotionally charged ideas could be discharged and relief experienced.

The phenomenon of catharsis is not as simple to explain in psychological terms as the figure of speech would indicate. The pressure of talk in a two-party situation sometimes seems to stem from a sense of guilt and a wish to confess, but at other times it represents a compelling need to establish contact with someone who will listen, who will "understand," who will accept without rebuff the productions of a prickly, lonely individual who has not expediently managed his long-accumulated frustrations and bitterness. This tendency to relieve "pressure" verbally is a familiar phenomenon, whatever its full explanation, and facilitates the *beginning* of an analysis.

Sooner or later, however, the confessions and confidings of which the early flow of communications consists begin to include material that the patient had not been aware of any need to discuss. He remembers the analyst's assurance, explicit or implicit, that no ill consequences will result from his communication of these confidences, that everything he says will be considered only tentative and completely confidential, and he tries to believe it. Indeed, he does come to believe it in time, but he soon gets into the position of "betraying" himself and implicating others. He finds himself telling tales out of school and admitting things he had previously denied— perhaps even to himself. So, whereas at first he had been relieved by the diminished pressure of his confessions, now new pressures develop because of them. Not only guilty secrets but aggressive and perverse fantasies are voiced which carry in their wake fears of retaliation or punishment. This tends in turn toward "clamming up."

Thus the patient seems to suffer simultaneously from a yearning to "get well" and a compulsion to defend himself against any change in his life adjustment, uncomfortable though it may be in many respects. He had found certain coping devices with which he "made do," after a fashion. Now he begins to wonder whether it might not be better to suffer the familiar pains and aches associated with these old methods rather than face the dangerous possibilities of a new and *perhaps* better way of handling himself. He knows that *probably* what he fears in the new situation is less dangerous than he supposes, and the rewards better than he imagines. He tells himself that his fear is *probably* based on misapprehensions. Nevertheless, the fear is there; the doubt is there; the hesitation is there. And they remain for a long time.

Thus, from the very beginning of the psychoanalytic treatment, every patient, in spite of his cooperativeness and eagerness to do whatever he is told in order to "get better," is at the same time partially "on the defensive." He unintentionally but purposively obstructs the very process upon which he counts so heavily to benefit him. He may obstruct it so effectively as to terminate it soon after it has begun. One of my early cases was very illuminating to me in this respect, and I have often used it as a teaching example. A young man had achieved a reputation for brave and dashing military exploits. For this, and because he was handsome and well-to-do, he was a romantic figure and a popular man about town. His sexual relations with his wife were a disappointment to both of them, and he began psychoanalytic treatment for this and some other symptoms. The early weeks of his analysis brought a sincere contrasting of the world's impression of him with his own realization of weakness. This encouraging phase was succeeded by a period of slowed up production culminating in a dream. In this dream he was exploring a house that looked very good on the outside. But as he went further through the halls of this interesting and handsome building he came to a corner of one room where he stopped short, horrified. For on the floor in that corner lay something dreadful, disgusting, terrible— "too awful to look at. Perhaps it was a decaying dog, a cur, a beast of some sort. Yet it was something that belonged to me." He could not bring himself to go down and to look at it but turned and fled from the building.

A few days later the patient wrote that he was feeling better and believed he would discontinue his analysis.

More often the resistance is less abrupt and violent, but develops in a certain rhythm or pattern that continues with fluctuations throughout the analysis. The psychoanalyst soon becomes familiar with its peculiar forms and manifestations in each case. In a way the analysis of each patient is a kind of never-ending duel between the forces impelling recollection, repetition, and expression *and* the forces and devices of resistance. It is no wonder that resistance almost becomes personified for some analysts and that they tend to equate it with the disease process.

Resistance, of course, is *not* a disease, not even a pathological process. It is not something that crops up occasionally to "impede" the course of treatment; it is omnipresent. In Freud's words, "Every step of the treatment is accompanied by resistance; every single thought, every mental act of the patient's, must pay toll to the resistance, and represents a compromise between the forces urging towards the cure and those gathered to oppose it."[48] It is a fascinating, dramatic production, on a par with the creation of a dream, in that the patient's resistance makes use of his typical defenses and more stable character traits. Or, to turn it around, his defensive repertoire is used in the service of resistance.

Some analysts have become so intrigued with the phenomenon of resistance that they have based their entire rationale of interpretation—a topic which we shall take up later—on the principle of fighting the resistance with insight. This seems to many of us to be somewhat of an overemphasis upon one important aspect of the process.

There is also a tendency among some analysts to think of resistance as something "bad"—that is, something to be regarded as an obstacle. Freud himself, in the early days, felt this way. It is significant, however, that Freud had the strong impression even while he was at Bernheim's Clinic that resistance could not be ordered out of existence by the therapist. He recoiled at Bernheim's charge that the patient was "countersuggesting." It is to be credited to Freud's uncanny sensitivity to the dynamics of human behavior that he early recognized that the content of a wish is only one part of an intrapsychic conflict. In 1910 he wrote:

> The idea that a neurotic is suffering from a sort of ignorance, and that if one removes the ignorance by telling him facts (about the causal connection of his illness with his life, about his experiences in childhood, and so on) he must recover, is an idea that has long been superseded, and one derived from superficial appearances. The pathological factor is not his ignorance in itself, but the root of this ignorance in his *inner resistances*; it was they that first called this ignorance into being, and they still maintain it now. In combatting these resistances lies the task of the therapy. Telling the patient what he does not know because he has repressed it, is only one of the necessary preliminaries in the therapy. If knowledge about his unconscious were as important for the patient as the inexperienced in psychoanalysis imagine, it would be sufficient to cure him for him to go to lectures or read books. Such measures, however, have as little effect on the symptom of nervous disease as distributing menu cards in time of famine has on people's hunger. The analogy goes even further than its obvious application, too; for describing his unconscious to the patient is regularly followed by an intensification of the conflict in him and exacerbation of his symptoms.*68

Analysis of the patient's resistances, then, allows the patient to realize the conditions, past and present, that maintain his dilemmas and unhappiness.

The phenomenon of resistance is one of Freud's greatest discoveries, and by his own definitive statement is one of the essential or basic planks of psychoanalytic theory. When we say that Freud

* This citation is one that young (and some older) analysts should read and *remember*. The glibness of some interpretations made in the name of "insight therapy" belies any grasp of Freud's message here.

"discovered" resistance we mean that he brought to the attention of physicians that in psychological medicine resistance is a factor that cannot be ignored and that can be dealt with in certain ways. Clinicians have known for centuries that something seems to impel patients under treatment to resist efforts to cure them. But the traditional attitude of medicine throughout the centuries has been to ignore this opposition, to treat it with equanimity, as Osler said in his classical essay. The dentist does not lose patience with a man whose tooth has stopped aching after an emergency appointment has been arranged. The (good) surgeon does not get angry with a struggling child who dreads the lance. The reluctance of such patients to accept treatment is ascribed to fear, in the hands of which they are considered helpless. Freud showed us that resistance is more than fear, that it is a force comparable perhaps to the inertia discovered by Newton to reside in all matter, a reluctance to change position or direction. The suffering patient submitting himself to our professional services at no mean expense in time, pain, and money seems to be demonstrating how much he wants to get well. But there are always indications that he is a man divided against himself and that he does not *wholly* want to get well! He also wants to stay sick! Freud's genius was reflected in his discovery that this paradox has deep meaning, that the conflict is of the essence and not a mere complicating nuisance, and that the intelligence is our best weapon against it.

There is a curious obverse side to the resistance coin. This is the amazing credulousness with which patients will commit themselves to strangers and almost transparent quacks in exchange for fantastic promises of benefit. People will commit large sums of money and submit to heroic and painful manipulations or take dangerous nostrums merely because they are told to do so by an individual whose sole claim on their compliance is a self-proclaimed effectiveness. This illustrates the irrational wish to believe just as resistance represents the irrational wish not to believe.

Resistance as it is used in psychoanalytic theory may be defined then as *the trend of forces within the patient that oppose the process of ameliorative change.* It is not the analyst who is being resisted; it is the process within the patient of making unconscious material conscious or of letting it become conscious that the analyst is encouraging. This makes resistance seem almost equivalent to repression, which is not correct because the latter is too restrictive a word. Resistance is more accurately identified with defensive processes in general.*

Clinically, resistance can be seen in a myriad of forms. Sometimes it is a mere concealing of acts and facts, sometimes an increased forgetting instead of an increased remembering, sometimes a tardiness or an absence, sometimes a prolonged silence. Enacting the events of a memory that does not come to mind as such is a form of resistance called *acting out*; indeed, one criterion of the end of an analysis is when acting out is largely replaced by remembering in the ordinary sense. There are also the forms of intellectualization, cataloging, dawdling, "emoting" instead of thinking and talking. There is a resistance of erotization, of which we shall speak in more detail shortly. There is a resistance of new symptom formation, psychological or somatic, as if to proclaim that the analysis is increasing rather than diminishing the patient's afflictions. (Ferenczi called this *passagere* resistance.)

In the appendix of *Inhibitions, Symptoms and Anxiety*,[54] under the heading of "Modifications of Earlier Views," Freud reformulated his concept of resistance as a defensive action undertaken by the ego to buttress the repression it maintains to protect itself and to defend this repressive function against the dissolving effect of "insight." Freud compared resistance to such things as pity, conscientiousness, and cleanliness in obsessional neuroses, where there is a reinforcement or exaggeration of an attitude opposite to that of the instinctual trend relative to the situation. Similarly, even when given the opportunity in the course of treatment, "It is hard for the ego to direct its attention to perceptions and ideas which it has up to

* Compare with our formulation the following statement of Freud's: "The unconscious, that is the repressed material, offers no resistance whatever to the curative efforts; indeed it has no other aim than to force its way through the pressure weighing on it, either to consciousness or to discharge by means of some real action. The resistance in the treatment proceeds from the same higher levels and systems in the psychic life that in their time brought about the repression. But since the motives of the resistances, and indeed the resistances themselves, are found in the process of the treatment to be unconscious, we are well advised to amend an inadequacy in our mode of expression. We escape ambiguity if we contrast not the conscious and the unconscious, but the coherent ego and the repressed."[48]

now made a rule of avoiding, or to acknowledge as belonging to itself impulses that are the complete opposite of those which it has made its own."[54]

FIVE CLASSICAL TYPES OF RESISTANCE

In the essay just mentioned, Freud listed five types of resistance. The first of them he called *repression resistance*, which comes from the persistent, automatic, normative tendency of the ego to try to control dangerous tendencies by blocking them off. The ego has the habit, so to speak, of solving its problems in this way as far as possible, and it resists the process of "free thought" and ventilation of preconscious memories lest the change upset the homeostatic balance and permit the emergence of *dangerous* tendencies. It is the ego's lifelong "business" (in part) to hold back certain things from expression, and this is automatically extended to the analytic situation, especially when the expression of previously *repressed* impulses (as distinguished from *suppressed* material) becomes likely to occur.

The second type of resistance is listed by Freud as *transference resistance*. Like the familiar defense resistance, transference resistance resurrects with the analyst the nature of older relationships, which are now experienced rather than recalled. Its clearest manifestations occur because of the analyst's "abstinence," his refraining from gratifying the increasingly regressive wishes of the patient. It thus, in part, expresses the patient's resentment at not getting from the analyst the expected response; it bespeaks the mounting frustration and anger of disappointment. We prefer to call it *frustration resistance* or *revenge resistance*. It is as if such a patient were sulking or, to put it more urbanely, as if he had become less than eager to try to please the analyst, and almost too angry to want to tell him anything. We shall discuss this at more length presently.

Third, there is the *epinosic gain resistance*, which has to do with the reluctance of the ego to give up the advantages that have accrued to the patient as a whole as a result of an illness. These secondary-gain resistances are related to the repression resistance just mentioned in that they reflect ego activities.

The fourth variety of resistance listed by Freud emanates, he believed, from the Id; he called it *repetition-compulsion resistance*. It was the last to be discovered. As Freud put it, "We find that even after the ego has decided to relinquish its resistances, it still has difficulty in undoing the repressions,"[54] despite the rewards and advantages we have (by inference) promised the ego if *it* will give up *its* resistances (the three types just listed) . This period of strenuous effort that the ego makes following its decision to relinquish them is called *working through*. This is carried on *against* the resistance of the repetition compulsion, "the attraction exerted by the unconscious prototypes upon the repressed instinctual process."[54]

Fifth, there is a *superego resistance*, which derives from the feeling of need for punishment. This may be a socialized form of the preceding type, but one that is very characteristic of human beings in our culture and era. "I do not deserve to get well; it is fitting that I should suffer (some) ." This is the inexpedient but partially effective way in which guilt feelings are atoned for and kept in a kind of spurious balance, which resists change.

To summarize, Freud suggested that there is resistance derived from unconscious fear (repression resistance) ; there is resistance derived from disappointed expectations in the analysis (transference resistance) ; there is resistance derived from inertia, false prudence, and short-sighted opportunism (secondary-gain resistance) ; there is resistance derived from self-directed aggression on the basis of a deep biological pattern (repetition-compulsion resistance) ; and there is resistance derived from the feeling that one should continue to suffer in propitiation (superego resistance) .

Freud enlarged these ideas in 1937, in one of his last essays "Analysis Terminable and Interminable."[47] In this paper he distinguished resistances that reflect defensive operations of the ego, such as projection and displacement, from resistances that arise from the nature of the psychic apparatus and that are etiologically independent of conflict. Resistances that arise from the nature of the psychic apparatus include adhesiveness of libido, mobility of the libido, loss of plasticity (for example, in advancing age) , and resistances from the sense of guilt (corresponding to the superego resistance mentioned in the *Inhibitions, Symptoms and Anxiety*. Freud also mentioned the role of some nuclear conflicts in impeding the cure: penis envy in women and passivity conflict in men.

Resistance derived from any or several of all of these sources may appear in various clinical forms. We have already referred to such familiar expressions as silence, tardiness, evasion of the basic rule, and so on. There are certain more comprehensive categories which deserve fuller treatment, especially acting out and erotization.

ACTING OUT RESISTANCE

Acting out is a term applied to an extremely common phenomenon occurring to greater or lesser extent in all analyses. It is the tendency to substitute an act or series of acts for episodes that the analysand cannot remember or at least fails to report. In other words, the patient remembers not in words, but in behavior and thus repeats a piece of language behavior. "He repeats it without, of course, knowing that he is repeating it."[61] This is an extremely effective kind of resistance since, like a dream, it offers some discharge of tension. It is like charades played between two parts of the ego.

This phenomenon has become of increasing importance in psychoanalysis since the recognition as potentially analyzable of many of these individuals afflicted with various so-called "character disorders." Fenichel[31] defined this form of resistance somewhat elaborately as "an acting which unconsciously relieves inner tension and brings partial discharge to warded off impulses (no matter whether these impulses express directly instinctual demands or are reactions to original instinctual demands, *e.g.*, guilt feelings) ; the present situation, somehow associatively connected with the repressed content, is used as an occasion for the discharge of repressed energies; the cathexis is displaced from the repressed memories to the present derivative, and the displacement makes this discharge possible."

Some patients are much more prone to the use of this type of resistance than others, and numerous explanations for the propensity have been suggested: strong oral phase disturbances and fixation; strong narcissistic needs; some kind of constitutional hyperactivity; special trends toward dramatization derived from exhibitionism; scoptophilic impulses and a strong belief in the magic of action.

The latter two were suggested by Phyllis Greenacre,[83] who carried her thinking about the matter further to the hypothesis that the common genetic situation that tends to produce such tendencies consists in a *distortion in the developmental relationship of speech and action.* Acts may not always speak louder than words, but in most of us they do speak first. The essence of Greenacre's theory is that the patient who tends to act out continually is one who had inhibitions of speech in early life that encouraged relatively more motor discharge. In the course of his therapeutic regression in psychoanalytic treatment, the patient resumes those forms of expression with which he had originally felt most comfortable.

There is a tendency on the part of some analysts to refer to any social misbehavior on the part of the patient during his treatment as "acting out." It would be better if some of this were differentiated as "acting up" or "acting in" or just "acting"! For certainly not all behavior that the analyst doesn't approve of can be put in the category of acting out. Furthermore, as Fenichel suggested and as we can also confirm, some analysts provoke and enjoy or encourage dramatic acting out in their patients and even find reason to ascribe benefit to it. The patient, they say, is overcoming his inhibitions and is gaining the courage to do what he should have done long ago. He is abreacting. We would again quote from Greenacre:

This seems quite occasionally the problem of young and inexperienced analysts, but may also occur among analysts who themselves tend to act out, either directly or in an inhibited form, and to enjoy this vicariously in their patients. This may be of greater frequency and importance than one might at first think. It occurs among analysts who display no overt acting out but who react as some severely restrained adults who enjoy and tacitly applaud the impulsive behavior of their children who dare to do what they themselves have not been permitted. This is seen strikingly in the parental attitudes which form the background of many impulse-ridden psychopaths. An attitude of overanxiety on the part of the analyst about the patient's acting out is frequently sensed and reacted to by the patient, who then unconsciously gratifies his sadism as well in the acting out and gets a spurious sense of power and independence through it. If the analyst behaves in either of these ways to any appreciable degree, acting out will continue no matter how much its specific content is interpreted.[83]

Aside from correcting the countertransference effect or the technical ignorance of the analyst, the standard attacks on this type of resistance consist in the interpretation of the behavior as resistance, the identification of the nature and meaning of the particular acts, and as a last resort the forthright prohibition or at least deprecation of the acts. Meanwhile there is the hope that the patient will not get himself into too much trouble prior to such growth in the strength of the ego as is sufficient to control such impulses. As Greenacre says, "Since in its very nature acting out is ego-syntonic and the patient is not aware of its destructive nature, it comes to the attention of the analyst in most instances after its occurrence (if at all), and sometimes is not reported or only indirectly."[83, 84]

Some young analysts are reluctant to express their disapproval or their notion of the unwisdom of certain kinds of behavior lest they seem censorious or moralistic and thus violate the "rule" of nonjudgmental detachment or even discourage their patient from communications. Others fear being exploited by the patient and progressively forced into a position of giving continuous guidance. Many of them hesitate to discuss with the patient their mutual awareness that both of them are members of the same social order and that they have long institutionalized their disapproval of this kind of behavior or recognized its implicit dangers. Other analysts overlook and fail to deal with the patient's unconscious or dimly conscious wish to have the analyst interfere in his behavior.

EROTIZATION RESISTANCE

We come now to the second of the two special forms of resistance requiring more particularization. There comes a day when the patient undergoing psychoanalysis realizes—in spite of its expensiveness in time and money, in spite of its dreariness and the bitter tears and memories it evokes—that in a curious way he enjoys it. This pleasure is quite apart from the symptomatic relief the treatment may have afforded him. It is a subtle, secret, pleasurable sensation. It may arouse slight uneasiness lest it appear to justify the accusations of unsympathetic outsiders that what certain patients want is not cure but treatment and that what some psychoanalysts want is not to cure but to treat. There is a germ of truth in this, of course, but there is much more to erotization than this.

Every patient's first and most important motive, we assume, is to be relieved of his symptoms. He is prepared to wait awhile for this result, and he expects the treatment, like all medical treatment, to be more or less unpleasant. Like the man who submits to a surgeon, he tells himself that the ultimate gain will be worth the unpleasantness of the treatment.

Almost from the beginning of psychoanalytic treatment, despite its unpleasant features, there is some conscious pleasure in the process. The opportunity to talk freely, to confess, to boast, to explain oneself, to be listened to sympathetically—this is no ordeal, but quite the contrary. The symptoms may abate or they may continue —for the present it doesn't matter. The narcissistic pleasure of contemplating and communicating oneself to an audience carries the process forward, and would continue it awhile even with no definite relief implied. This has been made amply clear by the work of Roethlisberger,[172] Carl Rogers,[174] and others.

Gradually, however, and quite independent of the dawning of some of the misgivings and disappointment discussed earlier, there comes a time when we (analysts) begin to observe that the patient is talking on, telling us memories, fantasies, dreams, and experiences, not so much to please or relieve himself as to try to please *us!* As we saw in the previous chapter, this wish to please and to be found pleasing proceeds to great lengths or, better to say, depths. The patient is often aware of this motive and will acknowledge it frankly. It is almost invariably a repetition of an effort he has made with not one but many people in his life, beginning perhaps with one of his parents. The analyst has probably begun to represent to him some of these earlier objects. Soon definite patterns of trying to please, failing to please, resenting the lack of appreciation, and other variations will appear, as we have seen.

In addition to these transference aspects, we should examine the resistance feature of these phenomena. Certainly, seeking to please others is no fault. The wish to please the analyst may indeed be a motive that facilitates the treatment at first, for no cases are more difficult to treat than those individuals who do *not* want to please the analyst even at the start. Nevertheless, it can develop into a form of resistance that becomes more and more apparent as such. It can easily turn around and become a wish to *displease* the analyst, to hurt or provoke him; this *too* is resistance. *Everything done for the sake of the effect upon the analyst* may be considered not only the illustration of a repetitive pattern, but *prima facie* evidence of resistance. This is clear enough when such things take the form of attempts to bribe the analyst or seduce or anger him, but it is also true in the more subtle forms. This does not mean that the material offered in this effort is worthless, but when pleasing or displeasing the analyst becomes the preeminent motivation for the delivery of material, resistance is dominant.

How is it that the wish to please the analyst is at the same time a motive power for the continuance of the analysis and a resistance? The explanation is that for the patient to fasten upon the analyst as the object of his daily efforts is, of course, obviously irrational. The analyst is only a means to an end, and not an end (object) in himself. Now, of course, the phenomenon of transference demonstrates that the analyst always represents in the unconscious of the patient someone he (the analyst) is not. And that "someone" cannot be affected by the patient's efforts to please or displease the analyst.

Furthermore, it is as if the patient were saying, "I want you to want me to get well, and to make me well; therefore I will try to please you, in order that you will do so." The patient forgets that in reality he pays for the analyst's help with money and not with good behavior or with psychoanalytic material, which assist, but do not reward, the analyst. The object of the treatment is the patient, not the doctor, who requires no special pleasing. A surgeon cannot operate on a patient intent upon paying him compliments or kissing his hand. The surgeon will only be embarrassed and annoyed; the analyst must be neither, but he must see through the conscious to the unconscious meaning of the effort.

One can look at these phenomena from the standpoint of social appropriateness. The purpose of analytic therapy is to bring buried, unconscious trends into consciousness, and in order to do this we encourage a "regression" in the several respects described in the preceding chapter. This regression regularly leads to increasing inappropriateness of "reactions" and fantasy behavior on the part of the patient. We expect it. In the regression the patient "wants" certain inappropriate things and seeks to obtain those things in various ways. We, his analysts, want him only to *see* that he wants them, to see that he once wanted them and failed to get them, to see why he failed, to see what better he could do. But instead of just seeing this, he *feels* it—and tends to express his feelings not merely in words, not merely in description of his sensations, dreams, and symptoms, but by gestures, symbolic acts, attitudes, and general programs of action modified, of course, to some extent by the healthy residuum of his ego.

The feeling on the part of the patient that he is doing something to please the analyst enlarges to a feeling that the analyst is getting pleasure from treating the patient. To give pleasure affords pleasure and the patient begins to enjoy pleasing, a pleasurable emotion quite aside from his lessened tension. Feelings of gratitude to the physician for listening, for showing interest in his problem, for protecting him in a way, for being kind to him in spite of his disagreeableness are now complemented by his feeling that he, the patient, is now gratifying the analyst.

Thus, in spite of its uncomfortable aspects, there arises a certain "illegitimate" pleasure in the analytic process. This pleasure may be felt only as a vague "spiritual" satisfaction, but it often becomes involved in the process. This involvement may be reflected in physical sensations, symptoms, and somatic changes.

This *erotization of the analytic situation* is a major form of resistance. The patient unconsciously tends to convert the analysis into an erotic experience corresponding to one of his deeply buried infantile wishes usually in respect to his relations with the parent.

Here is an example. A woman patient had developed strong feeling of dependency and helplessness, together with fantasies that the analyst could—were she sufficiently in his favor—perform a miracle and reconstruct her anatomically, psychologically, socially, and otherwise. She was sure that he was or would be greatly pleased to learn that she had discontinued her relations with a lover and also that she had ceased to gratify herself sexually by manual manipulation. She began to hint, with some embarrassment, that her present satisfactions (*i.e.*, with the analyst) were preferable and sufficient for her—indeed, a little more than merely sufficient. She found it difficult to speak, she said; she much preferred to listen to *him* speak. The verbal material that she communicated to him, whether or not it pertained to sexual matters, seemed to her to be an offering to him, a proffered gift, as if she were offering her body. Whether she spoke or whether she listened to his brief comments, sensations of mounting eroticism were experienced until she would plead to have the analyst speak to her—to say anything, just so she could hear and enjoy his voice. Her associations to this equated his voice sounds in speech with coital thrusts.

Fantasies of and expressed wishes for physical sexual gratification from the analyst are frequent, but sometimes the patient will go beyond these to vivid sensations of its occurrence for which, as in the example cited by Freud, the *patient* may run away in a panic (*e.g.*, Dora) , if, indeed, the *analyst* doesn't! (*e.g.*, Anna O.) .

The case cited, like Freud's, was an unusual and extreme one, and the situation should have been detected by the analyst before it had reached that degree of development and, by interpretation, controlled. This is not always possible, as Freud himself reported. Freud believed that erotization resistance always indicates some need for interpretation. It results from the patient interpreting (misinterpreting) the invitation to think and say "anything" to be a seduction by the analyst. "You tempt me—then frustrate me," he thinks (and often says) . Thus the frankly sexual dream often means, "You are not interpreting (*i.e.*, exposing) my resistance fast enough. You are letting me get away with something."

In nearly every analysis there is some degree of this erotization resistance, with physical sensations experienced always with a degree of shame and guilt feelings. Hence there is usually at the same time a struggle to suppress them. The struggle is not entirely conscious; the whole process of talking about the experience has a general tendency to diminish both kinds of feeling, since one object of analysis is to translate physical sensations and physical urges into words and images.

More subtle forms of this resistance are very common indeed.

The experience of pleasure may not be so definitely phallic. It can be observed in the early stages of analysis, for example, in oral forms; and in the middle stages of analysis in oral, anal, and even cutaneous modalities. It is proper to say, we think, that the analytic process may be sexualized or eroticized in all of the ways in which the patient as a developing child experienced physical pleasure: anally, orally, and so on. We have suggested that we can say that the analytic process is at various times *oralized, analized, phallicized,* and *genitalized* and to the extent that this occurs in any of the forms, it retards the analysis and must be regarded as resistance.

Oral erotization of the analysis, for example, is observable in some patients for whom speech—whether they do the talking themselves or merely drink in the words of someone else—has a high "libidinal value," as we used to call it. For some patients every word of the analyst is a pearl; and their own words are spoken as if they were minting gold coins with their lips. More frequently observable are aggressive oral tendencies, detectable both in the spitting or biting or flooding delivery and in the content (*e.g.,* food, drinking, smoking, kissing) of the material. The analysis proceeds on the pattern of nursing, of periodic feedings, and disappointments regarding appointment hours, interpretations, and other matters are experienced as painful "weanings."

Similarly, erotization of the analysis according to *anal* modalities results in a variety of phenomena derived from childhood experiences and emotional constellations developed during them. On the one hand, there may be a great overestimation of giving and receiving gifts, attempts to bribe the analyst, attempts to get special privileges from him. On the other hand, a typical (verbal) constipation syndrome may develop, with or without the equivalent of flatus production. It is often obvious that a patient is repeating on the couch the type of performance characteristic of him on the chamberpot many years previously—straining, groaning, and making much effort to demonstrate to the analyst that he is trying very hard, but all in vain, or with a pitifully meager production. This may be preceded or even followed by the equivalent of a diarrhea and the sort of material that can be interpreted as defecation *for* or *upon* the analyst. A patient may act as if to say, "I will not move my bowels for you—unless, etc."; or "See, I move my bowels for you," or "I would if I only could . . . please help me," or "Help me get started," or "Please give me an enema," or "Shit on you!"*

What we used to call "enema resistance" may be changing now that the children are so rarely subjected to forcible enemata and perhaps the designation of the phenomenon should be changed to the "soapstick" or the "suppository" pattern of resistance. Whatever it is called, it is very common and quite unmistakable. The patient will not begin talking until the analyst has made a remark or questioned the silence or something of that kind, after which the patient will talk freely. Some patients will protest that they cannot go on or cannot get started unless the analyst says something or, as they often put it (with richly overdetermined meaning) until the analyst *does* something.

Another manifestation of anal erotization of the analysis used as a resistance mode is the use of foul language, overvivid descriptions of offensive scenes and experiences, vulgar and disagreeable words and pictures. Material of this kind is sometimes "discharged" with particular reference to parental prohibitions. Young psychoanalysts sometimes find satisfaction in hearing such material, believing it to be somewhat comparable to the paradoxical satisfaction evinced by a surgeon whose incision is followed by a flow of foul-smelling pus. But the surgeon's satisfactions do not prevent him from recognizing the offensiveness and neither should the psychoanalyst's!

Incidentally, the psychoanalyst who is under the impression that he facilitates an analysis by using vulgar language that the patient is "more likely to understand" is doubly deceived. The patient will indeed correctly understand that the psychoanalyst is lowering himself instead of maintaining a standard to which he, the patient, may aspire to reach. Because the patient discharges psychological flatus is no reason for the psychoanalyst to do so.

In *phallic* erotization of the analysis the patient's behavior and material illustrate the dominance of adolescent fantasies that the genital organ and its activities and sensations are the totality of existence. And since the analyst's penis is unconsciously or consciously fantasized to be like the father's, the greatest of all, it be-

---

* In a study of anal erotism, my brother William Menninger[144] collected many illustrations of this symbolic language. [K.A.M.]

comes the primary object of the patient's desires. Obtaining this genital organ for himself becomes a central fantasy; he becomes preoccupied with fantasies of seducing, inspecting, peeking at, or castrating the analyst. His behavior may carry out reflections of this phallic preoccupation in promiscuity, masturbation, and otherwise.

What might be called a *genital* erotization of the analysis is represented by more mature and less narcissistic, even though unrealistic, fantasies of marrying the analyst or of having a child with him or her.

Any of these erotizations may involve more or less somatic compliance, *e.g.* "punishment" may appear in the form of sore throat, constipation, colitis, or dyspepsia. Genitourinary system complications of many kinds are frequent, such as polyuria, urinary retention, impotence, urethritis, dysmenorrhea, and amenorrhea. I have reported several instances of this. In one, a very severe coryza and other symptoms of a "bad cold" were a part of a total oralization of the analytic procedure.[138] In some other cases, urinary and uterine involvement were recognizable.[136, 140, 141] Indeed, some of our earliest insights into psychosomatic involvements and mechanisms were derived from the observation of these resistance phenomena in the course of psychoanalytic treatment.

One cannot expect an *orderly* appearance of these erotization techniques of resistance; however, a patient will often use first the type he has used habitually or characteristically. But, even the most "oral" character will sooner or later try the effect of "anal-izing" the analysis, and later of phallicizing it. And, as explained, erotization of the analysis, whether done symbolically, verbally, or somatically, is always resistance, because it substitutes the means for the end. It always says, "I want what I want when I want it, and I think this is the way to get it—not your way. For your sake I will try but I don't want to change my ways or pleasure. I want treatment that gratifies, not improvement that requires renunciation."

One final point about this erotization resistance: The analyst should never forget the aggressive component involved in it. Indeed, he should realize that the erotic wish and display act as a disguise for the hidden aggression underlying them. The analysand is asking for something improper and—by our standards—immoral. It is immoral in the same sense that giving morphine to an addict would be immoral. The thing wanted is self-destructive, and hence to yield to the importunity, no matter how urgent, is to assist in *hurting*, not helping the patient; and the patient *knows* this. Hence all erotization is an attempted distraction and seduction, a wish to remain ill and to hurt the analyst in revenge (for his alleged seduction of the patient) as well as himself (the analysand) in propitiation.

This is the place to mention what it would be better if we did not have to mention; namely, the fact that patients sometimes report that they were given physical gratification (or manipulation) by a previous therapist. He may or may not have been a psychoanalyst. It may or may not have actually happened. If it did, such patients are very poor subjects for psychoanalytic treatment. They spend endless hours trying to work through the problem, "Can *this* doctor also be seduced?" or, as they may put it, "Will this doctor also violate his Hippocratic Oath?"

The young psychoanalyst should never forget, however, that he has no real evidence that what the patient describes ever happened. A patient's fantasies can be very vivid. As psychoanalysts we are obliged to listen to it sympathetically, open-mindedly. We have to assume for the moment that it may have been true, at least it seemed to the patient to have been true. We can be sorrowful that one of our colleagues betrayed his oath, but we must also remember that this could only have happened if the patient unconsciously wanted it to happen, and we must help him or her to see this and to take his responsibility for what he is now trying to reenact with us in a new situation. It is all the more important for us to be doubly faithful to the ideal and doubly aware of the aggression and resistance represented by the phenomenon of the attempted seduction via the appeal for help.*

In the psychoanalysis of some men one not infrequently encounters the fantasy that is referred to ironically as the wish to make all girls happy. This stems from a childhood feeling of wanting to please mother in a sexual way, of wanting to do more for mother

---

* I recall a patient who regarded herself as a *femme fatale*; she maintained that two physicians, a psychotherapist of world renown, and a priest had successively turned professional situations into sexual affairs with her. She denied to the end (of the interview) any responsibility for these affairs.

than father did or could do, and extending this wish to other women who seemed to be available and presumably desirous. For some individuals this characterizes the patient's most conspicuous activities, for example, in the case of Don Juan, who was continually "pleasing" *and* frustrating women. In these (see Robbins,[171]) the hostile element is clearly apparent.

Acting out and erotization are two common clinical forms of resistance, but there are, as we know, many other forms. Resistance might be divided into consciously felt opposition and opposition occurring with the best of intentions, so to speak. For some patients it is necessary to pretend to be skeptical or independent. Others will consider it only their temperamental makeup that leads them to dawdle and delay. Some patients will insist that they never could talk spontaneously and use this fact as an excuse for not communicating thoughts, dreams, and reports of behavior. Sometimes resistance will take the form of lying, sometimes simply of not telling. More such items could be mentioned but they are all details. The important thing to see is that resistance is something that exists, that operates, that opposes change, that is aggressive, and that is self-defeating.

Some colleagues—*e.g.*, Kaiser[104] and Reich[164]—equate resistance with aggression, holding that if a patient's attention is called to how he is avoiding a communication that he wants to make, how he is behaving in order to *avoid* communicating—in short, how he is resisting—then it is not necessary for the analyst to expend any effort on specific interpretations of the content of the material behind the resistance. The patient is expected in the analytic situation to acknowledge and describe many suppressed or repressed impulses—not to yield to them. It is as if the analyst said, "These impulses are acceptable, insofar as they are verbalized, translated into speech." But the patient has difficulty in doing this—he feels constantly impelled to put some of them into action or else to hold them back. But he does communicate some of them—by words, by gestures, by postures, and by acts.

It was Kaiser's position that it is only necessary to point out the difficulties and inaccuracies of the communication. An experienced listener can recognize when there has been a substituted idea or substituted form in the communication. When certain impulses attached to certain ideas meet with the repressive barrier of the ego, there is a tendency for the impulse to split off from the idea and attach itself to a more acceptable, substitute idea which is, in a sense, a counterfeit. This quality of counterfeitness or phoniness can be detected and if it is pointed out to the patient, he becomes alerted and, so to speak, "goes into action." He attempts to explain it, and although this explanation will no doubt be chiefly rationalization, it will be closer to the original idea. In this way, by constantly pointing out the artificiality and ungenuineness of the material, the analyst eludes the resistance and assists the patient to come closer and closer to telling the truth, the whole truth, and nothing but the truth—at least in regard to the impulses.

The deficiencies of this one-sided approach have been pointed out carefully by Fenichel[30] and others. We agree with Fenichel, although in some types of cases Kaiser's technique has considerable usefulness, especially in the earlier phases of an analysis.

SOME THOUGHTS IN RECAPITULATION

The manifestations of resistance and their rationalization are many and devious, as we have illustrated in this chapter. They will take the form of love and anger, seeking to please and seeking to displease, new physical symptoms and new psychological symptoms, overly "bad" behavior and overly "good" behavior. The patient insists that he wants help, *but* it is so costly and time consuming. He wants to cooperate, and follow instructions to associate freely and tell what comes to his mind, *but* this is so embarrassing; besides, it might involve someone else who hasn't been consulted. He wants to please the analyst and show his appreciation for what is being attempted and he seeks the analyst's favor and even his love, but accepting love is dangerous and entails unknown consequences. Better to stay aloof, or even to hate.

Anyway, there is some reason for resentment, after all; the analysis is costing lots of money, and what has the patient to show for it? Still, one can hardly bite the hand that feeds him. It may be that "all these things" happened to him once, that he had such yearnings and such frustrations, *but* they seem hardly relevant today; maybe they are not even true. Maybe he just imagined them, *and* "I am so used to my muddlings and misery—do I really want to give it all up?"

As the patient gradually, perhaps even timidly, moves forward with an increasing sense of independence and abandons some of his unrealistic expectations of the analyst, and other infantile modes of thought, he sometimes hesitates for a long time at the threshold. "Am I really ready? Can I really give up my analyst? It is possible that I shall fail after all? Won't I perhaps relapse?"

In the next chapter we shall come back to some practical aspects of resistance as they appear in connection with the analyst's interventions in the process.

VI

INTERPRETATION AND OTHER INTERVENTION

Voluntary Participation of the Party of the Second
Part in the Psychoanalytic Treatment Situation

TO RECAPITULATE, THE THEORY OF CLINICAL PSYCHOANALYSIS THAT HAS
been presented describes it as a two-party contractual relationship
in which one party approaches another to obtain or get assistance in
effecting a change; the party of the second part responds affirmatively
by setting up a situation in which he can listen uncritically and relatively silently to verbal communications of the party of the first part
for an indefinite number of limited (hourly) periods. First a little
frightened, then progressively relieved and grateful for the opportunity of communicating to a sympathetic listener the nature and
details of his suffering, the patient takes increasing advantage of the
privilege. As he proceeds, however, there develop in him on the one
hand certain reservations, doubts and reluctances and on the other
mounting expectations that, as a result of the information he has so
freely communicated to the analyst, the latter will respond with ex-

124

planations, prohibitions, instructions, consolations, or other verbal magic that will resolve difficulties and relieve suffering and disability. The analyst does not make this expected response, and there is a gradually increasing dissatisfaction and resentment in the patient that induces him to revert to less and less disguised forms of the reactions characteristic of his childhood.

These childhood patterns of behavior transferred to the contemporary world are most clearly seen in the analytic process itself, although to some extent they will be visible in the patient's everyday behavior. They are, in essence, infantile methods of attempting to gain infantile objectives and in the psychoanalytic relationship they become the body of the transference and of the resistance. The patient's life style is epitomized in what he wants and tries to get from the analyst and the ways in which he tries to get it.*

The patient—the first party of the contract—is only partly aware of this regression at first, but he increasingly recognizes—sometimes with help from the analyst—that his behavior toward the analyst and others is a repetition, even an exaggeration, of his method of behaving at one time toward his parents. Whenever it is clear to the analyst that the patient *almost* grasps such a connection or repetition, or almost perceives the meaning of a constellation of events, when, in short, the patient shows that he knows something but doesn't realize that he knows it—at such a point the analyst may intervene in the process like an accoucher assisting the delivery of a baby. He can restate what the patient has told him, and in a way that the patient will see that is his own product. (For young analysts it is sometimes deflating, if not a little irritating, to have a patient say that he knew this all the time.)

When resistance constantly and persistently blocks the progress of analysis, it is always good to interpret first the fact that there is evidence of such resistance, that such and such things constitute this evidence. If or when the patient can see this, he can be guided into

---

* Haley humorously and somewhat satirically describes psychoanalysis as "a dynamic psychological process involving two people, a patient and a psychoanalyst, during which the patient insists that the analyst be one-up while desperately trying to put him one-down, and the analyst insists that the patient remain one-down in order to help him learn to become one-up. The goal of the relationship is the amicable separation of analyst and patient."[89]

a search for the reasons for the resistance. The analyst should never expect an immediate, correct answer to the question, "Why?" The patient may not know; may not *yet* know. Give him time. The answer will come.

After a time, in spite of resistance manifested in many ways, including the exhibition of hostile feelings, fantasies, and even acts toward the analyst, the patient increasingly admits into consciousness certain "new" facts, new understandings, and correspondingly, new attitudes. With these the process of regression is reversed, the patient begins to grow up again and to see himself more nearly as others see him, the ideal wistfully cited by Robert Burns.

We might ask ourselves why it is, theoretically, that the turning point in the course of the regression is ultimately arrived at in just this way. There will no doubt be numerous turning points, successive ups and downs. But gradually the trend is toward recovery; the ups exceed the downs, *i.e.*, the infantile patterns are replaced with more mature objectives and behavior. But why? Why does it happen so? Is it to be ascribed to an accumulated mass pressure of more and more insight? Is it a reaction to a particular crucial event or secret that the patient finally discovers, as Freud originally thought? Or does the patient, after acquainting himself sufficiently with the unprofitable, expensive, self-destructive way in which he has behaved, begin to seize the opportunity for a better "deal" for himself, a better life style? In this enactment he and his analyst may detect some of the "forgotten" conditioning, the damaging situations and events, the partial reminiscences that have deleteriously affected his life. Sometimes the model comes to mind of an archeologist digging in a pit for the relics of a vanished civilization; there comes a time when more and more digging recovers less and less material, but a reconstruction outside is now possible.

Or is the reversal trend something like awakening gradually from a deep sleep, which we do in spite of the fact that it is pleasant and requires no effort to remain asleep? The hypnotized patient similarly seems to show a spontaneous tendency to return to his own habitual states of mind and ways of behavior. Acute episodes of psychiatric illness that tend to disappear promptly may serve the purpose of enabling normal patterns of adjustment to be resumed more comfortably.* Is the psychoanalytic regression something like these?

We might as well confess right off that we do not know. We only know that usually—not always—the direction of the regressive tendency does ultimately cease, the trend reverses, and the psychological material produced by the patient assumes a more and more adult form. The infantile objectives are given up for more realistic and mature ones, and the techniques likewise undergo a progressive modification in the direction of maturity.

In the early days it was assumed that this came about because of some particular thing the analysand had discovered—this was the "repressed trauma" or "complex." The analyst assisted the patient through the critical sticking point responsible for the *neurotic* regression, around and beneath which the *treatment* regression was assumed to have taken him. There was a conviction that the clear and full recollection of half-remembered but actual traumatic experiences freed the patient from haunting and crippling derivatives of them (Freud and Breuer).[65] Then the credit began to be ascribed to the explosive release of pockets of unhealthy emotion in the form known as *abreaction*. This was regarded as some kind of riddance of an irritating "substance" from the psychological system. Next the prevalent mode of thought was that the therapeutic effect was to be attributed to the psychological disciplining involved in the so-called working-through process, about which we shall have something to say later. After this, insight became king for a short time, followed by the theory of cure through elimination or modification of and reconciliation with the superego.

There were other explanations, or perhaps we should say emphases. Freud's dictum, "Where Id was, there shall Ego be," was variously interpreted to mean the making conscious of significant, unconscious material; extending the "boundaries" or domain of the (observing) ego; abandoning the fixation points of immature development; and no doubt many other things, depending upon the conceptual model of the personality and the psychoanalytic process held

---

* I have elsewhere expanded this idea that regressive and explosive discharge may serve constructive purposes of the ego by forestalling more extensive personality disintegration. (See Menninger and Mayman.[136] Cf. Laing.[116])

by the interpreter. This pithy formula, previously referred to, merits a closer look. It implies that self-understanding and self-reflection are instruments of self-change. As Loewald has stated, "Our psychic organization tends to increase its range and level of functioning by virtue of the investigation itself, or on the other hand to become disorganized. Disorganization and higher organization often go hand in hand, the balance or confluence of the two may be precarious or disrupted, but they are part and parcel of the investigative process itself. By the opening up of channels of intrapsychic and interpsychic communication our psychic life is altered. . . ."[126]

Along with some of these went the tacit assumption that a deconditioning process occurred, for which Alexander[1] later coined the phrase "corrective emotional experience," implying that, with analytic enlightenment, the mature ego became able effectively to rearrange the distribution and investment of instinctual energies that had been so *dis*advantageously made by an immature ego. The unsolved dilemmas of childhood are not so unsolvable to the more sophisticated and experienced ego, which can handle them when helped merely to look at them and see them more realistically.

It is very likely that *all* of these things occur during the course of an analysis and that all of them participate in the therapeutic effect. We can view the matter somewhat comprehensively if we return to the model of the partly sick, partly regressed ego. We have assumed that the relatively normal, healthier part of the ego could in a sense detach itself and observe the various stages through which the more mobile regressing part of the ego successively passes. We assume that this alter ego is like "the saving remnant of the House of Israel," the steadfast portion or core of the personality, which has been overwhelmed and temporarily defeated by the willfulness and intransigency of *another part* of the personality, another part of the ego. Emergency compensatory maneuvers then seem to be necessary to preserve ego integrity. This healthy part of the ego is the ally of the therapist and experiences vicariously and somewhat detachedly what the "unhealthy" part of the ego experiences directly. The healthy part of the ego gradually gains strength at the expense of the afflicted ego. One can say that they tend thus to become united again or that the healthy part of the ego prevails and absorbs the other, a tendency that reflects a regulatory principle of synthesis, called by Freud "the synthetic function of the ego." Or one could imagine that the regressive ego tends to shrivel up and disappear.

THE ANALYST'S INTERVENTION

With some such model in mind of the waxing and waning of the regression, we can approach the problem of what constitutes the theoretical and functional participation of the psychoanalyst. Where does he come in? Precisely what is his function in bringing about the "improvement" of the patient, the regression and the return from it? How does he establish a working partnership with the intact ego? To be sure, he sets up the remarkable situation in which the regression experience can occur, and enters in to what Greenson likes to call a "therapeutic alliance with the healthy part of the patient's ego."[86] We have seen that he has a very considerable *involuntary* participation as the silent center and subject of the patient's fantasies. But is this *all* he does? Has he no *voluntary* duties?

In theory, it *might* be possible to defend the thesis that barring exceptional difficulties, the passive contributions of the analyst are sufficient to fulfill the contract. The patient contributes *his* function by following the basic rule, supplying "material." But beyond getting the patient started in the right direction (*i.e.*, of regression) and giving him some assistance in acquiring the habit, so to speak, of free association, what reason is there for the analyst to make any verbal contributions? Will not the regression run a course and return automatically to a *status quo ante*, and be succeeded or replaced by a progression?

It is helpful to discuss the possibility of a psychoanalytic therapy proceeding from beginning to end without the analyst ever having said a word. Of course, he would contribute to it by his consistency of appearance, attention, interest, and audience. But would not the patient, by virtue of the experience itself, gradually overcome his resistances enough to learn what the deeper meaning of his behavior was and decide how much of it he could relinquish, how much he could alter, and how much better off he would be to do so?

In *practice*, of course, it never happens. Even if it were theoretically possible, it would require an unjustifiably long time. The analyst should, in the interests of economy of money, time, and suffering, shorten the process if it is possible. We believe it is possible.

Haley's satirical remarks on this are appropriate:

> Perhaps the most powerful weapon in the analyst's arsenal is the use of silence. This falls in the category of "helpless" or "refusal to battle" ploys. It is impossible to win a contest with a helpless opponent since if you win you have won nothing. Each blow you strike is unreturned so that all you can feel is guilt for having struck while at the same time experiencing the uneasy suspicion that the helplessness is calculated. The result is suppressed fury and desperation—two emotions characterizing the one-down position. The problem posed for the patient is this: how can I get one-up on a man who won't respond and compete with me for the superior position in fair and open encounter. Patients find solutions, of course, but it takes months, usually years, of intensive analysis before a patient finds ways to force a response from his analyst. Ordinarily the patient begins rather crudely by saying something like, "Sometimes I think you're an idiot." He waits for the analyst to react defensively, thus stepping one-down. Instead the analyst replies with the silence ploy. The patient goes further and says, "I'm *sure* you're an idiot." Still silence in reply. Desperately the patient says, "I said you were an idiot, damn you, and you are!" Again only silence. What can the patient do but apologize, thus stepping voluntarily into a one-down position? Often a patient discovers how effective the silence ploy is and attempts to use it himself. This ends in disaster when he realizes that he is paying twenty dollars an hour to lie silent on a couch. The psychoanalytic setting is calculatedly designed to prevent patients using the ploys of analysts to attain equal footing (although as an important part of the cure the patient learns to use them effectively with other people).[89]

We should separate the actual from the exaggerated aspects of this description. What is omitted here is the cooperative venture, the alliance[86] of analyst and patient in the treatment process. Viewed only as a series of maneuvers divorced from its meaning context, psychoanalytic treatment, like all human behavior, can be reduced to absurdity. Nevertheless, Haley does have a point in that the treatment process can be shortened in quite a number of ways.

The realistic facts that time is money and that treatment costs both are a definite facilitation. This is why some analysts prefer to hand the monthly or weekly statement of their charges to the patient in person. They consider it helpful to say, by this act, "This is reality. This is what it costs you to 'indulge' in retrospection and regression." There is an implication here that the patient tends to linger in his regression and exploit his resistances; about this we have been explicit in the chapter on resistance. We know that many patients who pay less than an appropriate amount tend to make the analysis more expensive for themselves by various kinds of delay.

But the psychoanalyst expedites the process of recovery in other ways. He takes a hand in circumstances where the balance of forces in the conflict tends to bring about an impasse or an obsessional prolongation of the process. He points to the existence or possible existence of connections and implications and meanings that tend to elude the patient. He reminds the patient of forgotten statements or he confronts him with a discrepancy, a self-contradiction, a misrepresentation, or an obvious but unrecognized omission.

In this way the patient is assisted more rapidly to objectify, visualize, and understand the meaning of the place of various bits of his behavior, emotion, memory, fantasy, and experience. A few words from the analyst can assist the patient to integrate new material about himself with the main body of his conscious self-knowledge. They enable him to see clearly what he could not see before and to feel things he could not feel before by confirming or verbalizing his discoveries. This is called insight giving, clarification, confrontation, synthesis, or other categories of function, all lumped under the term *interpretation* (or, better, *intervention*).

Interpretation is a term loosely applied by (some) analysts to every voluntary verbal participation made by the analyst in the psychoanalytic treatment process. We dislike the word because it gives young analysts the wrong idea about their main function. They need to be reminded that they are not oracles, not wizards, not linguists, not detectives, not great wise men who, like Joseph and Daniel, "interpret" dreams—but quiet observers, listeners, and occasionally commentators. Their participation in a two-party process is predominantly passive (and partly involuntary); their *occasional* active participation is better called intervention. It may or may not "interpret" something. It may or may not be an interruption. But whenever the analyst speaks he contributes to a process, a process we have described elaborately. (Of course, his silence also contributes and, of course, he *does* help to interpret dreams.)

In a contribution by Ekstein,[27] stress is similarly put not on interpretation as such but on the interpretative process, the patient's communication, and the analyst's interventions. Ekstein relates our theory of technique to recent advances in ego psychology, developing a model of interpretation derived from Rapaport's model of thinking.[160] The baby's emergency cry is the precursor of communication, taking place at a stage when there are no true object relationships, and this quasi-communication is responded to by the mother's "interpretation," which meets the need of the infant and eases the tension state. This primitive communication and interpretation will later be replaced with symbolic communication, but the need for direct action and for direct gratification will continue to exist. The psychoanalytic patient, for example, may accept a specific interpretation but later express through a dream his feeling that the interpretation was a rebuke, or, perhaps, an oral gratification. The regression facilitates the patient's experiencing words not only on the level on which they are meant by the analyst but also on a different, more archaic level.

The extraordinary dependence of psychoanalytic therapy upon verbalization has given rise to renewed study by psychoanalysts of the functions of speech and of communication in general. Why is a memory made more vivid by recounting it? Why are emotions sometimes recognized only when they are described? Why is naming or characterizing something so effective in conceptualizing it? Why are connections between buried memories, symbols, events, and so on best "seen" when they are formulated in words?*

The cry, the gesture, the play of infancy and childhood have communication functions, relating no doubt chiefly to primary process needs. They are gradually (perhaps never completely) surrendered in favor of various symbols. In the course of the regression in psychoanalytic treatment, there are constant evidences of shifts from

---

* Loewenstein,[128] Nunberg,[150] Cassirer,[17] Hartmann,[91] Sapir,[177] Kris,[113] Beres,[9] Ruesch,[176] Brown,[16] and others have made important contributions to this topic, which students and interested readers should consult.

one to another level of communication in the psychoanalytic "dialogue."

It is for this reason that the analyst at times cannot use the classical form of interpretation but must use more primitive forms of intervention. An example of such primitive intervention is the method described by Madame Sechehaye[182] in which gratification and interpretation are joined. Even in classical analysis as Ekstein remarks, we speak frequently about the "giving" of interpretations, and it is suggested here and there that a patient "cannot swallow" or "does not want to stomach" an interpretation we offer.

These different interventions are actually but precursors of interpretation proper. The authors and Ekstein feel strongly identified with Bibring's[13] view concerning the hierarchy of therapeutic principles leading up to clarification and interpretation (suggestion, manipulation, abreaction, clarification, interpretation). Therapeutic interventions are justified and can be thought of as interpretative steps if they lead to interpretations of unconscious material, unconscious defensive operations, warded-off instinctual tendencies, hidden meanings of behavior patterns and their unconscious interconnections. Technical interventions that prepare for such interpretations should be considered a part of interpretative action.

From the beginning of an analysis, matters arise that require the active participation of the analyst. The patient may not speak loudly enough to be understood. He may incompletely or obscurely describe a historical matter of some anamnestic importance about which fuller information is desirable. Or he may make obscure statements that the analyst does not understand at all (and should not pretend to). Or he may be so overburdened by his fears, embarrassment, self-reproach, and so on that he bogs down completely and has to be helped out.

In the early stages of analysis, too, it is often important to ask questions occasionally about details or other matters of fact touched upon in the material, to inquire about the patient's feelings about an item, or to ask at appropriate points for an explanation of something or to call attention to apparently contradictory statements. Inquiry is apt to be overdone by young analysts, who are impressed with the stimulating effect of asking the impossible—*i.e.*, "Why?" This can easily become a cheap and irritating "trick." But if it is not overworked, and if the analyst will remember that no one can ever honestly answer this question and that it serves chiefly to evoke chains of rationalizations and false reasoning that lead only indirectly to the truth, it has a valuable place. Other standard questions are, "What occurs to you about that?" "What associations do you have to that?" "What do you think?"

There is often considerable value in indications on the part of the analyst that the communication offered by the analysand is being followed, and followed, without pressing the word too far, *sympathetically*. The interjection of such exclamations as "Really" (in the sense of mild astonishment), "Naturally!" (in the sense of a certain reaction being a very understandable one), a mild groan—when genuinely felt—to indicate sympathetic deploring of a tragic situation, a chuckle at an appropriate time in connection with an amusing episode, is often very useful especially early in the analytic treatment. They are useful because they convey to the patient the feeling that the analyst is there—listening, following, participating in the communication, and trying to understand. They can be overdone, but so can the perpetually frozen silence that some imagine to be appropriate.

This is quite aside from the necessity for the analyst to cough or sneeze, to move in his chair, and, in short, to act like the living human being that he really is in spite of the fantasies entertained by the patient. Perceptible fragments of his behavior are bound to be seized upon by the patient and utilized either as evidences that the analyst is interested or that he is not. These behaviors of the analyst are used in the service of the transference. Yet they are nonetheless real and do convey attitudes that give uniqueness to each particular psychoanalytic relationship. Gill[75] has proposed that such concrete behaviors should not be ignored or passed off as only transference; they should themselves—as the essence of the interpersonal aspect of the analytic endeavor—become a focus of analytic scrutiny as a force perhaps equal to the transference.

As the analysis goes along and the patient begins to expect some material contribution, there begins what is actually a mutual testing. The analyst is testing the analysand's capacity for frustration, while the analysand is often testing the analyst's forbearance. The process passes out of the first stage, in which the frustration is minimal, into a second stage, in which it gradually mounts. The analyst should remember that this mounting frustration must not, in the average patient, be permitted to go unchecked to the point of explosion. He should recognize that after the sense of frustration has begun to develop, the silence of the analyst is felt by the patient as unkind, essentially hostile. This quality of hostility must not develop too rapidly, and the frustration tension must be maintained at an optimal level—*i.e.*, a bearable and only *gradually* increasing level. Otherwise, it will be just as Freud hinted when he remarked, dryly, that one cannot analyze a patient who is no longer there.

Of course, on the other hand, if the contributions of the analyst were as sufficient as the patient wanted, there would be no frustration but paradoxically, a direct but ultimately disappointing gratification. There would be no progressive recall, the repressive barrier would not be penetrated, and unconscious material for the most part would not be reached.

What is probably meant by those who use the expression "handling the transference," which we consider to be a most reprehensible and improper phrase, is this tactical maneuver of maintaining the frustration at an optimum level. From it has arisen such jargon as "dosing the interpretations" and "giving the patient a little libido." These are clumsy and inelegant expressions, but the idea behind them is clear and sound. The patient continues to expect response from the analyst, despite the fact that numerous interventions have occurred during the earlier parts of analysis, and if this frustration tends to become too great for him to endure, this can be diminished by interventions on the part of the analyst. These do not necessarily "interpret" anything. They may be only in the nature of confirmations of something the patient has said, which is appreciated by the patient as a reassurance and hence a helpful participation. All he may have been needing, actually, is some indication that the analyst accepts him in a measure, accepts what he is saying, likes him a little bit in spite of his importunities and his infirmities.

OPTIMUM TIMING

Interpretations and other interventions are most effective at that point when the frustration tension is mounting to what the analyst believes to be too *painful* a degree, and must then be administered with parsimony—the least necessary quantity of help should be given the patient. To do otherwise tends to upset the desired optimum level of frustration tension by a swing in the opposite direction. It is, so to speak, too reassuring to the patient. It diminishes the internal incentive for him to plow forward. The analyst's participation, consequently, should be as simple, specific, accurate, and laconic as possible.

The question constantly arises in practice as to how the analyst can be sure when the optimum level of frustration tension is being threatened so as to use the best timing for his interventions. After some years of experience, this comes intuitively. This is a discouraging comment for students, and since this is, after all, a manual on theory, we shall try to offer some theoretical guidance.

Freud said that ". . . two conditions are to be fulfilled before it [interpretation] is done. First, by preparatory work, the repressed material must have come very near to the patient's thoughts; and secondly, he must be sufficiently firmly attached by an affective relationship to the physician (transference) to make it impossible for him to take fresh flight again" (*i.e.*, to repress again).[62, 68]

In line with this, and with the theory we have outlined, one looks for evidences of change in the nature of the patient's material in the direction of increasing negative features. It is difficult to put this in a simple way without oversimplifying it, but it is as if a patient, despairing of winning the approval of the analyst, is impelled almost to test or tempt his tolerance; he is actuated, too, by resentment that he is struggling to repress. He begins to loosen, to almost fling from him, material he has hitherto carefully guarded and concealed. But he has no sooner discharged this aggression than he recognizes certain implications in having done so. As his momentary penitence arises, it can be exploited by the obstetrical functioning of the analyst, who assists him in delivering the larger body of the material. Furthermore, by inference the analyst commends the patient for what he expected to be punished for. It is helpful to some young analysts to have it put thus: One "tells" a patient what the patient *almost* sees for himself, that is, when he almost knows what he doesn't know he knows, and one tells him in such a way that the patient, not the analyst, takes the "credit" for the discovery.

Our position is in agreement with that of Gill[74] in his insistence—perhaps a bit dogmatically, it is true—that characteristic for psychoanalysis is the reduction of the regression or transference neurosis by techniques of interpretation alone. This means that we *do not* favor attempts to "handle" the transference by artificially assuming various roles or making artificial manipulations in the conditions of treatment, and so on. It is true, as Gill points out, that unceasing processes of affective, nonverbal communication go on between the analyst and the patient, but the ideal is to go on with the analyzing of the patient's material until the nonverbal interchanges have been converted into explicit verbalizations and have been understood by interpretation.

Perhaps in this connection we should say a word about what it is now customary to call *parameters*, after Eissler.[23] These are procedures that deviate somewhat from the basic model of psychoanalytic technique. An example of a parameter would be a definite command or prohibition or some general advice on a specific problem. Such additional or alternate devices are warranted if they fulfill certain conditions: They must be used only when the basic model technique really does not suffice; they must never exceed the least necessary intervention; they must be used only when they finally lead to their self-elimination; and the effect of the parameter on the transference relationship must never be such that it cannot be abolished by interpretation.*

The distinction between psychoanalysis and psychoanalytically oriented psychotherapy, with particular reference to this matter of interpretations, is clearly stated by Gill:

> [A psychotherapist] does not foster a regressive transference neurosis, since he does not employ the devices which would lead to this, but on the contrary actively discourages the development of such a transference by conducting the interview more like a social interchange of equals, by avoiding free association, by emphasizing reality rather than fantasy, by creating an atmosphere of temporariness and similar measures. He observes various elements of transference developing anyhow—which he correctly calls transferences rather than a transference neurosis—and he may or may not interpret these. If they become obtrusive and seem to be hindering the treatment, or if he

* For a discussion of the use of questioning as a parameter, see Olinick.[153]

sees an opportunity to make a valuable point by interpreting a piece of transference he will do so. But if the transference is reasonably positive and desirable and behavioral changes are occurring or if evidences of hostile transference seem too hot to handle, he will remain silent about it and permit the transference to persist unresolved.[74]

KINDS OF INTERPRETATION

For decades there has been a running debate between proponents of *resistance* interpretation, proponents of *transference* interpretation and proponents of *content* interpretation. From our point of view this can be dismissed in a sentence: All three are necessary at different times.*

For what is it that we—we of the second part—want of the patient?

We want him to see himself. We want him to see that as a result of his being a human being who came into contact (long ago) with other human beings who were not perfect, and as a result of misunderstanding certain things then and being misunderstood by certain people, he experienced pain and fright from which he tried to protect himself by devices that he still continues to use not from present necessity but from a kind of habit. We want him to see that he persists in the same unprofitable formulae of adaptation. We want him to see that he expects the wrong things from the right people and the right things from the wrong people. And, finally, we want him to see that he doesn't want to see it, that he wants to get well—in a way—but is afraid to; that he wants to change, but fights against it. He must see that these unprofitable ways of adaptation bring a modicum of gratification both of early infantile wishes (their primary gain) and of contemporary wishes (their secondary gain). It is the gratifying aspect of these patterns, largely unconscious, that helps to maintain them. Indeed it is these gratifications that are so difficult to recognize and renounce.

Which of these things to point out at a particular moment depends on which of them is most accessible to the patient's con-

* See the discussion of this in connection with resistance in general, pp. 101ff.

sciousness and to the analyst's consciousness at that time. The analyst's attention hovers over the verbal productions of the patient. His extending area of awareness and the direction of the trend of inquiry are watched. If he keeps "in tune" with the patient's unconscious, he *knows* (or comes to know) when to speak.

One thing we certainly should *never* do is to tell the patient what is in his unconscious long before he has any capacity for grasping the significance of such oracular diagnostic incisions. All interpretation begins by a kind of preparatory process. The patient will have communicated so much detail that he will have lost sight of the obvious connections—if indeed he ever saw them—between events and feelings and attitudes. These connections will be apparent to the analyst if for no other reason than that he gets something of a bird's-eye view of the whole. He knows too that there are internal reasons for the patient's not seeing these connections, and hence just pointing them out starts a corrective process. Usually the patient is intrigued by the discovery, surprised, pleased, and curious. It is not necessary for the psychoanalyst to impute hopeful prospects to these early discoveries; the patient does so spontaneously (although Fenichel feels that we should take advantage of opportunities to "bribe" him to go further[33]) .

Having identified some connections or certain common elements in a considerable number of events in the patient's life or items in the material presented, the next step is to further the preparation for additional interpretation. Sooner or later, the analyst is in a position to say something like this: "This thing, then (this trick, this experience, this defense, this defeat) happens to you repeatedly; it seems to happen especially to you. You seem to have something to do with its happening. Perhaps it doesn't just *happen*, possibly you actually contribute to bringing it about. You have done it before. Perhaps you have some hidden purpose behind it, once valid, perhaps, but no longer so. This can be seen as what Fate has done to you; let us look now at what you do with your Fate!"

Such an "interpretation" is always a "blow" (to one part of the ego, not to the observing part) even when it is enlightening and freeing. It seems to the patient like a stone, when he has asked—or hoped—for bread. It contains hope although it often seems critical, and not comforting. It is as if the query, "If thy child asks for bread, wilt thou give him a stone?" were answered thus: "If my child asks for the moon, I'll give him a telescope."

An interpretation of this kind usually facilitates or pushes forward the psychoanalytic process. But sometimes the patient's indigenous and intrinsic negativism will seize upon any "justification" to delay and defeat the process of treatment. It is not unusual that, in such a moment of attempted clarification as we have described, the patient will block. He doesn't "get it"—or, it sounds pretty, but what does it mean? He forgets, theorizes, digresses, dawdles. He isn't quite able to accept (see) what he is now almost face to face with.

RESISTANCE INTERPRETATION

Instead of rubbing his nose in it, so to speak (which he will find his own ways to avoid), one proceeds then to the *analysis of the resistance*. First, one points out that such resistance exists; then one points out how it manifests itself; then one points out its obvious purpose (and, of course, if one doesn't know what its purpose is, then the patient's cooperation has to be enlisted in that search). In general, of course, the purpose is to avoid seeing what is, to one part of the ego, unpleasant truth. But this purpose may be further obscured by various transference patterns; the patient may be testing, defying, or seducing the analyst.

It is important to emphasize here that defenses and resistances are recognized as shifts in thoughts and actions, as ebbing and flowing in attitudes and counter-attitudes. These thoughts have a dynamic component—the wishes and motives. Every resistance or defense—"counter-cathexis" in the energy language of psychoanalysis —is directed against a wish or a goal and therefore takes the form of a goal-diverting action, thought, or affect. The unconscious nature of the counter-wishes makes the resistance unavailable to awareness. Further, these counter-wishes are themselves gratifying and wish-fulfilling. Part of the interpretative process, then, consists in analyzing the wishful character not only of the impulse defended against, but of the wishful impulses that are part of the resistance structure. Such wishes and motives become apparent in the unfolding of the transference neurosis and in the quality of the interaction with the analyst.

It is true that in the process of interpreting the resistance, we frequently behold new and unexpected material appearing spontaneously. But we feel the way a modern obstetrician feels in regard to the use of low forceps in deliveries. One can, to be sure, merely wait for a softening of the perineum, as it were, and the removal of any mechanical obstructions, and then wait for contractions of the uterus to force out the fetus. But one can save a great deal of time and suffering by assisting in the delivery by gentle traction. This is approximately what one can do in analysis. But one must remember to do it with gentleness. There is pain involved for the patient in these changes just as there is in an obstetrical delivery. The shattering of the narcissistic armor, as it has been called, can be exquisitely painful. The patient's capacity for pain tolerance is probably what is reflected in his frustration tolerance, which, in turn, reflects his self-esteem and its vulnerability. (See Kohut.[111])

And this develops the necessity for working through, or elaborating the sphere of the material. For it is an empirical fact that the same general type of material and the same general type of resistance appears in the analysis time after time—although in various contexts—to the considerable dismay of the young analyst who feels that, having accepted everything, the patient has relinquished his insight for the same old illusions.

No analysis is carried on in a vacuum; patients being analyzed are still living out their lives. They encounter daily experiences which may or may not be of their own doing but some of which disturb their equilibrium again and again and induce new retreat to old defenses. Resistance will often cover with the same obliviousness the repetition of the old pattern, so that "all that was won by painstaking labor seems to be forgotten. . . . We have to begin (over and over) again from the beginning."[33] Sometimes reminding the patient of the previously identified resistance will effect a change; usually it is not sufficient. He will often resume his former state of resentment or depression or provocativeness or whatever.*

* A cartoon in *The New Yorker* some years ago by Kindl showed a middle-aged man on the couch saying to his doctor, "Don't you think, Doctor, in view of my marked improvement, I might resume my affection for my mother?"

Some interpretations or explanations have to be repeated many times. Resistance never evaporates or flies away; it has to be consistently and persistently analyzed throughout every analysis. It often appears as if the patient had never heard the analyst's previous interpretation. This necessity for working through, for the analyst to repeat interpretations until they are taken hold of, is a reflection of the extension of the neurosis into many different aspects of or events of the patient's life. His defensive structure isolates these events from one another, so that he is not aware of the common tendency running through them. In the language of some learning theorists, the "transfer" or "spread of effect" of the insight from one situation to other situations is limited or blocked. In Freud's words, "One must allow the patient time to get to know this resistance."[61] Hence the necessity for repeating the interpretations as the patient repeats his neurotic behavior in different contexts.

In some patients more emphasis needs to be given to resistance interpretations, and in others more help is necessary in the reformulation, delivery, and integration of the material. Some analysts concentrate much of the analytic work on the destructive (*i.e.*, aggressive) elements in the patient's material. "Point out the aggression," they advise, "and the healthy erotic expression and growth will follow naturally." True, perhaps, but complicated by the fact that all acts contain evidences of both positive ("erotic") and negative ("aggressive") wishes and motives, fused and/or defused in varying degrees. The "bound" and concealed aggression must sometimes be dissected and sometimes left alone.

TRANSFERENCE INTERPRETATION

To a considerable extent both resistance and content are constantly apparent in the transference relationship. The analyst plays the part of various characters in the patient's life, and consequently, all resistance interpretation and all content interpretation will probably involve the analyst in one of his roles. Sometimes it is particularly helpful to the patient to have this transference role pointed out in connection with the way in which it is being used to slow up the process. To please the analyst the patient will do certain things or not do them; or to displease the analyst he will sometimes do them or not do them. Interferences and retardations that retard the analytic work can frequently be best approached or viewed from the standpoint of their transference meaning. Some analysts become very adept in perceiving and interpreting "transference resistance" and even concentrate exclusively on it.[104] Most analysts are constantly aware of the transference aspect of interpretation and make use of it specifically only when it is conspicuously present in an episode or phase of the treatment. For the most part transference interpretation occupies a conspicuous part of the psychoanalytic process in that both analyst and patient are engaged in exploring the "transference neurosis" both in its resistance and in its content manifestations. It is the interpretative exploration of the "transference neurosis" that provides one of the distinguishing features of psychoanalysis.

CONTENT INTERPRETATION

We may seem to have neglected or at least postponed discussion of content interpretation. Have we forgotten, someone may ask, that the psychoanalyst has a responsibility to assist the patient in gaining insight? Such a question implies that the analyst must at some point become a Joseph or a Daniel and tell the patient what certain obscure things mean.

In the psychoanalytic literature of the past few decades there have been two extreme positions in regard to how this should be taught. Wilhelm Reich[164] believed that a systematic, highly structured program of interpretation could be outlined with procedures spelled out in a one-two-three order, just as one might plan an appendectomy. At the other extreme was the position of Theodor Reik,[167, 168] who felt that psychoanalysts were handicapped by such theorizing, reflecting, and planning. He liked to put emphasis on the purely intuitive factors, and his books *Surprise and the Psychoanalyst* and *Listening with the Third Ear* contain excellent material to illustrate his thesis. They are good not only in content but in spirit. Just as one has to shut one's eyes to some of the strange digressions in Reich's book, so one must shut one's eyes to Reik's polemics against knowledge and thinking. Both authors are helpful in elaborating the details of technical practice.

Although I (K.A.M.) do not visualize or formulate the process quite as Reich did, my didactic and written expositions are more in line with his thinking, whereas my practice, I suspect, is more in line with that of Reik, so eloquently described long before Reik by Ferenczi:

> One gradually becomes aware how immensely complicated the mental work demanded from the analyst is. He has to let the patient's free associations play upon him; simultaneously he lets his own fantasy get to work with the association material; from time to time he compares the new connexions that arise with earlier results of the analysis; and not for one moment must he relax the vigilance and criticism made necessary by his own subjective trends.
>
> One might say that his mind swings continuously between empathy, self-observation, and making judgments. The latter emerge spontaneously from time to time as mental signals, which at first, of course, have to be assessed only as such; only after the accumulation of further evidence is one entitled to make an interpretation.[34]

It is a popular notion that the major content of analytic material is dreams and, accordingly, the reader may expect us to discuss here something of the technique of dream interpretation. Unfortunately dreams do *not* constitute the bulk of any psychoanalysis; we say "unfortunately" because they are, as Freud said, the royal road to the unconscious and assist greatly in identifying trends of unconscious thought and intent. They are, so to speak, the special gifts or nuggets of an analysis and surface as a rule only occasionally in most analyses. When they do, they deserve attention and, if possible, interpretation, and this is often the heart of the interpretative function. But sometimes they do not appear at all, and this too must be examined.

The interpretation of dreams is itself a large and recondite subject to which we cannot do justice in a schematic outline of theory such as this. We shall discuss it briefly a little later but the student is strongly advised to make a special study of this topic using several of the excellent treatises available.

A GRAPHIC MODEL OF THE TREATMENT PROCESS

My own difficulty as a student was that with all the formulations and explanations and illustrations, I never felt quite certain that I knew where my analysands were going. This will sound strangely naive to analysts who have acquired competence and self-confidence, who have learned how to fit pieces of new information in at the proper places in their own conceptualizations or reject them as unimportant. But the young candidate has the tender memory of his own recent tumultuous couch experiences, plus vast amounts of reading, plus various kinds of partially assimilated instruction. No wonder he is confused when his patient comes in day after day, piling Pelion on Ossa, until all notion of the structure of the process is lost. To mix metaphors, one can well say that he cannot see the woods for the trees. In supervisory work from time to time I have the candidate review all the material from the beginning in order to get a grasp of the ebb and flow of trends, of the regression, the repetition, the general form of resistance, but more particularly to get a concept of the analytic process as a whole.

One reason for the difficulty encountered by the student is our lack of an adequate systematic model or schema of the psychoanalytic process to which the student can attach his new ideas and experiences. Several such models have been proposed.

About thirty years ago, quite unfamiliar with Reich's ordering, I devised a conceptualization of the psychoanalytic treatment process that I found useful for myself and useful in teaching. Subsequent expressions of appreciation from former candidates encouraged me, so I shall record it here as best I can, although it is much easier to present it orally with the use of a blackboard and various colored chalks.

I ask the students to try to think abstractly of the life-course of a child who is ultimately to become a psychoanalytic patient. I ask them to represent his birth as a dot, his life-course as a line. From the "dot" the line extends forward into the future. The influence of parents, siblings, circumstances, and events will combine with the constitutional and instinctual factors to determine the precise direction that the subsequent life-course takes.

Were this to be a "normal" healthy, ideal life, perhaps the diagram of its subsequent course could be shown as it appears in Figure 10.

Or it might turn out that as his life developed his goals changed, but for the better. Assuming that G^2 represents an im-

FIGURE 10

provement of some kind, over and above an acceptable "normal" life objective (or series of objectives) represented by G^1, another schematic course of development is illustrated in Figure 11.

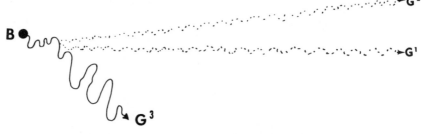

FIGURE 11

But the life that we are about to diagram is, by definition, that of an individual who was deflected from his goal—*i.e.*, to him an acceptable and approved goal—in a disappointing and unsatisfactory (regressive) direction to a "false" goal (G^3). We might diagram it as in Figure 12.

FIGURE 12

Our theory holds that such deflections toward an improper goal, or "false goal," come about through the early acquisition of wrong techniques of dealing with the opportunities and dangers of life. It holds too, that these wrong techniques of living developed in response to handicaps, injuries, painful experiences, gross misunderstandings, bewildering opportunities, and other "traumata" of the early formative period. On our diagram we can indicate these as X^1, X^2, X^3, and X^n (Figure 13).

What is not shown specifically in the diagram is the fact that the patient may have passed beyond the G^3 goal, seemingly over-

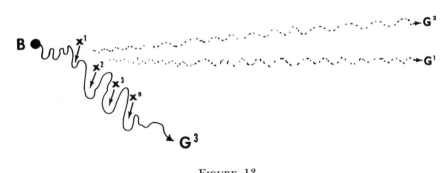

FIGURE 13

coming the bad start, only to regress back to it in the face of new difficulties.

Now we shall introduce the *treatment* factor into our diagram. When the conflict becomes unendurable, the struggling, baffled "victim" of fate, circumstance, and error reaches a point (the star in Figure 14) where he is impelled by pain or fear to seek help. Fortunately for our schema, he is brought into contact with a psychoanalyst and begins psychoanalytic treatment. This can be shown in the diagram by setting up a new sphere or area of activity quite distinct from the patient's past or contemporary life. The treatment is to bring a turning point into his life, but the turning point will not be visible immediately.

With the establishment of a relationship with the psychoanalyst, our subject as a "patient" begins to lead not a double life but a triple life. On the one hand, he continues relationships with his family, friends, employers, employees, and all the other elements of his work-a-day world. This, as we know, is an incomplete, partial, "superficial" existence. Beneath it is a conflictual trend of existence, of which he is only vaguely conscious but which expresses itself in various ways.

For one hour a day, in the secret chambers of the psychoanalyst, he looks upon a subterranean, long concealed and scarcely recognized aspect of himself. He perceives this buried portion of his mental life as a prominent but submerged extension of his infancy and childhood. During that hour he recalls wounds and sorrows and long-nourished but frustrated desires, and as he reminiscently experiences them, he revalues them and gives to them a new place in his thinking. Gradually their power and numbers diminish and come increasingly under the control of his maturing intelligence.

In Figure 14 we have tried to show the next stage in the schema. Psychoanalysis has begun (*A*) and the psychoanalytic situation in the patient's life develops. Simultaneously a reality situation exists (*R*) and beneath it is the pathological conflict extending forward from the infancy situation, injuring and crippling the normative trend.

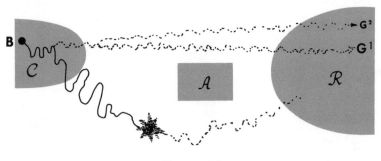

FIGURE 14

Day after day as the analytic treatment proceeds and as it's scope enlarges, memories of days long gone are recalled and related to contemporary events, feelings, and emotional reactions within the treatment situation. A parallel or reciprocal correspondence—not an exact one, to be sure, but a significant one—can be inferred as existing between the "steps" or progress in the analysis, the steps of demoralization or inhibition or fixation or whatever most characterized the unhappy childhood, and the steps of improvement in the contemporary adjustment. (For this and the subsequent discussion, see Figure 15.)

When the depth of the regression has been reached, the patient tends to improve in his adjustments to life and more wholeheartedly and concertedly to strive toward the "good" goal of comfortable and productive achievement. This refers to the patient's *life* goal, not the treatment goal, although the latter is here assumed to be the achievement of the former. The goals of psychotherapy, including analysis, may not always be so simply stated, and actually vary considerably as Gill has reminded us eloquently.[78] The theoretical goals of psychoanalysis may be variously formulated; Freud did so repeatedly, most clearly perhaps thus:

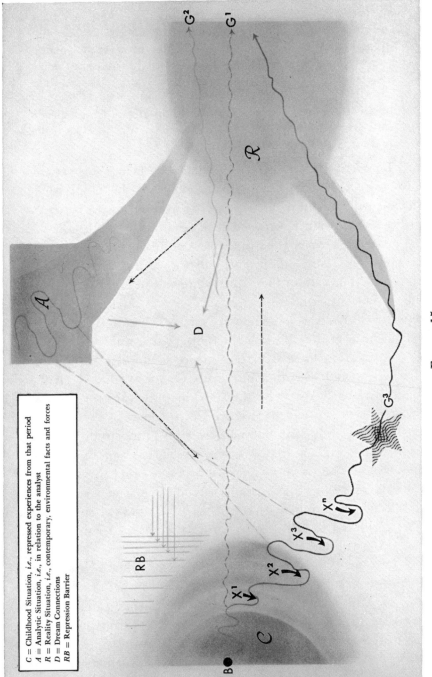

C = Childhood Situation, *i.e.*, repressed experiences from that period
A = Analytic Situation, *i.e.*, in relation to the analyst
R = Reality Situation, *i.e.*, contemporary, environmental facts and forces
D = Dream Connections
RB = Repression Barrier

FIGURE 15

It may be laid down that the aim of the treatment is to remove the patient's resistances and to pass his repressions in review and thus to bring about the most far-reaching unification and strengthening of his ego, to enable him to save the mental energy which he is expending upon internal conflicts, to make the best of him that his inherited capacities will allow and so to make him as efficient and as capable of enjoyment as is possible. The removal of the symptoms of his illness is not specifically arrived at, but is achieved, as it were, as a by-product if the analysis is properly carried through.[67]

Theoretically each step in the analysis brings the patient one step closer to reality and one step closer to the point when the analysis will no longer be necessary, as reflected in the patient's real life by steps toward improvement in relationships with others. Both the process of recovery and the process of psychoanalysis tend toward the same end point, although actually they will not terminate simultaneously. The area of the patient's life and interests represented by the analytic situation will grow smaller and smaller, ultimately to disappear, while the contemporary reality situation will enlarge and extend, in a greater freedom for object attachment and creativity.

In addition to this correspondence of steps in the progressive changes (analytic situation and reality situation), there is an approximate parallelism between the steps in the treatment process and the steps representing the original development of the illness—*i.e.*, the sequence of deviant or *downward* steps in the original childhood or infantile situation. These are roughly images or replicas of one another, the one moving toward illness, the other toward recovery. I always point out how logical it would be to assume that the *first* recollections of an analysis are the *earliest* (traumatic) experiences (X^1), followed by the recollection of the *second* traumatic experience (X^2) and then the third, and so on, to X^n.

Of course, we all know that this is not the way it goes at all. Indeed, it is apt to be just the reverse of this, speaking very generally. It is the many *more recent* disappointments, pains, and heartbreaks that are first recalled—and then the less recent and on back to the more remote. Thus as the analysis goes further ahead, the recollection goes further back, but in a quite unpredictable order of recall.

These recollections of earlier events that correspond with contemporary experiences are not the primary objects of the patient's search. They merely "occur" to him in connection with experiences in the *two* contemporary situations—the analytic and the reality. They are like reference material in a library—they back up and explain the reflections of contemporary reality problems as the latter appear in the analytic situation. As we shall see, there is more order-liness and meaningfulness to this recollection of the genetic experi-ence than this implies.

But at first, as we all know, the patient tends to make the analytic situation reciprocal to his reality situation. The outside world has been unkind, and he expects from the analyst the opposite of unkindness. The outside world frightens him; from the analyst he wants reassurance. But gradually, of course, failing to find coopera-tion from the analyst in developing this reciprocity, the patient tends to deal with the analyst in the same way that he has disad-vantageously dealt with people all of his life (from B to G^1).*

But *now* there is a corrective element. We have indicated the tendency toward correction on the chart by stepwise movement away from the false toward the true goal (G^3 toward G^1) but we haven't said what determined it. What *is* the corrective factor?

It will be recalled that we discussed earlier in this chapter various theories explaining the improvement resulting from psycho-analytic treatment. Everyone agrees that something "happens," that changes in personality structure and function do occur, but we do not know why they do. We concede the importance of what we call *insight* in the process of recovery, but whether it is a product or a provocation of the change we cannot be sure. But just what is insight?

We define insight as the recognition by the patient

1. that this or that aspect of his feeling and attitudes, this or that technique of behavior, this or that role in which he casts other people, is *of a pattern*;
2. that this pattern, like the footprint of a bear that has lost certain toes in a trap long ago, stamps itself with every step of his life journey; it is present in his contemporary reality situation relationships, and it is present in his analytic relationship;

* Cf. reference 59.

3. that this pattern originated for a reason that was valid at the time, and persisted despite changes in some of the circumstances that originally determined it;

4. that this pattern contains elements that are offensive and injurious to others as well as expensive and troublesome to the patient.

Insight is not just seeing that something in the analytic situation is similar to something in childhood, or seeing that something in childhood is reflected in the activities of his contemporary situation, or seeing that something in his contemporary situation is a reflection of something in the analytic situation. In the proper sense of the word and in the useful sense for psychoanalytic technique, *insight is the simultaneous identification of the characteristic behavior pattern in all three of these situations, together with an understanding of why they were and are used as they were and are.**

As Lowenstein put it,

> The interest of analysis does not, as it is sometimes erroneously thought, focus on the past alone, but on the inter-relationship between past and present: the influence of the past upon the present and, paradoxical though it may sound, of the present upon the past. The paramount role which the analysis of transference plays in psychoanalytic technique is based on this particular interconnection we find between the past and the present in human life.[128]

DREAM INTERPRETATION

We represent this on the diagram (Figure 15), which connects the three areas—childhood, contemporary environmental reality, and psychoanalytic situation—and forms a triangle, the triangle of insight. A fortuitous feature of this diagrammatic scheme is that the triangle encloses an area that, for heuristic purposes, serves as a place to indicate the dream (D) as a packaged product of the timeless unconscious. Dreams become studiable and understandable in

---

* Richfield[169, 170] has remarked that the voice of the intelligence is not only soft, but speaks with two voices; that is, there are two kinds of insight, based on the fact that there are two kinds of knowledge, two different ways in which we can know things, illustrated by the ways in which we know alcohol and the way we know strychnine (Bertrand Russell). "What Reid and Finesinger[165] have called 'dynamic insight,' the 'intellectual *summum bonum* of analysis,' actually may be achieved by the effective timing of both fundamental kinds of insight in an appropriate order governed by the peculiarities of each case."

the analytic situation when the analyst receives them as gifts and coded messages. They are like the Rosetta stone, containing parallel columns, as it were, in terms derived from the analytic situation, the reality situation, and the childhood situation. Hence it is that the dream has been called the *via regia* to the understanding of the unconscious, and the passkey to the identification of the characteristic pattern-complex of the personality.

"Dreams, then," said Erikson, "not only fulfill naked wishes of sexual licence, of unlimited dominance and of unrestricted destructiveness; where they work, they also lift the dreamer's isolation, appease his conscience, and preserve his identity, each in specific and instructive ways."[29]

"As Erikson outlines it," comments Ekstein, "the dream reflects the life cycle of the dreamer: his present phase and the related infantile phase, his psychosexual and psychoaggressive fixations and arrests. It reflects the social process, the collective and ego identity, and defensive and integrative mechanisms of the ego organization."[24]

The importance of dream interpretation to psychoanalytic therapy was recognized by Freud from the very beginning, and it has not diminished with the passing of time and the accretion of experience. The theory of dreams, their recollection and interpretation is really the basic theory of technique, of which all these pages are but an elaboration. *The Interpretation of Dreams* is the Magna Carta of psychoanalysis and the theory is spelled out therein quite fully.

This is precisely the reason we do not discuss here more specifically the details of dream interpretation.* In practice *and* in teaching we have always leaned heavily upon dream interpretation and regard its evasion or neglect by young analysts as an indication of some incompleteness in their training. Dreams serve the psychoanalyst as core-drilling samples serve the geologist—except that our samples are spontaneous! They are coded communications from the

---

* Thomas N. French[44] has undertaken an intensive examination of psychological processes in the light of psychoanalytic discoveries and conditioned-reflex theory. The second of the five volumes in this study is devoted entirely to the theory of the dream and its interpretation in psychoanalytic treatment with special reference to recurring patterns and sequences in different dreams of the same person. He relates these patterns to behavior patterns of the patient.

unconscious, which in that form can elude the repression barrier. When they are translatable, they—with the aid of association—illuminate and clarify whole areas of obscurity in the life history, the clinical picture and the transference situation.

THE ORDERLY SEQUENCE OF MATERIAL

One explanation or description of the way the gaining of insight furthers the progress toward recovery is that the realm and freedom of the ego are extended when insight pushes back the barrier of repression and enlarges the area of self-knowledge. This can be shown schematically in our model by a vertical line anterior to the bulk of the childhood zone. As the process develops, this repression barrier (*RB*) will be repeatedly approached and increasingly penetrated for the recovery of forgotten material. In effect, the line is moved progressively further and further "back"—*i.e.*, to the left.

Along with this progressive regression in the recall of the forgotten and repressed, the correlation process continues, so that the patient is, so to speak, at one moment recalling something from the past, the next moment reporting an attitude toward the doctor and, the next moment, a fantasy (or dream) that identifies the similarity of all three areas.

There is usually a vague general order in the apparently unstructured presentation of analytic material from these several areas. In the beginning of an analysis the patient will often describe some of his contemporary unhappiness and perhaps give a certain anamnestic resume proceeding from the reality situation back to his childhood. "This happened to me today," he will continue, "just as it did so often when I was a child, for example when. . . ." This is what we designate a *clockwise* direction of the order of presenting material; it is typical of good psychiatric histories and of psychotherapy, but not of good psychoanalysis except in the very early stages.

In a "properly going" analysis, on the other hand, the patient will usually describe, for example, an aspect of the *reality* situation that he finds to be unpleasant, and from this go to certain aspects of the *analytic* situation, which he may find either pleasant or unpleasant, but probably pleasant in contrast to the unpleasantness of the reality situation. Under the aegis of this pleasant aspect of the analytic situation his mind reverts to childhood, and he recalls something from that area—neither the earliest nor most recent thing but something related. From this area he soon turns again to the present, to something in the contemporary reality situation, and a cycle will have been completed. (Formula: Reality situation —► Analytic and/or transference situation —► childhood situation —► Reality situation —► Analytic and/or transference situation —► etc.)

Example: "My wife *never* has dinner ready when I get home from work. She always keeps me waiting. Of course, you do too sometimes. But that isn't so serious; I don't wait long. I don't know why I made that little jab at you. I used to tease my mother that way sometimes, ungrateful little cuss that I was. I would accuse her of things she was innocent of. My mother would go to great lengths to see that I got enough to eat. I remember the lunches she made for me when I came home from school. My wife wouldn't even—and yet I don't reproach her much. Maybe I'm afraid to. Yes, I think I'm afraid to criticize her. I seem to have more courage about criticizing you than I do my wife; I almost hunt things to find fault with you about."

Any analyst will recognize other things here than the point we wish it to illustrate, which is that the patient successively goes from the contemporary situation to the analytic situation, thence to related aspects of the childhood situation, thence to the reality situation and on around the circle in the same *counterclockwise* direction (as in Figure 15). This is the typical, proper, and correct sequence. We have support for this proposition from Freud's general advice that analysis should proceed from the so-called surface to the so-called depth.[53, 62]

But if successive material tends to move from the depths directly to the present moment, *i.e.*, in what on our diagram is a clockwise direction, something is wrong. Thus any analyst would recognize that a patient who talked in the following way was in some kind of serious resistance difficulty:

"You keep me waiting here. I wonder why that is. Don't you want to see me? My wife keeps me waiting, too, always does. I say nothing—afraid to, I guess. My mother never kept me waiting; she'd have lunch ready for me when I got home from school—never any waiting, like here. Why *do* you keep me waiting?"

In this example, the flow of the material is in the wrong direction (Analytic → Reality → Childhood → Analytic). It should roll forward with time along the lines actually experienced and not along trackless, traceless orbits extending from childhood to the analytic situation.

Another common manifestation of resistance is reflected in the tendency for the flow of material to get "stuck" or "hung up," as it were—the "broken record" type of resistance, we call it. A patient will become preoccupied with childhood material, for example, and mull it over and over without insight or progress. The resistance in this case usually has to do with facing something in the contemporary reality situation, and this can be pointed out to the patient and the process moved forward a step. But a patient may also become preoccupied with the reality situation—"reality resistance," as it is sometimes called. In such a case the resistance is usually against recognition of something in the analytic situation, and the patient has to be moved on, so to speak, in that direction. Instead of "How does that operate in your contemporary life?" the analyst would now say, "Is that perhaps reflected in your relationship to me?" But the patient may also become stalled at the point of preoccupation with his *analyst,* and an erotization of the analytic situation. Correction consists, then, in pushing the patient into the past as it were, directing his attention to the fact that "what you feel toward me is a reflection of something that was once attached to some other person, long ago. But who?" or "Can you recall ever having felt just this way before?"*

Another way in which the flow of material gets hung up is not on one-point stickiness or resistance or perverseness but on an obsessional seesawing back and forth between any two points. Some patients will incessantly jump from a reality problem to the analytic situation, back to the reality situation, back to the analytic situation, and so forth; never a word is heard about the infantile period. Other

---

* It was Ferenczi who once said that if the patient talks about the present, he should be directed to the past, and if he talks about the past, he should be directed to the present. Our schema is actually only an amplification of the principle implied in this comment of Ferenczi's.

patients will speak exhaustively about the infantile period and from that to the analytic situation for a while, perhaps making numerous correlations but never once (or at least not consistently) bringing in the factor of contemporary reality. Such a patient will speak at length about his resentment of a baby brother born two years later than himself and compare this with a new patient the analyst has just taken or with changes in his job status, without mentioning his own children, perhaps even the recent birth to his wife of a new daughter. In this kind of resistance the young analyst is sometimes at a loss as to where the turning back occurs. If he follows this diagram he need not be (allowing, of course, for certain exceptions for which no rule can be devised).

To take a final look at our schematic diagram, one can say that the cyclic process of comparison, correlation, recollection, correction, etc., seems to move forward totally—bodily as well as contracting intrinsically. The depth of recall increases, the repression barrier recedes, the analytic situation begins to vanish by absorption into the reality situation, and the patient's progress approaches the ideal goal. Perhaps the Socratic ideal of knowledge—correctly knowing things about oneself and one's world and seeing them objectively, past and present—might be designated the goal of the treatment. But this is only true if with such knowledge goes the appropriate emotional reaction and the sense of freedom for the investment of the creative and constructive powers derived from the life instinct.

In concluding this chapter on the intervention function of the analyst, we am well aware of how sketchy, one-sided, and incomplete it is. But it does contain devices and formulations that many have found useful. They have enabled us to convey to the aspiring analytic candidate a belief that there is an orderliness even in the disorganized unconscious material with which he is to deal, and a certain orderliness, too, in our methods of dealing with it. This helps him to gain confidence in what he is doing as a therapist. Later he can fit into the scheme the many other views and facts and theories that his reading and experience will supply, or he can drop it from his memory. Glover, in his well-known questionnaire survey, discovered a wide variation in the use of "interpretation," its form, timing, quantity, depth, order, and content by practicing analysts. We probably all do it somewhat differently.

VII

TERMINATION

Severance of the Contract
between the Two Parties

WE HAVE DESCRIBED PSYCHOANALYTIC TREATMENT AS A CONTRACTUAL relationship in the course of which one party assists a second party in a self-evaluation. The ego of the subject undergoes a functional splitting or division of duties such that one part of it observes another part progressively abandoning façades of being healthy, mature, realistic, and secure. This observed part (or set of functions) of the ego is to some degree immature, inhibited, unrealistic, and inefficacious in its functioning—hence the patient's need for treatment. But under scrutiny, more of the immaturity, inhibition, and inept functioning becomes apparent, particularly during the daily fifty-minute treatment periods. In this process even some previously healthy ego functions become (temporarily) impaired.

During the rest of the day the regression is kept in abeyance or under cover through dominance of the *healthy* ego functions. And at all times this regression, of whatever degree, remains under the scrutiny of the intact portion of the ego, a scrutiny that is supported and assisted by the psychoanalyst. Along with this scrutiny we may assume that there goes the soft, weak voice of intelligent self-counsel.

Though often ignored and resisted, it is *persistent*. Ultimately it is listened to and heeded.

But when *is* "ultimately"? The familiar question, "How long does psychoanalysis last?" (heard so often inside and outside of analysis) is, at the beginning of an analysis, a practical question that has to be given a theoretical answer, whereas toward the end of an analysis it becomes a theoretical question to which a practical answer is usually given.

It seems incredible that after fifty years of psychoanalysis there should be such a vast difference of opinion as to what even the average length of analysis is or *should be*! The three months of analysis advocated by Otto Rank proved to be a farce for some and a tragedy for others. On the other hand, we all know patients who have been in analysis for ten years or more, which seems similarly tragic or farcical. These differences may reflect differences in the goals of treatment or mistakes in the assessment of analyzability. In the early days of psychoanalysis a disappearance of symptoms indicated a recession of the illness. Today we no longer regard this as an adequate criterion for the termination of treatment. The patient who has adequately recovered from an illness with the aid of psychoanalysis will not have become his old self again; rather he has become (we trust) an enlarged, an improved, indeed a *new* self. But it is hard to say in advance how long this will take.

THE TURNING POINT

In the description of regression (the "transference neurosis") we discussed the general shape of the curve described by the successively lower levels reached. When does the descent cease and the ascent or progression toward "normal" begin? One may pore through the hundreds of articles on technique and on the psychoanalytic process and find few forthright discussions of this question.* In the long-ago days of our discipline, it was a cardinal principle

---

* Among these few are Ekstein's contribution[25] and a panel discussion at the American Psychoanalytic Association meeting in 1969.[39] The Chicago Psychoanalytic Institute has for many years held a seminar on termination of analysis, first under the leadership of Maxwell Gitelson and later under that of Joan Fleming.

that once the painful, traumatic events of childhood were fully recalled, extracted like splinters from a child's finger, the chronically
festering wounds healed and the patient recovered promptly, to live
happily ever afterward, we hoped.

But as we became more sophisticated—or at least more com-
prehending—in our notions of etiology and therapy, we spoke less
and less in these surgical terms of extracting or evacuating or recovering painful memories. But we did not put anything in the place of
that simple model. One reads very little about the process of recovery, of re-regression or progression or reconstitution or reconstruction. (We are not even sure what best to call it.) Ekstein[26] and
Reider[166] inquire into how it is that the observing part of the ego,
the healthy part, the stable part, as we assume, becomes enlarged and
strengthened by accretions from the formerly affected part. As this
occurs, increasingly, the emergency makeshifts can be abandoned.

Every clinician is familiar with the symptomatic evidences of
these shifts in the balance—the little day-to-day victories that mean
so much to the discouraged, wistful patient. The soft but persistent
voice of the intellect, the new awareness of self-defeating tendencies,
the increasingly clearer vision of the practical benefits of better
reality adaptation, the fear of repeated pain, the pull of opportunities, the fruits of better techniques of winning love, the new-found
courage to try new ways—with all these the steadily cumulative
burden of the cost of treatment in time, effort, and money combined
turns the direction of the curve from downward to upward, from
regression to progression. And there is clearly the increasingly perceived example of the psychoanalyst himself—his poise, patience,
fairness, consistency, rationality, kindliness, concern, and his *real*
love for the patient.

The change in direction from regression to progression seems
to take place through a change in conviction or belief on the part of
the patient. He has presumably gotten as far from reality as possible
and doesn't like what he finds. We cannot quite say that he isn't
satisfied; it might be more accurate to say that he is satisfied that he
cannot be satisfied by going further in that direction. He has seen
that in many respects he had never grown up, but maintained
childish attitudes and longings, reaching back into his earliest childhood, which interfered with his present-day life. He comes to see

without equivocation that above everything else in life he wants to love and be loved, he realizes that he can give love and can get love and also that he can hate and fight effectively when necessary, *e.g.*, in self-defense or in defense of a worthy cause.

Suppose we go back to the very beginning of our theoretical propositions and recollect what it was the patient came for. He came to be relieved of certain distress or certain disability; these were his symptoms. He came, as we diagrammed it, with the proposition, "I want the analyst to *cure* me." (See Figure 6.)

The analyst promised to assist him in getting relief from some of his distress and to set up a treatment program. Then, in the course of this treatment, wherein he was to lose these symptoms, the patient began to discover that his symptoms had a purpose, that he was not so anxious to lose them but that he was, at the same time, anxious to have something else and was impelled, moreover, to use some very astonishing techniques to do so. He wanted to be loved, and to be able to love, but there were unconscious obstacles to both.

The regression induced by the treatment exposed these facts and brought about changes in his goals. At the peak of the regression, at its greatest depth one might say, the patient was aware that he was both blissfully gratified and acutely unsatisfied. Then he began to recognize that in certain respects he would always be unsatisfied, compared to his resurrected memories and fantasies. But he also came to realize that his present dissatisfactions need not be as great as his poor techniques had brought about. He progressively approached a point where he could say, in no spirit of sulking or sour grapes:

"I have gained much from this experience; I am still gaining from it. But the law of diminishing returns is operative, and the question is now whether what I have yet to gain will outweigh the practical inconvenience and expense of my continuing to come for my daily sessions. I have my analyst's friendship and I have his example. I have his point of view toward illness. What I *thought* I wanted from him was in part a childish fantasy, which I renounced. In the sense of wanting to love and be loved, I realize I can obtain these satisfactions in more likely places and with more appropriate techniques than I have ever used, or than I used during the experience with my analyst. By not giving me what I thought I wanted from him, the analyst gave me what I most needed; namely, a better self-understanding, a better capacity for discrimination, greater tolerance for unavoidable dissatisfaction, a clearer view of my needs. In a symbolic sense, the analyst has given me himself, and I felt free to take his gift. I do not need his help any more. I have gotten what I paid for; I can do for myself. I can assume a mature role in preference to one of expectant pleading; I can substitute hoping for despairing, enjoying for expecting, giving for taking. I can endure foregoing what must be foregone and accept and enjoy, without crippling guilt, such pleasures as are accessible to me. I have acquired, reluctantly, the knowledge of my temptation to substitute self-scrutiny for self-correction, and to analyze rather than striving to alter the situation. The knowledge that there is no real complete independence for anyone, that we are all mutually dependent, tempts my passivity, but I have lost the fear of being dependent on another occasionally."

Every analyst is happy when a "terminating" patient is able to say something like this and mean it. Many are able to say it; some do say it. But we also recognize that there is no such thing as a perfect analysis, a perfect analyst, or a perfect analysand and would be the first to agree with Glover's designation of the myth of the completely analyzed person.[81]

And so, as Marion Milner [145] drily remarked, "Although there is perhaps no such thing as a completed analysis, patients do sooner or later stop coming to analysis." The daily sessions with the analyst cease by mutual agreement. This is variously referred to as "finishing the analysis," "discontinuing the analysis," "terminating the analysis," "interrupting the analysis," "getting through with the analysis," and so forth. The controlled contractual relationship terminates in respect to *the successive daily sessions.* The process of self-analysis continues automatically with increasing freeing and expanding of ego functions, for many months—and even years— following the cessation of visits. It is understood that the analyst will stand by for a period of time, in case the decision regarding a proper date of interruption of the contract has been faulty, and lend assistance if trouble develops. Most analysts make it a practice to make themselves available to a former patient for occasional conferences following the analysis and even for some years thereafter.

In all the discussions of termination in the literature (which are actually not very numerous) there is scarcely any mention of the simple question of *why* an analysis must end. Indeed, Ferenczi[35] played with the idea that perhaps it need not end but could (ideally) go on indefinitely. But does this not imply that the analysis as such is more important than the result? Does it not imply that discovering more and more about onself is increasingly profitable? Is the law of diminishing returns inapplicable to this process?

Both the analyst and analysand are sometimes tempted to evade the question of termination. We shall not stress here the counter-transference of the analyst or the unanalyzed reluctance of the patient to leave, but merely point to the general factor of inertia. Some patients have nothing so interesting to do as to continue their self-study, and some analysts seem to think they cannot do better than to permit this! They may both be right.

Ferenczi answered his own question by saying that in most analyses an end point is reached which is perfectly evident to both the analyst and the analysand, that the analysis wears itself out, as it were, and is thus over and done.[37] But this is an intuitive rather than a theoretical criterion.

Balint formulated the theoretical question involved here thus:

> Is health a natural state of equilibrium? Do processes exist in the mind which—if hampered and undisturbed—would lead the development toward that equilibrium? Or is health the result of a lucky chance, a rare or even an improbable event, the reason being that its conditions are so stringent and so numerous that the chances are very heavily weighted against it? . . . Roughly there are two camps [in the ranks of analysts].
> . . . (1) [There are] those who think that mature genitality [mental health] is not simply a chance sum-total of a motley mixture of component sexual instincts but a function *per se* [and] that health is a natural equilibrium; [for these] the termination of a psycho-analytic cure is a natural process. (2) The other camp [holds that] health, the termination of an analysis and mature genitality are similarly the result of the interplay of so many forces, tendencies and influences that one is not justified in assuming governing natural processes.[4]

We understand Balint to be attempting to restate the problem represented by Hippocrates' concept of a *vis medicatrix naturae*.

Do the forces of nature tend to make the patient well when the something adventitious that instituted the "disease" is removed? Experience would say sometimes yes, sometimes no; some wounds heal and some gape too large. Freud discovered, and all analysts must constantly remember, that in the case of mental illness the wound is partly self-inflicted and self-maintained; that which is adventitious is largely self-created.*

Certain broad generalities of theory about the spontaneous dissolution of the transference, the reversal of the regression, the increased objectivity of the patient, and so forth have long been current. Perhaps such descriptions of changes in the patient are the best we can do at present. It is an inescapable fact that if certain pressures are relieved symptoms sometimes disappear, and the sense of "recovery," of increased well-being, and relative "independence" force practical considerations to the fore. "The well man hath no need of a physician"—*i.e.*, hath no need to continue treatment.

One practical aspect regarding termination, rarely mentioned, relates to the calendar and the vacation custom. Could the statistics be gathered accurately regarding the dates of termination of analyses over the United States, there would, we think, be a startling preponderance of patients getting well enough to terminate their analyses at the beginning of summer, when many analysts take their vacation. Most analysts are very conscientious about not interrupting their work any more than necessary, or not interrupting it prematurely because of their personal convenience, but vacations are a problem because they involve the analyst's family plans. Patients sometimes say ironically that they ought really to avoid having their illnesses in the summertime!

Estimates of healthiness cannot, however, be based solely upon the patient's subjective appraisal. These are important, but so are the opinions of society and of the analyst! In a two-party contract, such as psychoanalytic treatment, the analyst has access to his own observations and to the patient's judgment regarding the degree of

* My own point of view in this problem of recovery has been dealt with more extensively in *The Vital Balance*.[143] It is my belief that one cannot definitely distinguish the process of "recovery" from the process of "disease"; these are two aspects of the same thing. I would answer Balint's first question with a "yes," but I would remind my readers that there are those who dispute this, on good grounds. [K.A.M.]

"recovery" but much less access to the opinions of friends, relatives, children, or to the judgment of a more objective or differently equipped colleague. Insofar as he knows them, the analyst cannot ignore the known discrepancies in these various judgments. If neither the patient nor the analyst is satisfied, the contract has obviously not reached a proper termination or interruption point. Nevertheless, for practical and irrelevant (to the analysis) reasons—the illness of the analyst, serious financial problems for the patient, illness in the patient's family necessitating a geographic move, and so on— it may become necessary to terminate it. In such cases there is no precise rule of conduct; more analysts would try to leave the opportunity open for the patient to return to him as soon as possible or to assist the patient in finding another analyst as soon as that would be possible.

Sometimes the analyst is satisfied that the analysis has gone as far as it profitably can, but the patient is *not* satisfied. This doesn't happen very often, and it usually means that the analyst has come to the conclusion that one of these interminable or irresolvable problems exists that cannot ever be fully analyzed. Freud discussed them at length in his profound although somewhat pessimistic final paper, "Analysis Terminable and Interminable."[47]

More frequent is the situation in which the patient is satisfied with the results of the analysis and wishes to discontinue it, but the analyst is not so satisfied that he has reached his potentialities. The analyst attempts to point to the progress remaining to be made, problems not yet solved, attitudes and techniques that could be improved upon; but these the patient refutes or minimizes. This is easily recognized as resistance, but it is not always easily resolved, even with that recognition. An actual physical flight from analysis is more apt to occur during the early months than during the latter months, but every one of us has seen some of the latter,* to our dismay and, if the truth be told, to our considerable anger and sorrow. It would be an interesting psychoanalytic research to follow up a number of these abruptly departing patients who leave "against advice," and see whether in the long run their judgment was perhaps

---

* The expression "flight into health" is ascribed by Balint to Freud, but Eduardo Weiss credits it to Tausk. For the references to these sources, and the discussion of the topic, see George F. Train.[196]

actually better than that of the analyst or, to put it another way, whether the best thing for them to have done in the circumstances was to have evaded the discovery of that final knowledge about themselves, which they perhaps could not have borne.

Ideally, of course, the situation is one in which the analyst is satisfied with the results of the many months of work together, the patient is satisfied, and reports from friends and associates are favorable. The analyst believes that the patient has achieved his goal—*the goal* of aiming confidently and competently now, for a "better" goal—and the patient feels that he can go on learning by himself. In a moment we shall speak of some of the criteria for such a conviction. But this is a good place to speak again of the fact that both the patient and his analyst undoubtedly have blind spots in this regard, and their best efforts to be objective about the matter are sometimes defeated thereby. It is obviously impossible for them to ask the social environment at large what opinion it may have, but sometimes there are representative figures whom it is not impossible to consult.

However, this is a delicate matter. The patient cannot very well go around asking people if he seems to be doing better! Nor, on the other hand, can the analyst expect much outside evaluation (although he may receive some gratuitously).

CRITERIA FOR DETERMINING THE APPROPRIATE POINT OF DISCONTINUANCE

We have implied that both the analyst and the analysand do have certain criteria upon which they base their conclusions that maximum therapeutic benefit has been probably obtained and that termination of the contract may be effected. What are these criteria?

Many authors have written on this subject* (although it is an interesting commentary that nearly every author who does so begins by saying that very little has ever been written on it). In 1950 a whole issue of the *International Journal of Psychoanalysis* was given over to the topic. Some writers feel confident that it can all be reduced to a few simple points; we mention this to indicate our disagreement. For example, Melanie Klein thought it sufficient that

* See Hurn[99] for a short clear article with a lengthy bibliography.

"the patient's relations to the external world be sufficiently strengthened to enable him to deal satisfactorily with the situation of mourning arising at this point." But what is "satisfactorily"? Wilhelm Reich and even Fenichel[33] thought that the achievement of strong orgastic potency was the essential criterion. The disappearance of the infantile amnesias was considered the index by many of us in the earlier days, although just how we could tell that something negative—*i.e.*, amnesia—is absent poses a problem!

Most analysts today rely upon a rather wide variety of criteria for assistance in forming a conclusion that is, at best, approximate, uncertain, and perhaps always partly opportunistic. Everyone agrees that the purpose of the analysis is to enable the individual to deal "better" (*i.e.*, more maturely) with his internal and external problems. Does he demonstrate that he is consistently competent to do this unassisted and unwatched, as it were? One hopes for a subsidence of symptoms or for a better tolerance of them.

In addition to the disappearance or mitigation of the symptoms, what other indications have we that the disintegrative trends have been arrested and the self-destructive techniques and purposes replaced with constructive ones? What is the evidence for the achievement of a better personality integration?

One swallow does not make a summer. The clinical improvement of psychoanalytic patients represented by the successive abandonment of the phases of regression is like birds returning in the spring—first, the one swallow, then a few bluebirds perhaps, and then a flock of warblers. The patient begins to "feel" better and *do* better. He has more ups than downs, although there are still lags and snags, digressions and delays. But he moves toward new ways, new vistas, new goals. There is a progressive shift from infantile passivity to adult activity, from the assumption that love is something taken to the realization that love is also something given, from the passive expectation of being loved "for one's own sake" to the active satisfaction in giving love without the requirement of a *quid pro quo*.

We wish to emphasize that even through what the analysand feels as unending renunciation—renunciation to a degree that makes him cry out that analysis takes away some of his dearest treasures—he senses the indication for and the beginning feeling of obligation and responsibility and a capacity for restitution. One must pay the piper. The long indulgence in infantile fantasies and infantile modes of behavior entail their guilt feelings, some of them appropriate. However much fun the growing child may have in his playroom, he must ultimately pick up his toys. The environment has indeed been injured. It has been smeared, depreciated, hurt, and sometimes destroyed. There is restitution to be made and there is now an increasing capacity for this through the release of creative ambitions and creative activities. The butterfly must emerge from the crawling, devouring, or sleeping stages of larva and pupa.

In a general way, we can say that better relationships with himself, better relationships with others, and better utilizations of work, play, and other sublimations indicate such a satisfactory adjustment.

Let us discuss these somewhat more specifically.

RELATIONS WITH SELF

"Better relations with one's self" means in our theoretical model, that the ego split is mended, the observing part and the regressive part being once more "united" and harmonious. Nacht (joining many a nonanalytic philosopher) describes it as being at peace with oneself.[148] The trend toward depersonalization will have been reduced to a minimum. In a practical sense it refers to the self-estimate that the patient consciously develops and manifests in his relations to others.

With respect to the ego-ideal, one ordinarily sees an elevation of goals as gauged by our cultural standards. On the other hand, in many patients the level of aspiration has been entirely out of balance with attainable goals, and in such individuals the apparent goals and ideals will have been lowered but the likelihood of achievement increased. This does not imply any reduction or change in the value system, of which more will be said later.

The fate of the superego in the analyzed patient has been much discussed in the literature. For a long time it was held that after having been projected upon the analyst, it was gradually but completely eliminated and its function replaced by conscious judgment and perhaps a strengthening of the (conscious) ego-ideal. It was more or less assumed that the superego was "destroyed" and disappeared with the separation from the analyst.

It is pretty well agreed now that this was oversimplified and extreme. Indeed, some patients seem to demonstrate an increased strength of the superego after analysis. It is really naive to think that value judgments and attitudes can be left to "pure" reason. Many of them have to be made and will continue to be made unconsciously, at the behest of the superego, which should be considered a useful function, causing trouble only when it is ill-formed and ill-functioning (like the gall bladder). Typical of the majority of our patients, perhaps, are cases in which the superego has acted with capriciousness or cruelty or gross corruptibility, or all three. Certainly these attitudes and expectations of the superego make for illness, and hence to the extent that the superego is represented by such functioning we would consider a criterion of the successful effects of the analysis that the old superego would have disappeared. The practical effect of this is a *sense of greater freedom, a capacity for more joy in life, a cessation of various compulsive activities,* and a *diminution of the tendency to depression.**

RELATIONS WITH OTHERS

It is in the relationships of the patient to other people that we usually see the most conspicuous changes. Quantitatively one expects a widened range or a deepened intensity, or both. We can only speak in a general way of an improvement in the affective satisfactions derived from these relationships through a correction of too little or too great diversity or restriction.

Qualitatively, of course, we expect to see mature, so-called "genital" patterns of sexuality replace the various immature and overly self-centered modes that characterize "illness." The achievement of such maturity appears in a diminution of ambivalence toward, and improved relationships with, not only the spouse but with the offspring and also with those who in a sense represent *foster*

* The benign, loving, and beloved aspects of the superego have been explored by Schafer.[179]

offspring. Maturity has no need to pursue satisfactions for childish wishes. The "analyzed person" either comes to realize that they can be gratified without such exertions as he had previously made, or that he has no further feeling of need for such gratification, or that there is no prospect of gratifying them and hence they must be renounced without regrets. Having worked this through, the analyzed person is no longer in competition with his own children and with all those who represent his own children. Instead of competing with them, he can now take over his actual role of parent and give to them what they need. This is reflected in a greater pleasure in being with the children, better judgment in making decisions in regard to them, greater patience with them, increased interest in what they are interested in, and so on. And, by extension, this is reflected in a greater interest on his part in all those peoples of the earth who are weaker or needier than he. One may say that *Agape* has increased at the expense of *Eros*.* At any rate, the outside world will very properly continue to judge the efficacy of psychoanalytic treatment in considerable measure by its indirect effect, that is to say, the way in which the former patient deals with those about him. If his analysis was successful, *their* lives, too, will be improved.

The relationships with the actual parents, if they are living, usually show much improvement, simply because the unconscious elements of hostility and longing attached to events of days long past have been exposed and decimated. Many patients find that the parent whom they had preferred less now becomes the more interesting. Either parent may have possessed so many unlovable and unacceptable traits in actuality that the patient's continued tolerance of them could be described as more neurotic than realistic. In such instances the ability to sever intimate relations with the parent and deal with him at a distance and more objectively is a great improvement.

The relations with the spouse are considered by many analysts to be the most definitely indicative criterion, representing as they do the expression of the patient's formalized heterosexual adjustment. However, paradoxically enough, the sexual aspects of marriage will, in many instances, have a diminished rather than an increased

---

* It may clarify some confusion in the student for us to point to the fact that Freud sometimes used *Eros* in the sense of *Agape*.

importance. (Naturally, this is not true of those cases in which there was marked sexual inhibition.) Phallic-stage propensities yield to genital-stage characteristics. Sexuality in the narrow sense becomes less important because sexuality in the wider sense becomes more important. Sexual relations are usually more satisfactory, more mature in type, freer from anxiety, and freer from overestimation or underestimation. It is misleading, indeed, to follow the thesis of Reich in regard to sexual potency, making the nature of the orgasm the most important criterion of a completed analysis and hence, by inference, of mental health. Neither psychoanalytic treatment nor life itself can be adequately envisaged in the concept of a frantic search for a better orgasm (a point of view unfortunately not limited to Reich[164] and Kinsey[108]).*

In the case of unmarried patients, one expects to see improvement in the love object choices in the direction of those most likely to fulfill the total needs of companionship, mutual love, parenthood, and mutual support. Usually this tends toward a marriage situation.

The attitude of both the married and the unmarried toward the principal love object will have changed in the well-analyzed individual from one dominated by possessiveness, opportunism, parasitism, dependency, and the like, to one dominated by the appropriate masculine or feminine attitude. The male patient will have tended to become more masculine in his attitudes, identifications, techniques, and object choices, and the female patient more feminine. On the other hand, however, neither will be unaware of or apologetic for those elements conventionally more characteristic of the opposite sex which have come to be an unchangeable part of his own personality. He will strive, rather, to adjust them to the reciprocal characteristics of the partner.

Both male and female members of the partnership will have established toward each other an attitude in which the welfare of the other is a concern of the greatest importance. To put it another way, the love object will have become an end, and not a means to an end. The husband will cease to use the wife as permissive mother or nurse or masturbational assistant; the wife will cease to use the husband as a slave or monster or personified penis.

* Karl Menninger, "Impotence and Frigidity from the Standpoint of Psychoanalysis." *Journal of Urology,* 34:166–183, 1935. See also *GP,* 8:67, Dec. 1953.

RELATIONS TO THINGS AND IDEAS

The relationships of an individual to the material things of the world constitute the essence of his sublimations of destructive energies unexpendable toward human beings (and animals). As a practical matter, sublimation takes the form of work, play, and thinking. In a general way, it is a criterion of success in analytic treatment that these aspects of life have improved and taken on more importance for the individual. By an improved work pattern, I mean an improved interest in work, a greater satisfaction in work for its own sake rather than as a means to an end, a greater skill, a greater efficiency. And with respect to play, improvement would mean a greater interest if play has been an inhibited modality and a lesser interest if play had occupied too much of the patient's life. In either case he should expect a greater satisfaction from the play and a minimum of guilt feelings connected with it. He should expect a higher degree of sportsmanship and a greater degree of social participation. Important, too, is the achievement of a proper balancing between work interests and play interests. Some people tend to work too much and play too little, some play too much and work too little, and some cannot do either. A trend in the direction of doing both and doing them in a proportion that is both satisfying and effective is usually a dependable criterion of improved integration. The result of this, of course, is an increased productivity and an increased creativity, an increased satisfaction to the individual and to others. (See chapters on work and on play in Reference 138.)

In the context of our [K.A.M.'s] proposals regarding the nature of sublimation,[138, 90] the improvements just described mean that the ego finds it increasingly possible to effect a neutralization of quantities of aggressive energy with a constructive infusion of "life instinct." In the place of brooding hate, self reproach, or flagellation, or the thinly disguised destruction of the peace or joy or property of fellow beings, the better integrated individual can now expend these energies in their useful disguises as competitive play and constructive work. We are so familiar with the phenomenon of improvement as represented by "getting a job" or "learning to play" or "playing for the first time in my life" that we might forget how logically indicative this is of the sort of change that is predicted by our theory.

Toward possessions and power one sees a change in attitude exactly opposite from that occurring with respect to persons. Whereas the healthiest and most mature object relation with a *human being* is one in which the other person is an end and not a means to an end, toward *things* it is ideal that they be regarded as a means rather than an end. If money, a car, a house, a business, or a position of power becomes a love object, adored for its own sake, it represents a substitute for a human love object and to that extent detracts from interpersonal relationships.* For this reason one might say that the result of an analysis is that one feels less possessive of one's possessions but can make better use of them.

Finally, one expects to see a disappearance or diminution of feelings of covetousness and power-seeking, not because these are "cardinal sins," but because they indicate an unrealistic attitude and a lack of capacity for satisfaction with those devices for sublimations and love that one already possesses or that one can, in the course of ordinary enterprise and adventure, obtain for oneself.

OTHER CRITERIA FOR TERMINATION

There are still other criteria for the termination of an analysis. There is, for example, that well-known criterion of an increased tolerance for personal discomfort. Surely in the minds of all psychoanalysts there will never be a more magnificent example of this

---

* Art objects, nature and its phenomena, and the expression of beauty generally constitute an exception to this rule concerning which we are at a loss to supply an explanatory abstraction. A rose, a painting, an essay, or poem are indeed adorable for their own sake as love objects and we doubt if they can be equated with, or derived from, human love objects. In this respect we may be somewhat heretical, since the standard teaching relates the rose to the breast, the sculpture to the penis, and so forth, but the sublimation becomes so complete or so isolated that for practical purposes such things fall into a different category. These issues touch upon the complex and often confused theory of narcissism. Involved are such considerations as whether these phenomena of love for people and objects and ideas can be conceptualized as quantitative variations in narcissistic libido or whether issues of qualitative difference must be introduced, or whether, as Klein[109] has suggested, they represent vital pleasures in their own right, equal in pleasure-giving qualities with physical sex.

aspect of healthy-mindedness than that of Sigmund Freud, who through nearly two decades of constant suffering rarely indulged himself with even so much as a tablet of aspirin. This is to say nothing of the fear, the grief, and the sorrow incident to his exile and the loss of his friends and many of his possessions. (See Ernest Jones.[102]) The implications of this for an interpretation of the "drug culture" and the prevalence of addictions to various chemical compounds seem obvious.

Discomfort may be physical; it is more often psychological. The latter can either be in the form of that curious uneasiness that we call anxiety or that equally curious discomfort that we call guilt feelings. It is important for young analysts, particularly, to avoid the error made by so many laymen to the effect that psychoanalysis "removes" anxiety and guilt. Psychoanalysis, let us hope, diminishes the anxiety aroused by unresolved unconscious conflicts, but it can never remove anxiety derived from exigencies and conflicts yet to develop. Psychoanalysis can indeed alleviate certain guilt feelings that are attached to the idea of an aggression that the individual never committed; it cannot remove guilt feelings properly attached to the aggressions that a person does commit or has committed. Many of the unconscious guilt feelings that people experience are attached to the wrong thing, and one of our objectives might be said to be to get the patient's guilt feelings attached to the "right" things.

Hence, instead of being free from guilt feelings and anxiety feelings, the psychoanalyzed person may have even more of both than the unanalyzed person, but he will know where they came from and what to do about them, instead of developing symptoms. He will know whether or not restitution can be made; whether or not penance is in order; whether or not easement can be found. And if they are not be be had, then he must have the courage to bear them.

The well-analyzed individual usually will have gained the maturity that enables him to endure failure. Success and failure are illusions in part, but a sense of failure may be a correct appraisal of a project. The point is that no failure is the end of the line; new goals, new programs, new endeavors lie ahead with the benefit of experience.

SUBJECTIVE VIEWS OF THE OUTCOME

It may perhaps seem to the analysand by now that psychoanalysis is a prodigious hoax. She did not lose her homely looks; he did not get a larger penis; he (she) was not given a baby by the analyst; he (she) was not absolved of guilt feelings for having mistreated a brother. He was merely shown that he would not be punished for crying; that there are other places to go for help for certain things; that he cannot have the moon but that he can have certain other satisfactions that he had considered equally impossible. In this sense psychoanalysis works to achieve a better discrimination in regard to what is good and what is evil, what is worth having or doing and what is not.* In this respect, psychoanalysis must be considered a kind of higher education, the aim of which, according to Arthur Morgan, is "to free us from whatever is trivial, chance, accidental, provincial and misleading in our earlier conditioning, and to replace it with what is true, significant, universal and in accord with the inherent nature of things."[147] Thus freed, we can substitute constructive action—or restraint—for wistful fantasy, awkward aggressiveness, or paralyzing indecision.

THE RELATIONSHIP WITH THE PSYCHOANALYST

Finally, criteria for the termination of analysis are discoverable in the transference situation. We have already discussed the changes in the individual and the changes in regard to his relationships with the outside world. His relationship to the analyst has been a special, peculiar, precious thing. In it he has relived all kinds of previous relationships. He has reacted to the analyst as if he were his mother, his father, his brother, his teacher, his sister, his wife. Gradually these illusions have tended to fade in intensity. The analyst becomes more and more just the analyst, "that doctor who has patiently listened to me." The patient begins to be a little bit more considerate of the analyst as a person for his (*i.e.*, the analyst's) own sake. This

---

* Hurn describes the terminal phase thus: "The terminal phase begins with the appearance of evidence . . . that the patient has significantly [!] accepted the impossibility of obtaining infantile gratification from the analyst: he has achieved an irreversible degree of resolution of the transference neurosis."[99]

objectivity toward the analyst increases and the magic omnipotence of the great man begins to diminish. In fantasy this is sometimes conceived of as his death; in a more constructive formulation it represents replacement by a friend, a friend with his own infirmities, his own interests, his own problems, but with a record of consistent and faithful efforts to be helpful. In this way the termination of an analysis often carries with it the thought expressed by Tennyson: "I hope to see my Pilot face to face, when I have crossed the bar."

From another standpoint the termination is less a period of mourning than a period of rejoicing. "The King is dead. Long live the King!" The patient feels, as Balint has put it, that he is going through a kind of rebirth to a period of new life. He has arrived at the end of a dark tunnel, and he sees light again after a long journey. He is almost afraid to feel grateful, lest it be construed as an evasion of gratification, as it well may be. But not entirely, for he has gotten more than he bargained for, more than he paid for, and he will pass its benefits on to someone else.

"It is a deeply moving experience. The general atmosphere is of taking leave forever of something very dear, very precious—with all the corresponding grief and mourning . . . mitigated by the feeling of security, originating from the newly won possibilities for real happiness. Usually the patient leaves after the last session happy but with tears in his eyes and—I think I may admit—the analyst is apt to be in a very similar mood."[4]

Fleming commented that there is a significant difference between separation involved in the termination of an analysis and many other separations during the psychoanalysis. The latter are likely to be regarded by the patient as imposed by external factors, as involving being left, rather than leaving. The termination-separation takes on meaning in that it is the patient who is leaving the analyst "in a two-fold sense; he is widening the gap in their actual contact and is also giving up an old anachronistic relationship."[41]

METHODS OF TERMINATION

A short discussion is relevant about the methods of terminating the analysis, once it has been decided upon, or rather about the theory behind the methods.

When the analyst feels that the point of maximum benefit is approaching, based on criteria discussed, he should begin to look for expressions of a similar opinion from the patient. If he hears them, he may incline to concur with the patient. Perhaps he answers with "Why not, indeed?" Or he may comment to the effect that there seems to be no objection to the possibility of his finishing. He lets the inference be that it is not indicative of resistance for him to begin to think (talk) about an ending of the treatment. Sometimes this is a matter of rumination for weeks or even months. If no "protest symptoms" appear, we gradually begin to speak in more definite terms as to just when it might be, and observe his reactions to this. If he suggests that it might as well be tomorrow, one may remark that usually there is some advantage in a little longer time than that to analyze the reactions to the prospect. If he asks outright how soon he could finish, we are apt to ask how soon *he* thinks, and if he suggests a month or two months, one can indicate concurrence with that as a possibility.

We are always careful to say something like, "Yes, I think you could finish by then," in order to make it clear to him that this is what we think he *could* do; what he is *going to do* we cannot predict. Sometimes we are very explicit in these latter words. "From what I see of you now it looks to me as if you have the capacity for working out the few remaining difficulties by about such a date and from then on could handle your affairs alone." All one can say is how it looks to me, to the analyst, but he does not actually know; therefore we say "I think." Furthermore, his unconscious motives may decide that the analysis is too good a thing to be given up or that it has more material that should come out. In that case, he can't—or doesn't want to—finish by such and such a date, but we don't know that he can't finish.

The main thing is for the analyst to remember that he doesn't know everything and that the patient's unconscious pressures are, in the last analysis, going to settle things. If the analyst, for reasons of opportunism or mistaken judgment, or necessity, ends the analysis too abruptly, he will hear about it.

The patient's repressive processes sometimes hold out buried material as long as possible, hoping that the analysis will overlook its existence, so to speak, and that he (the patient) can endure the repression. On the other hand, this may lead to continued high tension in the ego. Some patients, once the date of termination is more or less tentatively agreed on mutually, will suddenly become very much "sicker." Many symptoms will recur, as if the unconscious were protesting vigorously the arbitrary decision of the ego. Usually what is necessary is merely the postponement of the date another thirty or sixty days to get things straightened out. In some cases, a few symptoms which have recurred may remain, only to disappear completely after the patient has gone away.*

Now a final word on the countertransference problem. One must bear in mind, as we have tried to throughout this book, that there are two parties concerned in the psychoanalytic treatment contract, and that both have an unconscious as well as a conscious. We have already hinted that the termination may be more difficult for the analyst than for the patient. I [K.A.M.] recall one of my teachers apologizing for his weariness and disinterest in a supervisory session I was having with him by saying that he happened at that moment to have several patients who were just terminating their analyses and that this was always a very trying experience. As a young analyst who was wistfully hoping at that time for the ultimate termination of his own analysis, to say nothing of the successful completion of *one* patient's analysis *someday*, I felt this to be a most strange remark. It was difficult to conceive of so happy and fortuitous an event as a "trying" experience for the analyst.

Nevertheless all experienced analysts know how difficult the terminal period is. It is difficult because it is fraught with various uncertainties. Has the point of maximum treatment benefit been reached? Has the law of diminishing returns begun to operate? "Am I influenced in my inclination to terminate this patient's analysis by certain personal advantages—a new patient clamoring for my time, an impending vacation date, some slightly negative feelings toward this patient, some over-optimistic estimates of my success with him? Is the patient concealing behind the façade of improvement certain sinister seeds of psychic infection? Is the patient merely testing my

* Our colleague, Dr. Ishak Ramzy, comments: "After all, in the 'realistic' profession of being a psychoanalyst one should not expect the satisfaction of having done a 'perfect' job. Moreover if we have liberated the demons of hate, why should we expect them to bid us goodbye without a few wallops?"

perspicacity or is he perhaps flattering my vanity? Am I leaning over backward in my conservatism or perhaps even inflicting some mild punishment on this patient by delaying his separation from me? Do I really want to separate from this fine fellow now and see him no more? Am I perhaps favoring a perseverative continuance and an unconscious erotization of the process in him for certain gratifications which these afford me?"*

These are but a few of the questions that a conscientious analyst asks himself at such times. At no other period in the analysis are the countertransference phenomena so disturbing and so potentially dangerous. And it is a paradoxical truth—or at least we think it is a truth—that the less disturbing these thoughts are, the more dangerous the countertransference may be. An experienced colleague, Annie Reich, has well said:

> Sometimes analysts have a tendency to terminate analyses too early. Apart from expediency motives, there is frequently a narcissistic need to achieve results quickly which cannot tolerate the slow pace of analytic work. There are others who have a need to end relationships with patients soon before a danger situation in regard to their own badly controlled homosexual urges can arise; others, on the other hand, cannot give up a patient and enjoy the dependency situation. These countertransference difficulties, of course, should be eliminated in the analyst's own analysis. But the situation of ending an analysis is seldom one that comes to the attention of the training analyst, as we do not usually see our students that long. Of course, the underlying difficulty should show up in some other fashion.[163]

It is incredible—or it would be were it not for our knowledge of repression—to what degree the most highly proficient and competent analysts will fall into this countertransference trap, defending with the most transparent rationalizations their subsequent pursuit of or proprietary attitude toward their former patients. Many years ago, at the request of the president of the American Psychoanalytic

---

* Freud proposed that in those cases where, either because the patient becomes so attached to the analysis, and so persistent in his erotization of the process that he does not want to give it up or where the analysand keeps turning up more and more material that seems to go on forever and ever, the analyst may decide to announce that the analysis will stop on such and such a date. Whether successful or not, this is final, and there is nothing more to do about it once one has done it that way.

Association, I [K.A.M.] conducted a series of seminars at our Annual Meetings made up entirely of training analysts. Many valuable considerations were developed, but the signal contribution and conclusion of *all the discussions* might be framed thus: Unrecognized countertransference of an essentially destructive type, even though "positive" in form, is an ever-present threat to successful analysis, particularly a training analysis, and the only dependable remedy is the one recommended by Freud: repeated sessions of postgraduate analysis *of the analyst*. This recommendation has rarely been systematically followed.

THE UNSUCCESSFUL ANALYSIS

Finally, we must not fail to mention the termination of the unsuccessful case. It is a time-honored custom or, let us say, tendency, for doctors to take credit when the patient recovers and give the patients (or the intractable disease) the blame when recovery does not ensue. And sometimes it really is the patient's "fault," his rigidity, his fluidity, or his unconquerable fear.

We often start in so bravely with patients whose chief revelation to us in the deep pentration of their "illness" is the poverty of their egos, the frozen impenetrability of their character structures. Recall the case mentioned in Chapter V—for whom his analyst had such high hopes—who "couldn't bear to look at the 'it' which was himself"! Some of the cases that initially look the most promising disappoint us sadly. On the other hand, among the cases I [K.A.M.] count the most successful in my own experience, one was an ignorant (but not unintelligent) colleen, one was a long-standing physical invalid, a spinster, who is now a happy grandmother, one was a psychiatrist who had been rejected as unanalyzable by one of our greatest psychoanalysis teachers.

(I shall not here register my failures and my disappointments.) Annie Reich wrote wise and comforting lines when she said:

Frequently we do not fail completely, but we can bring about (only) partial mitigation of symptoms and strengthening of the ego. But the time comes when we have to face the fact that it does not make sense to go on. In these cases, it is my impression that a thorough working through of the reaction to the termination of the analysis as described above is not indicated. It is wisest, in these situations, to wait for a period when the ending of analysis seems to be least painful; when, for instance, suffering has subsided, when certain narcissistic gratifications are available. One could say with justification that this way of ending analysis is not really a psychoanalytic but a psychotherapeutic one. It may be so indeed, but it seems to be the most painless procedure.[163]

Freud devoted his last great contribution to an examination of this problem in his paper, "Analysis, Terminable and Interminable."[47] Rereading this paper annually should be almost a religious duty of the practicing psychoanalyst in order to foster the humility appropriate to his task.

THE SEPARATION

And so, at last, the stipulations of the psychoanalytic contract are fulfilled. The parties of the first and second part prepare to separate. The party of the second part has the satisfaction of having helped a fellow creature who was in distress. He has learned something—as one does from *every* case. He is better prepared for his next "contract," his next opportunity to be helpful and to do the work he knows best how to do. He may even have discovered something of value for other colleagues to know—some little or big contribution to science and to the world. How amazed Freud's patient Dora would have been to learn that she had been an agent for the relief of millions of people and for a revolution in psychology and psychiatry.*

Besides all this, the party of the second part has been paid in money by the party of the first part, who, we hope, will feel that he has indeed gotten his money's worth. But it may not be so easy for him to say *wherein* his gain has been. He is poorer and, we hope, wiser. But by the end of his analysis, he had learned that most of the things he hoped for he failed to get. Most of his expectations were never realized. Instead he only learned that one shouldn't expect to get certain things and then cry one's eyes out in disap-

* For some of the subtle gains and satisfactions of the analyst, see Szasz.[191]

pointment or scratch out other people's eyes in rage. So, as we suggested some pages earlier, the party of the first part may feel defrauded, "let down easy" but very expensively. And some who cannot complete their analyses feel exactly this way.

But the completed analytic experience does *not* leave one in that frame of mind. For, although it is true that his expectations were not met, his gains are *beyond* his expectations! He has learned to love and to be loved—and therein to live. This is his great gain.

Learning this simple thing, and recognizing it to be a universal principle of which his own personal experience is but an example, represents a beginning constructive identification of himself with the universe, with reality, with other people. No one ever gets as much love as he wants, no one gives as much love as he might. Choices can be made but choice involves the assumption of responsibility and the necessity for renunciation. But life is for living, and this attitude he has gained the courage to accept.

> I asked for all things, that I might enjoy life;
> I was given life, that I might enjoy all things.*

There is thus an implicit philosophy and ethic in the psychoanalytic experience, deny it who may. It is implicit that love is the greatest thing in the world. It is implicit that true love suffereth long and is kind, envieth not, is not puffed up, seeketh not its own (but the welfare of others), and rejoiceth not in iniquity but in the truth.

Thus the intangible gains of psychoanalytic treatment extend out into the universe. They are immeasurable. But the tangible values of the treatment contract have been achieved and balanced, usually to the satisfaction and betterment of both parties. The analyst has given, received, and learned; the patient likewise. Learning and improvement will continue autonomously, but the treatment is at an end. The contract has been fulfilled. The parties part company.

* From "Prayer of an Unknown Confederate Soldier," clipped from a newspaper by Dr. John E. Large.[117]

VIII

PERSPECTIVES

IN THE PRECEDING CHAPTERS WE HAVE TRIED TO PRESENT A CONSISTENT theory of what happens when two people engage in an interchange of the sort represented by psychoanalytic treatment. We have traced the vicissitudes of this experience with particular regard to the rationale of the therapist's intervention from the beginning of the process to its termination, at least to its indefinite interruption. As we have said, a process of consolidation will continue in the former patient but it will be autonomous.

Meanwhile, the therapist continues with other patients, and with each repetition of the process learns to handle some problems better, encountering some new problems with which he may or may not deal as well as he would like. Unlike the *treatment* of a particular patient, the *theory* of psychoanalysis does not come to an end; as with all scientific theories there is a continuous checking, revising, enlarging, extending.* The theory of therapeutic technique under-

* An exposition of the evolving nature of psychoanalytic theory is presented in Holzman.[98]

goes growth just as does the body of psychoanalytic knowledge.

The theory of technique as we have described it is clearly not congruent with the psychoanalytic theory of mental functioning. The latter is an inductive system derived from various data, especially psychopathological behavior modifications, patients' introspections, and objective correlations made during psychotherapeutic treatment. The psychoanalytic theory of mental functioning comprises such concepts as unconscious psychological processes, repression, projection, internalization and drive development—including psychosexual and psychoaggressive aspects and their interaction.

The theory of technique, on the other hand, is not inductive. It came about from a happy accident, a discovery made by Freud in the course of several years of trial and error in trying to unravel the meanings of his patients' neurotic suffering. His theory as we have described it is thus more in the nature of a rationale, an explanation of what it is that the psychoanalyst does on the basis of a clinical theory and an *ad hoc* rationalization for what the treatment accomplishes. This explanation makes use of a number of the concepts employed in the clinical theory, such as unconscious functioning, primary and secondary processes, regression, unconscious fantasy, the libidinal and aggressive qualities of interpersonal relations, the persistence of the past in the present and the tendency to repeat the past, and inter- and intrasystemic resistances. But the technique is not derivable from these concepts.

The technique of psychoanalytic treatment as it is currently practiced is not proposed as the only way of ameliorating neurotic suffering or even of carrying out a psychoanalytic study of a personality. Many therapeutic devices which have noteworthy effects can also be rationalized within the framework of psychoanalytic theory. The psychoanalytic therapist should therefore look encouragingly on responsible efforts to innovate, shorten, and improve the method of treatment. The circumspect introduction of new turnings in technique, if they help the patient, should be welcomed and studied. As long ago as 1925 Freud wrote:

> In scientific affairs there should be no place for recoiling from novelty. Science, in her perpetual incompleteness and insufficiency, is driven to hope for her salvation in new discoveries and new ways of regarding things. She does well, in order not

to be deceived, to arm herself with skepticism and to accept nothing new unless it has withstood the strictest examination. Sometimes, however, this skepticism shows two unexpected features: it may be sharply directed against what is new while it spares what is familiar and accepted, and it may be content to reject things before it has examined them. But in behaving thus it reveals itself as a prolongation of the primitive reaction against novelties and as a cloak of that reaction. It is a matter of common knowledge how often in the history of scientific research it has happened that innovations have met with intense and stubborn resistance, while subsequent events have shown that the resistance was unjustified and that the novelty was valuable and important. What provoked the resistance was, as a rule, certain factors in the subject matter of the novelty, while, on the other side, several factors must have combined to make the eruption of the primitive reaction possible.[64]

Even before the last major change that Freud introduced into the clinical theory—the systematic consideration of ego and superego aspects of functioning alongside that of the drives—he had made a number of modifications in psychoanalytic technique. For example, he advocated a more active role in the treatment of phobias than appropriate for the treatment of hysterical problems. The technique requires that the analyst recognize that the patient must confront and not avoid the anxiety of the phobia.

Take the example of agoraphobia; there are two classes of it, one slight and the other severe. Patients belonging to the first indeed suffer from anxiety when they go about alone, but they have not yet given up going out alone on that account; the others protect themselves from the anxiety by altogether giving up going out alone. With these last one succeeds only when one can induce them through the influence of the analysis to behave like the first class, that is, to go about alone and to struggle with their anxiety while they make the attempt. One first achieves, therefore, a considerable amount of moderation of the phobia, and it is only when this has been attained by the physician's recommendation that the associations and memories come into the patient's mind enabling the phobia to be solved.[66]

And regarding obsessional disorders he wrote:

In severe cases of obsessive acts a passive waiting attitude seems even less well adapted; indeed, in general, these cases incline to favor an asymptomatic process of cure, an interminable protraction of the treatment; in their analysis there is always the danger of a great deal coming to light without its affecting any change in them. I think there is little doubt that here the correct technique can only be to wait until the treatment itself has become a compulsion and then with this countercompulsion forcibly to suppress the compulsion of the disease.[61]

And he added: "You will understand, however, that these two instances I have given you are only samples of the new developments towards which our therapy is tending."

These considerations touch on the issue of the limits of psychoanalytic technique. There have been a number of efforts to widen the scope of psychoanalytic treatment and to use the technique for a variety of clinical conditions for which it had not previously been used. Some of these efforts have been singularly successful, particularly as practiced by their artificers, such as Aichhorn's work with some delinquents, Kohut's with certain narcissistically vulnerable people,[111] Anna Freud's with some homosexuals, Jacobson's[100] and Wexler's[202] with some psychotic patients, Knight's,[110] Kernberg's[106] and others' work with so-called "borderline conditions."*

Other departures in psychoanalytic techniques have taken as their starting point the apparent failures of psychoanalysis, by hypothesizing what might have gone wrong in the treatment. In some cases, we meet a formidable obstacle to amelioration despite apparent progress in recall, insight, and understanding of transference— the so-called "negative therapeutic reaction." At other times, where structural problems predominate, as in the major functional disorganizations, the techniques of introspection, interpretation, and reconstruction of the past *via* the transference, seem to be generally contraindicated and newer techniques, innovated by others, not psychoanalysts—such as drug treatment, behavior modification, benign didactic efforts, social restructuring—have a significant effect in bringing about social improvements in patients who might otherwise continue a regressive course.

---

* See also A. Aichorn, *Wayward Youth*, New York: Viking, 1935; A. Freud, Studies in Passivity, Pt. I: Notes on Homosexuality, in *The Writings of Anna Freud*, Vol. IV, New York: International Universities Press, 1968. Cf. the careful study of the "borderline conditions" by Grinker, Werble, and Drye.[87]

The effort to expand the scope of psychoanalysis is in the service of attempts to reform, to control, to ameliorate. As such, it represents what Schafer[180] has called the comic vision within psychoanalysis. The ameliorative thrust in psychoanalysis takes the form of efforts to revise, to freshen, to review, but not to remake (for that is impossible) a troubled life, and perhaps through those efforts to increase the patient's self-respect, to free him from crippling fixations and from regressive tendencies.

But these responsible and careful attempts to revise and expand the technique of psychoanalysis should be distinguished from the movement of fierce therapeutic enthusiasm that, in the name of *humanism*, seeks to reform and cure everywhere. In these efforts, as Schafer has observed, conflict is centered not so much within the person, as between the person and an obstructing society. The goal is reform, but the program is vague and unarticulated. The achievement is a kind of unambivalent existence without guilt, anxiety or remorse.

The psychoanalytic method, however, is not that panacea. It recognizes the inevitable resistances a person sets against self-change, the regressive pull of the transference, the tendency to act against one's broader self-interest for the sake of more or less transient satisfactions. While it values change and seeks to free a person from the troublesome traps of self-deceptions that have slowed personal growth, it acknowledges that anxieties and defenses, resistances and regressions, guilt and remorse, hurting and being hurt, are part of the human condition. In the context of the transference neurosis the patient repeats his self-defeating patterns—but with a difference. Through the abstinence of the analyst (see pp. 69–70) and through his interpretative interventions (p. 123ff) the patient is able to understand his own active, yet essentially unconscious, role in producing or bringing about his suffering and thus perceives his own real responsibilities, failings, and weaknesses. Psychoanalysis seeks to heighten one's self-awareness, and in this process the awareness of limits and the attunement to responsibility. This effort is clearly not fashioned to erase social evils or to offer the patient the promise of pervasive well-being.

Recently a number of new psychotherapies have appeared, some of which hold a promise of alleviating neurotic suffering, others of which direct themselves to retraining and reteaching. While all have to be evaluated in terms of their relative merits and their specificity, some may accomplish more alleviation of psychological pain in more people than classical psychoanalytic treatment can now do. This is an ironic state of affairs, for psychoanalysis was the first *rational* treatment, and the first to offer hope to people troubled in this way. That it may now be replaced by better, faster techniques may be seen in the perspective of history of most new and revolutionary ideas. The inventor of psychoanalysis was prepared for the possibility of such an eventuality. During the last decade of his life he wrote,

> I should like to add that I do not think our cures can compete with those of Lourdes. There are so many more people who believe in the miracles of the Blessed Virgin than in the existence of the unconscious. If we turn to mundane competitors, we must compare psychoanalytic treatment with other kinds of psychotherapy. . . . Analysis as a psychotherapeutic procedure does not stand in opposition to other methods used in this specialized branch of medicine; it does not diminish their value nor exclude them. . . . But [psychoanalysis] has its very appreciable limits. The therapeutic ambition of some of my adherents has made the greatest efforts to overcome these obstacles so that every sort of neurotic disorder might be curable by psychoanalysis. They have endeavored to compress the work of analysis into a shorter duration, to intensify transference so that it may be able to overcome any resistance, to unite other forms of influence with it so as to compel a cure. These efforts are certainly praiseworthy, but, in my opinion, they are vain. . . . The expectation that every neurotic phenomenon can be cured may, I suspect, be derived from the layman's belief that the neuroses are something quite unnecessary which have no right whatever to exist. Whereas in fact they are severe, constitutionally fixed illnesses, which rarely restrict themselves to only a few attacks but persist as a rule over long periods or throughout life. Our analytic experience that they can be extensively influenced, if the historical precipitating causes and accidental auxiliary factors of the illness can be dealt with, has led us to neglect the constitutional factor in our therapeutic practice, and in any case we can do nothing about it; but in theory we ought to bear it in mind.[57]

None of the new therapies, in our view, direct their efforts to the kind of internal psychological investigation that psychoanalysis calls for. In this search, utilizing the self-reflection of the patient and the empathic participation of the analyst, self-awareness broadens, thus contributing to change. The quality of mental functioning tends to change as well as our knowledge about the relationships to oneself, and to the myriad other objects, human and nonhuman, tends to become illuminated. How one has become constricted, weakened, bound, supported, or obstructed; how one has loved, hated, opposed, obeyed, helped, and hindered, as part of a response to inner conflicts—all of these are perceived in their historical and contemporary contexts.

This exploration is supported principally by the continued communication between analysand and analyst; an abiding empathic feeling permits both to endure the struggle of the analytic process, for such empathy binds them and even provides a modicum of gratification to them that helps keep a sense of perspective on the general posture of abstinence. The process of understanding continues, urged on by interpretation. Relations among events become clearer; new connections are established; some old links are broken; other links are seen in different contexts. Such a process is broadening, particularly when the patient takes into himself these new relationships, that is, internalizes them. He then becomes freer to use them in place of older stereotyped compulsive actions. Thus action based on infantile conflict sources is replaced by a higher level of action and thought that takes account of new relationships and a growing maturity.

The limitations of psychoanalytic treatment are determined in no small measure by the kinds of illness it seeks to influence. Freud said it quite succinctly: "You know already that the field of application of analytic therapy lies in the transference neuroses—phobias, hysteria, obsessional neurosis—and further, abnormalities of character which have been developed in place of these illnesses. Everything differing from these, narcissistic and psychotic conditions, is unsuitable to a greater or less extent" (p. 155).[57]

Thus classical psychoanalytic therapy and the classical theory of technique are limited to the amelioration of a relatively small number of people. Yet in our view it has an enormous potential in the education of those therapists and of others who seek to deal with the minds of troubled people, either as therapists or as researchers. The broadening of perspective, the forging of new links within one-self and the persistent task of self-scrutiny force an orientation toward knowledge and love of truth. Hence psychoanalysis as a therapeutic experience can well be recommended to physicians, psychologists, sociologists, social workers, anthropologists, historians, lawyers, political scientists, creative artists, clergymen, and others who concern themselves with the mind of man.

BIBLIOGRAPHY

1. Alexander, Franz, & Others. *Psychoanalytic Therapy*. New York: Ronald, 1946.
2. Allen, A. The Fee as a Therapeutic Tool. *Psychoanal. Quart.*, 1971, pp. 132–140.
3. Balint, M. On the Termination of Analysis. *Inter J. Psycho-Anal.*, 31:196–199, 1950.
4. Balint, M. *Primary Love and Psychoanalytic Techniques*. New York: Liveright, 1953.
5. Balint, M. and Balint, A. On the Transference and Countertransference. *Inter. J. Psycho-Anal.*, 20:223–230, 1939.
6. Barker, R., Dembo, T., & Lewin, K. *Studies in Topological and Vector Psychology, II*. Frustration and Regression, an Experiment with Young Children. Iowa City, Iowa: University of Iowa, 1941.
7. Bellak, L. & Smith, M. B. An Experimental Exploration of the Psychoanalytic Process. *Psychoanal. Quart.*, 25:385–414, 1956.
8. Benedek, T. Dynamics of the Countertransference. *Bull. Menninger Clin.*, 17:201–208, 1953.
9. Beres, D. Communication in Psychoanalysis and in the Creative Process: A Parallel. *J. Amer. Psychoanal. Assn.*, 5:408–423, 1957.
10. Berg, C. *Deep Analysis*. New York: Norton, 1947.
11. Berman, L. Countertransference and Attitudes of the Analyst in the Therapeutic Process. *Psychiatry*, 12:159–166, 1949.
12. Bexton, W. H., Heron, W., & Scott, T. H. Effects of Decreased Variation in the Sensory Environment. *Canad. J. Psychol.*, 8:70–76, 1954.
13. Bibring, E. Psychoanalysis and the Dynamic Psychotherapies. *J. Amer. Psychoanal. Assn.*, 2:745–770, 1954.

14. Bjerre, P. *The History and Practice of Psychoanalysis*. Boston: Badger, 1920, pp. 18–19.
15. Braatöy, T. *Fundamentals of Psychoanalytic Technique*. New York: Wiley, 1954.
16. Brown, R. W. *Words and Things*. New York: The Free Press of Glencoe, 1959.
17. Cassirer, E. *Language and Myth*. New York: Harper, 1946.
18. Deutsch, F. *Applied Psychoanalysis*. New York: Grune & Stratton, 1949.
19. Devereux, G. Some Criteria for the Timing of Confrontations and Interpretations. *Inter. J. Psycho-Anal.*, 32:19–24, 1951.
20. Dimascio, A., Boyd, R. W., & Greenblatt, M. Physiological Correlates of Tension and Antagonism During Psychotherapy. *Psychosom. Med.*, 19:99–104, 1957.
21. Durrell, Lawrence. Studies in Genius: VI. Groddeck. *Horizon*, 17: 384–403, 1948.
22. Edwards, W. The Theory of Decision Making. *Psychol. Bull.*, 51: 380–417, July 1954.
23. Eissler, K. R. The Effect of the Structure of the Ego on Psychoanalytic Technique. *J. Amer. Psychoanal. Assn.*, 1:104–143, 1953.
24. Ekstein, R. Psychoanalytic Technique. In *Progress in Clinical Psychology*, D. Brower & L. Abt, Eds. New York: Grune & Stratton, 1956, Vol. 2, pp. 79–97.
25. Ekstein, R. Psychoanalytic Theory and Technique. In *Progress in Clinical Psychology*, D. Brower & L. Abt, Eds. New York: Grune & Stratton, 1952, Vol. 1, pp. 249–267.
26. Ekstein, R. The Space Child's Time Machine: On "Reconstruction" in the Psychotherapeutic Treatment of a Schizophrenoid Child. *Amer. J. Orthopsychiat.*, 24: 492–506, 1954.
27. Ekstein, R. Thoughts Concerning the Nature of the Interpretive Process. In *Readings in Psychoanalytic Psychology*, M. Levitt, Ed. New York: Appleton-Croft, 1959, pp. 221–247.
28. Ellenberger, H. A Clinical Introduction to Phenomenology and Existential Analysis. In *Existence: A New Dimension in Psychiatry and Psychology*, R. May, E. Angel, & H. F. Ellenberger, Eds. New York: Basic Books, 1958.
29. Erikson, E. H. The Dream Specimen of Psychoanalysis. *J. Amer. Psychoanal. Assn.*, 2:5–56, 1954.
30. Fenichel, O. (1935). Concerning the Theory of Psychoanalytic Technique. In *Collected Papers of Otto Fenichel*, First Series. New York: Norton, 1953–1954, pp. 332–348.
31. Fenichel, O. Neurotic Acting Out. *Psychoanalyt. Rev.*, 32:197–206, 1945.

32. Fenichel, O. *Principles of Intensive Psychotherapy.* Chicago: University of Chicago, 1950.

33. Fenichel, O. (1935). Problems of Psychoanalytic Technique. *Psychoanal. Quart.,* 1941.

34. Ferenczi, S. (1928). The Elasticity of Psychoanalytic Technique. In *Final Contributions to Psychoanalysis.* New York: Basic Books, 1955, pp. 87–101.

35. Ferenczi, S. *Further Contributions to the Theory and Technique of Psychoanalysis.* London: Hogarth, 1926.

36. Ferenczi, S. (1909). Introjection and Transference. In *Sex and Psychoanalysis.* Boston: Badger, 1916.

37. Ferenczi, S. The Problem of the Termination of the Analysis. In *Final Contributions to the Problems and Methods of Psychoanalysis.* New York: Basic Books, 1955, pp. 77–86.

38. Fingert, H. H. Comments on the Psychoanalytic Significance of the Fee. *Bull. Menninger Clin.,* 16:98–104, 1952.

39. Firestein, S. K., Reporter. Problems in the Termination in the Analysis of Adults. *J. Amer. Psychoanal. Assn.,* 17:222–237, 1969.

40. Fisher, C. Studies on the Nature of Suggestions. Part I. *J. Amer. Psychoanal. Assn.,* 1:222–254, 1953.

41. Fleming, J. Quoted in: Problems of Termination in the Analysis of Adults. Panel discussion reported by Stephen K. Firestein. *J. Amer. Psychoanal. Assn.,* 17:222–237, 1969.

42. Fliess, R. The Metapsychology of the Analyst. *Psychoanal. Quart.,* 11:211–227, 1942.

43. Forsyth, D. *The Technique of Psychoanalysis.* London: Paul, French, Trubner, 1922.

44. French, T. M. *The Integration of Behavior.* Vol. I (1952), Vol. 2 (1954). Chicago, Ill.: University of Chicago.

45. Freud, A. The Ego and the Mechanisms of Defense. London: Hogarth, 1937.

46. Freud, A. *Psychoanalytic Treatment of Children.* London: Imago Publishing Co., 1946; 2nd Ed., 1947; 3rd Ed., 1951.

47. Freud, S. (1937). Analysis Terminable and Interminable. In *Standard Edition of the Complete Psychological Works of Sigmund Freud.* London: Hogarth, Vol. 23, pp. 209–254.

48. Freud, S. (1920). Beyond the Pleasure Principle, *S.E.,* Vol. 18, pp. 3–64.

49. Freud, S. (1912). The Dynamics of the Transference. *S.E.,* Vol. 12.

50. Freud, S. (1910). Five Lectures on Psychoanalysis. *S.E.,* Vol. 11, pp. 3–58.

51. Freud, S. (1905). Fragment of an Analysis of a Case of Hysteria. *S.E.,* Vol. 7.

52. Freud, S. (1904). Freud's Psychoanalytic Procedure. In *Die Psychischen Zwangersheinungen,* by Leopold Loewenfeld. Wiesbaden: Bergmann, 1904. Also in *S.E.,* Vol. 7.

53. Freud, S. (1910). The Future Prospects of Psychoanalytic Therapy. *S.E.,* Vol. 11.

54. Freud, S. (1926). Inhibitions, Symptoms, and Anxiety. *S.E.,* Vol. 20.

55. Freud, S. (1900). *The Interpretation of Dreams.* New York: Basic Books, 1955. Also in *S.E.,* Vols. 4–5.

56. Freud, S. (1916, 1917). Introductory Lectures on Psychoanalysis. *S.E.,* Vol. 16.

57. Freud, S. (1933). New Introductory Lectures on Psychoanalysis. *S.E.,* Vol. 22, 1964.

58. Freud, S. (1920). A Note on the Prehistory of the Technique of Analysis. *S.E.,* Vol. 18.

59. Freud, S. (1913). Papers on Technique. On Beginning Treatment. *(Further Recommendations on the Technique of Psychoanalysis I.) S.E.,* Vol. 12.

60. Freud, S. (1915). Papers on Technique. Observations on Transference Love. *(Further Recommendations on the Technique of Psychoanalysis III.) S.E.,* Vol. 12.

61. Freud, S. (1914). Papers on Technique. Remembering, Repeating and Working Through. *(Further Recommendations on the Technique of Psychoanalysis II.) S.E.,* Vol. 12.

62. Freud, S. (1912). Papers on Technique. Recommendations to Physicians Practicing Psychoanalysis. *S.E.,* Vol. 12.

63. Freud, S., (1904). On Psychotherapy. *S.E.,* Vol. 7.

64. Freud, S. (1925). Resistances to Psychoanalysis. *S.E.,* Vol. 19.

65. Freud, S. (1895 with J. Breuer). *Studies on Hysteria.* New York: Basic Books, 1957. Also in *S.E.,* Vol. 2.

66. Freud, S. (1919). Lines of Advance in Psychoanalytic Therapy. *S.E.,* Vol. 17.

67. Freud, S. (1923). Two Encyclopaedia Articles (A). Psychoanalysis. *S.E.,* Vol. 18.

68. Freud, S. (1910). "Wild" Psychoanalysis. *S.E.,* Vol. 11.

69. Fromm-Reichmann, F. Notes on the Development of Treatment of Schizophrenics by Psychoanalytic Psychotherapy. *Psychiatry,* 11: 263–273, 1948.

70. Fromm-Reichmann, F. Personal and Professional Requirements of a Psychotherapist. *Psychiatry,* 12:361–378, 1949.

71. Fromm-Reichmann, F. *Principles of Intensive Psychotherapy.* Chicago: University of Chicago, 1950; London: Allen & Unwin, 1953, p. 67.

72. GAP Symposium No. 3. *Factors Used to Increase the Susceptibility of Individuals to Forceful Indoctrination: Observation and Experiments.* New York: Group for the Advancement of Psychiatry, 1956.

73. Gedo, J. A Note on Nonpayment of Psychiatric Fees. *Inter. J. Psycho-Anal.,* 44:368–371, 1963.

74. Gill, M. M. Psychoanalysis and Exploratory Psychotherapy. *J. Amer. Psychoanal. Assn.,* 2:771–797, 1954.

75. Gill, M. M. Research in Psychoanalysis: A Perspective and a Proposal. Presented at Austen Riggs Center, Stockbridge, Mass., August 18, 1971.

76. Gill, M. M. Spontaneous Regression on the Induction of Hypnosis. *Bull. Menninger Clin.,* 12:41–48, 1948.

77. Gill, M. M. & Brenman, M. *Hypnosis and Related States.* New York: International Universities Press, 1959.

78. Gill, M. M., Simon, J., Fink, G., Endicott, N. A., & Paul, I. A. Studies of Audio-Recorded Psychoanalysis: I. General Considerations. *J. Amer. Psychoanal. Assn.,* 16:230–244, 1968.

79. Gitelson, M. The Emotional Position of the Analyst in the Psychoanalytic Situation. *Inter. J. Psycho-Anal.,* 33:1–10, 1952.

80. Glover, E. *Psychoanalysis.* 2nd Ed. London: Staples, 1949, p. 309.

81. Glover, E. Therapeutic Results of Psychoanalysis. *Inter. J. Psycho-Anal.,* 18:125–132, 1937.

82. Glover, E. *The Technique of Psychoanalysis.* London: Bailliere, Tindall & Cox, 1928; 2nd Ed. New York: International Universities, 1955.

83. Greenacre, P. General Problems of Acting Out. *Psychoanal. Quart.,* 19:455–467, 1950.

84. Greenacre, P. The Predisposition to Anxiety, Part II. *Psychoanal. Quart.,* 10:610–638, 1941.

85. Greenacre, P. The Role of Transference. *J. Amer. Psychoanal. Assn.,* 2:671–684, 1954.

86. Greenson, R. *The Technique and Practice of Psychoanalysis.* New York: International Universities Press, 1967.

87. Grinker, R. R., Sr., Werble, B., & Drye, R. *The Borderline Syndrome.* New York: Basic Books, 1968.

88. Haak, N. Comments on the Analytical Situation. *Inter. J. Psycho-Anal.,* 38:183–195, 1957.

89. Haley, J. The Art of Psychoanalysis, etc.: A Review of General Semantics. 15:190–200, Spring 1958.

90. Hartmann, H. Notes on the Theory of Sublimation. *Psychoanalytic Study of the Child.* New York: International Universities Press, 1955, Vol. 10, pp. 9–29.

91. Hartmann, H. Technical Implications of Ego Psychology. *Psychoanal. Quart.,* 20:31–43, 1951.

92. Hawthorne, N. *The Scarlet Letter.* New York: Pocket Books, 1948, p. 127.

93. Hebb, D. O. The Mammal and His Environment. *Amer. J. Psychiat.,* 111:826–831, 1955.

94. Hebb, D. O. The Motivating Effects of Extroceptive Stimulation. *Amer. Psychologist,* 13:109–113, 1958.

95. Heiman, P. On Countertransference. *Inter. J. Psycho-Anal.,* 31:81–84, 1950.

96. Hill, D. On the Contributions of Psychoanalysis to Psychiatry: Mechanism and Measuring. *Inter. J. Psycho-Anal.,* 52:1–10, 1971.

97. Hilles, L. A Clinical Management of the Nonpaying Patient. *Bull. Menninger Clin.,* 35:98–112, 1971.

98. Holzman, P. S. *Psychoanalysis and Psychopathology.* New York: McGraw-Hill, 1970.

99. Hurn, H. T. Toward a Paradigm of the Terminal Phase: The Current Status of the Terminal Phase. *J. Amer. Psychoanal. Assn.,* 19: 332, 1971.

100. Jacobson, E. *The Self and the Object World.* New York: International Universities Press, 1964.

101. Jelliffe, S. E. *The Technique of Psychoanalysis.* 2nd Ed. New York: Nervous & Mental Disease Publishing Co., 1920.

102. Jones, E. *The Life and Work of Sigmund Freud,* Vol. III. New York: Basic Books, 1957.

103. Jones, E. *Treatment of the Neuroses.* New York: Wood, 1920.

104. Kaiser, H. Probleme der Technik. *Internat. Ztschr. f. Psychoanal.,* 20:490–522, 1934.

105. Kant, E. Von der Macht des Gemüths, durch den blossen Vorsatz seiner krankhaften Gefühle Meister zu sein. *J. d. practischen Arzneykunde u. Wundarzneykunst,* 5:701–751, 1798.

106. Kernberg, O. F. Factors in the Psychoanalytic Treatment of Narcissistic Personalities. *J. Amer. Psychoanal. Assn.,* 18:51–85, Jan. 1970.

107. Kielholz, A. Vom Kairos. *Schweiz. med. Wschr.,* 86:982–984, 1956.

108. Kinsey, A. *Sexual Behavior in the Human Female.* Philadelphia: Saunders, 1953.

109. Klein, G. S. The Vital Pleasures. *Psychoanalysis and Contemporary Science,* Vol. 1. New York: Macmillan, 1972, pp. 181–205.

110. Knight, R. P. Borderline States. In *Psychoanalytic Psychiatry and Psychology.* R. P. Knight & C. R. Friedman, Eds. New York: International Universities Press, 1954, pp. 97–109.

111. Kohut, H. *The Analysis of the Self.* New York: International Universities Press, 1971.

112. Korzybski, A. *Science and Sanity.* Lakeville, Conn.: International Non-Aristotelian Library, 1948.

113. Kris, E. On Preconscious Mental Processes. *Psychoanal. Quart.*, 19:540–560, 1950.

114. Kubie, L. S. *Practical Aspects of Psychoanalysis.* New York: Norton, 1936. 2nd Ed. was published under the title *Practical and Theoretical Aspects of Psychoanalysis.* New York: International Universities Press, 1950.

115. Lagache, D. Some Aspects of Transference. *Inter. J. Psycho-Anal.*, 34:1–10, 1953.

116. Laing, R. D. *The Politics of Experience.* New York: Pantheon Books, 1967.

117. Large, J. E. *Think on These Things.* New York: Harper, 1954.

118. Leibniz, G. W. *Nouveaux essais sur l'entendement humain.* First published at Amsterdam and Leipzig in 1765.

119. Lewin, B. D. Dream Psychology and the Analytic Situation. *Psychoanal. Quart.*, 24:169–199, 1955.

120. Lewin, B. D. Sleep, Narcissistic Neurosis, and the Analytic Situation. *Psychoanal. Quart.*, 23:487–510, 1954.

121. Lievano, J. Observations About Payment of Psychotherapy Fees. *Psychiatric Quarterly*, 41:324–338, 1967.

122. Lifton, R. J. "Thought Reform" of Western Civilians in Chinese Communist Prisons. *Psychiatry*, 19:173–195, 1956.

123. Lilly, J. C. Mental Effects of Reduction of Ordinary Levels of Physical Stimuli on Intact, Healthy Persons. *Psychiat. Res. Rep.*, 1956, No. 6, 1–9.

124. Little, M. Countertransference and the Patient's Response to It. *Inter. J. Psycho-Anal.*, 32:32–40, 1951.

125. Loewald, H. On the Therapeutic Action of Psychoanalysis. *Inter. J. Psycho-Anal.*, 41:16–33, 1960.

126. Loewald, H. Psychoanalytic Theory and the Psychoanalytic Process. *Psychoanalytic Study of the Child*, Vol. 25, 1970, pp. 45–68. Quote from p. 56.

127. Loewenstein, R. M. The Problem of Interpretation. *Psychoanal. Quart.*, 20:1–14, 1951.

128. Loewenstein, R. M. Some Remarks on Defenses, Autonomous Ego and Psychoanalytic Technique. *Inter. J. Psycho-Anal.*, 35:188–193, 1954.

129. Lorand, S. *Technique of Psychoanalytic Therapy.* New York: International Universities Press, 1946.

130. Lorand, S. & Console, W. A. Therapeutic Results in Psychoanalytic Treatment Without Fee. *Inter. J. Psycho-Anal.*, 39:59–64, 1958.

131. Lorand, S. Regression: Technical and Theoretical Problems. *J. Hillside Hospital*, 12:67–80, 1963.

132. Macalpine, I. The Development of the Transference. *Psychoanal. Quart.*, 19:501–539, 1950.

133. Macalpine, I. & Hunter, R. A. *Schizophrenia 1677*. London: Dawson, 1956.

134. McGinley, P. *Love Letters*. New York: Viking, 1954.

135. Mearns, H. *Creative Power*. Doubleday, 1929.

136. Menninger, K. & Mayman, M. Episodic Dyscontrol. *Bull. Menninger Clin.*, 20:153–165, 1956.

137. Menninger, K. Impotence and Frigidity from the Standpoint of Psychoanalysis. *J. of Urology*, 34:166–183, August, 1935.

138. Menninger, K. *Love Against Hate*. New York: Harcourt, 1942.

139. Menninger, K. Psychological Factors Associated with the Common Cold. *Psychoanalyt. Rev.*, 21:201–207, 1934.

140. Menninger, K. Regulatory Devices of the Ego Under Major Stress. *Inter. J. Psycho-Anal.*, 35:412–430, 1954.

141. Menninger, K. Somatic Correlations with the Unconscious Repudiation of Femininity in Women. *J. Nerv. Ment. Dis.*, 89:514–527, 1939. Also in *Bull. Menninger Clin.*, 3:106–121, 1939.

142. Menninger, K. Some Observations on the Psychological Factors in Urination and Genitourinary Afflictions. *Psychoanalyt. Rev.*, 28:117–129, 1941.

143. Menninger, K., Mayman, M., & Pruyser, P. *The Vital Balance*. New York: Viking, 1963.

144. Menninger, W. C. Characterologic and Symptomatic Expressions Related to the Anal Phase of Psychosexual Development. *Psychoanal. Quart.*, 12:161–195, 1943.

145. Milner, M. A Note on the Ending of Analysis. *Inter. J. Psycho-Anal.*, 31:191–193, 1950.

146. Moloney, J. C. Psychic Self-Abandon and Extortion of Confessions. *Inter. J. Psychoanal.* 36:53–60, 1955.

147. Morgan, A. E. Learning to Learn. Quoted in *Manas*, 11:2, January 22, 1958.

148. Nacht, S. Introduction au colloque sur les criteres de la fin du traitement psychanalytique (Introduction to the Colloquium About the Criteria of the Termination of Psychoanalytic Technique). *Rev. Fr. de Psychanal.*, 18:328–336, 1954.

149. Nunberg, H. *Practice and Theory of Psychoanalysis*. New York: Nervous and Mental Disease Publishing Co., 1948.

150. Nunberg, H. (1932). *Principles of Psychoanalysis: Their Application to the Neurosis*. New York: International Universities Press, 1955.

151. Nunberg, H. Transference and Reality. *Inter. J. Psycho-Anal.*, 32:1–9, 1951.

152. Oberndorf, C. P. *A History of Psychoanalysis in America*. New York: Grune & Stratton, 1953, pp. 15–16.

153. Olinick, S. L. Some Considerations of the Use of Questioning as a

Psychoanalytic Technique. *J. Amer. Psychoanal. Assn.*, 2:57–66, 1954.

154. Payne, S. Notes on Developments in the Theory and Practice of Psychoanalytic Technique. *Inter. J. Psycho-Anal.*, 27:12–19, 1946.

155. Plotinus. *The Enneads.* A. Kirchoff, Ed. Leipzig, 1856.

156. Racker, H. The Meanings and Uses of Countertransference. *Psychoanal. Quart.*, 26:303–357, 1957.

157. Rado, S. The Economic Principle in Psychoanalytic Technique. *Inter. J. Psychoanal.*, 6:35–44, 1925.

158. Rado, S. Recent Advances of Psychoanalytic Therapy. *A. Res. Nerv. & Ment. Dis., Proc.* (1951), 31:42–58, 1953.

159. Rapaport, A. *Two Person Game Theory: The Essential Ideas.* Ann Arbor: University of Michigan Press, 1966.

160. Rapaport, D. *Organization and Pathology of Thought.* New York: Columbia University, 1951, pp. 689–730.

161. Rapaport, D. The Theory of Ego Autonomy. *Bull. Menninger Clin.*, 22:13–35, 1958. Also in *Collected Papers of David Rapaport.* M. M. Gill, Ed. New York: Basic Books, 1967, pp. 722–744.

162. Reich, A. On Countertransference. *Inter. J. Psycho-Anal.*, 32:25–31, 1951.

163. Reich, A. On the Termination of Analysis. *Inter. J. Psycho-Anal.*, 31:179–183, 1950.

164. Reich, W. *Character Analysis.* New York: Orgone Institute, 1933; 2nd Ed., 1945; 3rd Ed., 1949.

165. Reid, J. R. & Finesinger, J. E. The role of Insight in Psychotherapy. *Amer. J. Psychiat.*, 108:726–734, 1952.

166. Reider, N. Reconstruction and Screen Function. *J. Amer. Psychoanal. Assn.*, 1:389–405, 1953.

167. Reik, T. *Listening with the Third Ear.* New York: Farrar, Strauss, 1948.

168. Reik, T. *Surprise and the Psychoanalyst.* London: Paul, French, Trubner, 1936.

169. Richfield, J. An Analysis of the Concept of Insight. *Psychoanal. Quart.*, 23:390–408, 1954.

170. Richfield, J. The Role of Philosophy in Theoretical Psychiatry. *Bull. Menninger Clin.*, 17:49–56, 1953.

171. Robbins, L. L. A Contribution to the Psychological Understanding of the Character of Don Juan. *Bull. Menninger Clin.*, 20:166–180, 1956.

172. Roethlisberger, F. J. & Dickson, W. J. *Management and the Worker.* Cambridge: Harvard University, 1939.

173. Rogers, B. (tr.). *Fifteen Greek Plays.* New York: New York University Press, 1953, pp. 554, 564, 572–575.

174. Rogers, C. R. *Client-Centered Therapy*. Boston: Houghton-Mifflin, 1951.
175. Rubinstein, B. On Metaphor and Related Phenomena. In *Psychoanalysis and Contemporary Science*. New York: Macmillan, 1972.
176. Ruesch, J. *Disturbed Communication*. New York: Norton, 1957.
177. Sapir, E. *Language: An Introduction to the Study of Speech*. New York: Harcourt, 1921.
178. Schafer, R. *Aspects of Internalization*. New York: International Universities Press, 1968.
179. Schafer, R. The Loving and Beloved Superego in Freud's Structural Theory. *Psychoanalytic Study of the Child*, Vol. 15, pp. 163–188. New York: International Universities Press, 1960.
180. Schafer, R. The Psychoanalytic Vision of Reality. *Inter. J. Psycho-Anal.*, 51:279–297, 1970.
181. Schein, E. H. The Chinese Indoctrination Program for Prisoners of War. *Psychiatry*, 19:149–172, 1956.
182. Sechehaye, M. A. *Symbolic Realization*. New York: International Universities Press, 1951.
183. Sharpe, E. *Collected Papers on Psychoanalysis*. London: Hogarth, 1950.
184. Silverberg, W. V. The Concept of Transference. *Psychoanal. Quart.*, 17:303–321, 1948.
185. Solomon, P., Leiderman, H., Mendelson, J. & Wexler, D. Sensory Deprivation. *Amer. J. Psychiat.*, 114: 357–363, Oct. 1957.
186. Spitz, R. A. Countertransference: Comments on Its Varying Role in the Analytic Situation. *J. Amer. Psychoanal. Assn.*, 4:256–265, 1956.
187. Sterba, R. Character and Resistance. *Psychoanal. Quart.*, 20:72–76, 1951.
188. Stone, L. *The Psychoanalytic Situation*. New York: International Universities Press, 1962.
189. Sullivan, H. S. Conceptions in Modern Psychiatry. *Psychiatry*, 3:1–117, 1940.
190. Sullivan, H. S. The Theory of Anxiety and the Nature of Psychotherapy. *Psychiatry*, 12:3–12, 1949.
191. Szasz, T. S. On the Experiences of the Analyst in the Psychoanalytic Situation: A Contribution to the Theory of Psychoanalytic Treatment. *J. Amer. Psychoanal. Assn.*, 4:197–223, 1956.
192. Tartakoff, H. H. Recent Books on Psychoanalytic Technique. *J. Amer. Psychoanal. Assn.*, 4:318–343, 1956.
193. Tillich, P. *Kairos*. Darmstadt, Reichl., 1926.
194. Tolstoy, L. *War and Peace*. New York: Modern Library, 1931.
195. Tower, L. E. Countertransference. *J. Amer. Psychoanal. Assn.*, 4: 224–255, 1956.

196. Train, G. F. Flight into Health. *Amer. J. Psychotherapy*, 7:463–486, 1953.

197. Trosman, H. The Cryptomnesic Fragment in the Discovery of Free Association. *J. Amer. Psychoanal. Assn.*, 17:489–510, 1969.

198. van der Waals, H. G. "Narcistische" problematilk van het narcisme. *Psychiatrische en Neurolische Blaben*, No. 5/6, 1940.

199. van der Waals, H. G. Le Narcissisme. *Rev. Fr. de Psychoanal.*, 13:501–526, 1949.

200. Waelder, R. The Function and the Pitfalls of Psychoanalytic Societies. *Bull. Philadelphia A. Psychoanal.*, 5:1–8, 1955.

201. Waelder, R. Introduction to the Discussion [of] Problems of Transference. *Inter. J. Psycho-Anal.*, 37:367–368, 1956.

202. Wexler, M. The Structural Problem in Schizophrenia: Therapeutic Implications. *Inter. J. Psycho-Anal.*, 32:157–166, 1951.

203. Winnicott, D. W. Hate in Countertransference. *Inter. J. Psycho-Anal.*, 30:69–74, 1949.

204. Winnicott, D. W. Metapsychological and Clinical Aspects of Regression Within the Psychoanalytic Set-Up. *Inter. J. Psycho-Anal.*, 36:16–26, 1955.

205. Zetzel, E. R. (1958). Therapeutic Alliance in the Analysis of Hysteria. In *The Capacity for Emotional Growth*. New York: International Universities Press, 1970, pp. 182–196.

206. Zilboorg, G. *Sigmund Freud*. New York: Scribner's, 1951.

207. Zilboorg, G. Some Sidelights on Free Associations. *Inter. J. Psycho-Anal.*, 33:489–496, 1952.

INDEX

Abreaction, 127

Absences by analyst, 36–37

Abstinence of analyst, 7–8, 55–56, 187

Acting out episodes: failure to pay fees and, 32; as form of resistance, 107, 110–112; relatives of patient and, 33

Addiction to chemical compounds, 174

Additive treatment, 23

Adler, Alfred, 15

Agape, 170

Agoraphobia, 185

Aichhorn, A., 186

Alexander, Franz, xi, 46n, 128

Allen, A., 32n

Alterative treatment, 23

Amenorrhea as resistance in analysis, 119

American Psychiatric Association, x

American Psychoanalytic Association, x, 159n, 179–180

Anal erotization of analysis, 117–118

"Analysis Terminable and Interminable" (Freud), 8, 109, 165, 181

Appointments: fees and cancellation of, 32; frequency of, 7, 34–36; length of, 35–36

Aristophanes, 41

Aristotelian theory of complex causation, 49n

Arsphenamine, ix

"Art of Becoming an Original Writer in Three Days, The" (Boerne), 41

Associated ideas, 43

Balint, M., 163–164, 165n, 176

Behavior modification, 186

Bellak, L., 11

Berlin, teaching of theory in, vii

Bernheim, Hippolyte, 105

"Beyond the Pleasure Principle" (Freud), 81

Blitzsten, Lionel, xi

Boerne, Ludwig, 41

Bond, Dr. Earl, 71n

Borderline conditions, psychoanalytic treatment of, 186

203